THE SECURITISATION OF CLIMATE CHANGE

This book provides the first systematic comparative analysis of climate security discourses.

It analyses the securitisation of climate change in four different countries: the USA, Germany, Turkey, and Mexico. The empirical analysis traces how specific climate security discourses have become dominant, which actors have driven this process, what political consequences this has had and what role the broader context has played in enabling these specific securitisations. In doing so, the book outlines a new and systematic theoretical framework that distinguishes between different referent objects of securitisation (territorial, individual and planetary) and between a security and risk dimension. It thereby clarifies the ever-increasing literature on different forms of securitisation and the relationship between security, risk and politics. Whereas securitisation studies have traditionally focused on either a single country case study or a global overview, consequently failing to reconstruct detailed securitisation dynamics, this is the first book to provide a systematic comparative analysis of climate security discourses in four countries and thus closes an empirical gap in the present literature. In addition, this comparative framework allows the drawing of conclusions about the conditions for and consequences of successful securitisation based on empirical and comparative analysis rather than theoretical debate only.

This book will of interest to students of climate change, environmental studies, critical security, global governance, and IR in general.

Thomas Diez is Professor of Political Science and International Relations at the University of Tübingen, Germany. He is author/editor of numerous books, including, most recently, *A Different Kind of Power? The EU's Role in International Politics* (2014).

Franziskus von Lucke is Researcher in the Department of Political Science at the University of Tübingen, Germany.

Zehra Wellmann is Researcher in the Department of Political Science at the University of Tübingen, Germany.

PRIO New Security Studies
Series Editor: J. Peter Burgess, PRIO, Oslo

The aim of this book series is to gather state-of-the-art theoretical reflection and empirical research into a core set of volumes that respond vigorously and dynamically to the new challenges to security scholarship.

The Geopolitics of American Insecurity
Terror, power and foreign policy
Edited by François Debrix and Mark J. Lacy

Security, Risk and the Biometric State
Governing borders and bodies
Benjamin J. Muller

Security and Global Governmentality
Globalization, governance and the state
Edited by Miguel de Larrinaga and Marc G. Doucet

Critical Perspectives on Human Security
Rethinking emancipation and power in international relations
Edited by David Chandler and Nik Hynek

Securitization Theory
How security problems emerge and dissolve
Edited by Thierry Balzacq

Feminist Security Studies
A narrative approach
Annick T. R. Wibben

The Ethical Subject of Security
Geopolitical reason and the threat against Europe
J. Peter Burgess

Politics of Catastrophe
Genealogies of the unknown
Claudia Aradau and Rens van Munster

Security, the Environment and Emancipation
Contestation over environmental change
Matt McDonald

Securitization, Accountability and Risk Management
Transforming the public security domain
Edited by Karin Svedberg Helgesson and Ulrika Mörth

Commercialising Security
Political consequences for European military operations
Edited by Anna Leander

Transnational Companies and Security Governance
Hybrid practices in a postcolonial world
Jana Hönke

Citizenship and Security
The constitution of political being
Edited by Xavier Guillaume and Jef Huysmans

Security, Emancipation and the Politics of Health
A new theoretical perspective
João Nunes

Security, Technology and Global Politics
Thinking with Virilio
Mark Lacy

Critical Security and Chinese Politics
The Anti-Falungong Campaign
Juha A. Vuori

Governing Borders and Security
The politics of connectivity and dispersal
Edited by Catarina Kinnvall and Ted Svensson

Contesting Security
Strategies and logics
Edited by Thierry Balzacq

Conflict Resolution and Ontological Security
Peace anxieties
Edited by Bahar Rumelili

Biopolitics of Security
A political analytic of finitude
Michael Dillon

Security Expertise
Practice, power, responsibility
Edited by Trine Villumsen Berling and Christian Bueger

Transformations of Security Studies
Dialogues, diversity and discipline
Edited by Gabi Schlag, Julian Junk and Christopher Daase

The Securitisation of Climate Change
Actors, processes and consequences
Thomas Diez, Franziskus von Lucke and Zehra Wellmann

'*The Securitisation of Climate Change* is a welcome and important contribution to the literature. The authors provide detailed empirical analysis of the way securitisation practices play out in a range of national settings, and make the important point that the different forms of linking climate change and security are crucial to the types of practices securitisation encourages. In the process, this book not only provides much-needed empirical depth and theoretical nuance to literature on climate security, it also makes a broader contribution to debates about the construction of security – and the normative implications of this construction – in international relations.'

Matt McDonald, University of Queensland, Australia

'In addressing the great challenge of our time, *The Securitisation of Climate Change* brings unprecedented analytical sensitivity, nuance and breadth to the politics of climate change. Reflecting the fascinating diversity of securitisations exposed in their comparative study, the authors compellingly advance the conceptual and ethical frontiers of securitisation theory.'

Stefan Elbe, University of Sussex, UK

'*The Securitisation of Climate Change* is a great read for anyone seeking to understand how and why climate change gets connected to ideas of security. Cross-country comparisons provide a sophisticated look at the variation in ways that climate change security links are made by actors in different political, economic and social contexts. The authors provide some much-needed depth to existing debates while remaining accessible to readers.'

Nicole Detraz, University of Memphis, USA

THE SECURITISATION OF CLIMATE CHANGE

Actors, processes and consequences

*Thomas Diez, Franziskus von Lucke
and Zehra Wellmann*

LONDON AND NEW YORK

First published 2016
by Routledge
2 Park Square, Milton Park, Abingdon, Oxon OX14 4RN

and by Routledge
711 Third Avenue, New York, NY 10017

Routledge is an imprint of the Taylor & Francis Group, an informa business

© 2016 Thomas Diez, Franziskus von Lucke and Zehra Wellmann

The right of Thomas Diez, Franziskus von Lucke and Zehra Wellmann to be identified as authors of this work has been asserted by them in accordance with sections 77 and 78 of the Copyright, Designs and Patents Act 1988.

All rights reserved. No part of this book may be reprinted or reproduced or utilised in any form or by any electronic, mechanical, or other means, now known or hereafter invented, including photocopying and recording, or in any information storage or retrieval system, without permission in writing from the publishers.

Trademark notice: Product or corporate names may be trademarks or registered trademarks, and are used only for identification and explanation without intent to infringe.

British Library Cataloguing-in-Publication Data
A catalogue record for this book is available from the British Library

Library of Congress Cataloging-in-Publication Data
Names: Diez, Thomas, 1970- author. | Lucke, Franziskus von, author. | Wellmann, Zehra, author.Title: The securitisation of climate change : actors, processes and consequences / Thomas Diez, Franziskus von Lucke and Zehra Wellmann.Other titles: Securitization of climate changeDescription: Abingdon, Oxon ; New York, NY : Routledge, 2016. | Series: PRIO new security studies | Includes bibliographical references and index.Identifiers: LCCN 2015045912| ISBN 9781138956353 (pbk.) | ISBN 9781315665757 (ebook) | ISBN 9781138956346 (hbk)Subjects: LCSH: Climatic changes--Political aspects. | Climatic changes--Government policy. | National security--Environmental aspects. Classification: LCC QC903 .D55 2016 | DDC 363.738/747--dc23LC record available at http://lccn.loc.gov/2015045912

ISBN: 978-1-138-95634-6 (hbk)
ISBN: 978-1-138-95635-3 (pbk)
ISBN: 978-1-315-66575-7 (ebk)

Typeset in Bembo by Saxon Graphics Ltd, Derby

CONTENTS

List of illustrations viii
Acknowledgements ix
List of abbreviations xi
Note on translations xvii

1 Introduction 1

2 Analysing climate security discourses 13

3 The United States: climate change as danger to the state 36

4 Germany: ambivalent forerunner in individual security 65

5 Mexico: a case of politicised securitisation? 96

6 Turkey: no climate for change? 121

7 Conclusion: the politics of securitising climate change 145

References 154
Index 196

ILLUSTRATIONS

Figures

2.1	The space of politics and security	19
3.1	Network citation analysis (US case)	56
4.1	Network citation analysis (German case)	84
5.1	Network citation analysis (Mexican case)	111
6.1	Network citation analysis (Turkish case)	139

Tables

2.1	Important keywords distinguishing between the danger and risk dimension	16
2.2	A typology of climate security discourses	21

ACKNOWLEDGEMENTS

This book is the result of a four-year long process. It all started with Julia Grauvogel's idea to write her master's thesis under Thomas's supervision on the securitisation of climate change, and the idea quickly grew to turn this into a bigger comparative project that would make a substantial contribution to the securitisation literature. So Thomas and Julia applied for project funding from the German Research Foundation (Deutsche Forschungsgemeinschaft, DFG). Unfortunately, the reviewing process got delayed, and so by the time that news about the success of our proposal came in, Julia had accepted a job offer elsewhere and the project team had to be assembled anew. So while Julia moved from Tübingen to Hamburg, Franz did the same in the opposite direction, and he and Thomas were joined by Zehra, who then spent three years shuttling back and forth between her residences in Istanbul and Tübingen. The first round of thanks therefore goes to Julia, without whom this book probably would never have been written, and to the DFG for their generous funding (project grant number DI-1688/2-1).

When we started our work, we quickly realised that this was an issue that many colleagues had a strong interest in, and we benefitted from their constructive engagement with our numerous attempts to come to terms with what turned out to be a rather difficult conceptual framework. Among those providing us with their insights have been Didier Bigo, Ingrid Boas, Marieke de Goede, Nikki Detraz, Stefan Elbe, Rita Floyd, Hendrik Hegemann, Matt McDonald, Chris Methmann, Angela Oels, Lena Partzsch and Delf Rothe. Clemens Hofmann and Jan Selby allowed us to publish the first explication of our theoretical framework with some very rudimentary empirical illustrations in a special issue of *Geopolitics* that they edited, and we are very grateful to them and then *Geopolitics* editor Simon Dalby for the opportunity and for their rigorous and often challenging comments. We also benefitted immensely from the discussions in the International Relations colloquium in Tübingen, where Andreas Hasenclever and Matthias Leese in particular kept challenging us from opposite ends of the IR theory spectrum. Special thanks also go to our interview partners in the four countries of our research who provided us with feedback, experiences, anecdotes and background knowledge on the assumptions and findings of our study. Many parts of our analysis would not have been possible without the immense help from our student assistants: Schielan Babat, Thea Güttler, Leonie Haueisen, Benno Keppner, Miriam Keppner, Katharina Krause, Hanna Spanhel and Josefa Velten. A big thank you goes to you as well!

Last but not least, we owe apologies to our families and friends, who probably would have preferred us to spend time with them rather than on our ClimaSec project.

Tübingen
Thomas Diez
Franziskus von Lucke
Zehra Wellmann

ABBREVIATIONS

ABGS	Avrupa Birliği Genel Sekreterliği – General Secretariat of the European Union
AFAD	Başbakanlık Afet ve Acil Durum Yönetimi Başkanlığı – Prime Ministry Disaster and Emergency Management Authority
AFD	Agence Française de Développement – French Development Agency
AFES	Arbeitsgruppe Friedensforschung und europäische Sicherheitspolitik e.V – Peace Research and European Security Studies Working Group
AKP	Adalet ve Kalkınma Partisi – Justice and Development Party
ASP	American Security Project
ATASE	Askeri Tarih ve Stratejik Etüt Başkanlığı – Head Office of Military History and Strategic Studies
BMU	Bundesministerium für Umwelt, Naturschutz und Reaktorsicherheit – Federal Ministry for the Environment, Nature Conservation and Nuclear Safety (German Environmental Ministry) (renamed BMUB in 2013)
BMUB	Bundesministerium für Umwelt, Naturschutz, Bau und Reaktorsicherheit – Federal Ministry for the Environment, Nature Conservation, Building and Nuclear Safety (German Environmental Ministry)
C2ES	Center for Climate and Energy Solutions
CAN	Climate Action Network
CAP	Center for American Progress
CCAD	Comisión Centroamericana de Ambiente y Desarrollo – Central American Environment and Development Commission
CCC	Centro de Colaboración Cívica – Civic Cooperation Centre
CCCCC	Caribbean Community Climate Change Centre
CCS	Center for Climate and Security
CDM	Clean Development Mechanism
CDU	Christlich Demokratische Union – Christian Democratic Union

CENAPRED	Centro Nacional de Prevención de Desastres – National Centre for Disaster Prevention
CENTCOM	US Central Command
CEMDA	Centro Mexicano de Derecho Ambiental – Mexican Centre for Environmental Law
CESPEDES	Comisión de Estudios del Sector Privada para el Desarrollo Sustentable – Study Group for Sustainable Development from the Private Sector
CFR	Council on Foreign Relations
CIA	Central Intelligence Agency
CICC	Comisión Intersecretarial de Cambio Climático – Inter-ministerial Commission for Climate Change
CISEN	Centro de Investigación y Seguridad Nacional – Centre for Research and National Security
CLiSAP	Climate System Analysis and Prediction
CMM	Centro Mario Molina – Mario Molina Centre
CNAS	Center for a New American Security
CNBC	Consumer News and Business Channel
CNN	Cable News Network
CONAGUA	Comisión Nacional del Agua – National Water Commission
COP	Conference of the Parties
CPI	Climate Performance Index
CPRS	Coventry University Centre for Peace and Reconciliation Studies
CSIS	Center for Strategic and International Studies
ÇOB	Çevre ve Orman Bakanlığı – Ministry of the Environment and Forestry
ÇŞB	Çevre ve Şehircilik Bakanlığı – Ministry of Environment and Urbanisation
DHS	Department of Homeland Security
DIE	Deutsches Institut für Entwicklungspolitik – German Institute for Development Cooperation
DIW	Deutsches Institut für Wirtschaftsforschung – German Institute for Economic Research
DKK	Deutsches Klima-Konsortium – German Climate Consortium
DKRZ	Deutsches Klimarechenzentrum – German Climate Computing Centre
DMG	Deutsche Meteorologische Gesellschaft – German Meteorological Society
DOD	Department of Defense
DOE	Department of Energy
DOS	Department of State
DOT	Department of Transportation
DPG	Deutsche Physikalische Gesellschaft – German Physical Society
DPT	Devlet Planlama Teşkilatı – State Planning Institution

DSI	Devlet Su İşleri – State Hydraulic Works
ECC	Environment, Conflict and Cooperation
EEG	Erneuerbare-Energien-Gesetz – German Renewable Energy Act
EMCC	Eastern Mediterranean Climate Centre
ENACC	Estrategia Nacional de Cambio Climático 2007 – National Strategy on Climate Change 2007
ENCC	Estrategia Nacional de Cambio Climático 2013 – National Strategy on Climate Change 2013
EPA	Environmental Protection Agency
ESS	European Security Strategy
EU	European Union
EUISS	EU Institute for Security Studies
FAO	Food and Agriculture Organisation of the United Nations
FCO	Foreign and Commonwealth Office
FEMA	Federal Emergency Management Agency
FONDEN	Fondo Nacional para el Desarrollo Nacional – National Development Fund
FOPREDEN	Fondo para la Prevención de Desastres Naturales – Disaster Prevention Fund
FUNDAECO	Fundación para el Ecodesarrollo y la Conservación – Eco-Development and Conservation Fund
GCRA	Global Change Research Act
GBP	Pound sterling
GDP	Gross Domestic Product
GDV	Die Deutschen Versicherer – German Insurance Federation
GEF	Green Environmental Fund
GHG	Greenhouse Gas
GIZ	Deutsche Gesellschaft für Internationale Zusammenarbeit – German Federal Enterprise for International Cooperation (formerly GTZ)
GLOBE	Global Legislators Organisation for a Balanced Environment
HDI	Human Development Index
IASS	Institute for Advanced Sustainability Studies
IBB	İstanbul Büyükşehir – Istanbul Metropolitan Municipality
IfP-EW	Initiative for Peacebuilding – Early Warning Analysis to Action
IklimBU	İklim Değişikliği ve Politikaları Uygulama ve Araştırma Merkezi – Climate Change Politics Exercise and Research Center
INE	Instituto Nacional de Ecología – National Institute for Ecology
INECC	Instituto Nacional de Ecología y Cambio Climático – National Institute for Ecology and Climate Change
INEF	Institute for Development and Peace
IOM	International Organisation for Migration
IPC	Istanbul Policy Center
IPCC	Intergovernmental Panel on Climate Change
ISIS	Islamic State of Iraq and Syria
İTÜ	İstanbul Teknik Üniversitesi – Technical University of Istanbul

KADOS	Kadıköy Bilim Kültür ve Sanat Dostları Derneği – Kadiköy Science, Culture and Friends of Arts Association
KfW	Deutsche Kreditanstalt für Wiederaufbau – German Development Bank
KOSKI	Konya-based Agency for Water Supply
MAB	Military Advisory Board
MCC	Mercator Research Institute on Global Commons and Climate Change
MCII	Munich Climate Insurance Initiative
MDG	Millennium Development Goals
MGM	General Directorate of State Meteorology Services
MURCIR	Marmara Üniversitesi Uluslararası İlişkiler Araştırma ve Uygulama Merkezi – Marmara University Exercise and Research Centre for International Relations
NAFTA	North American Free Trade Agreement
NASA	National Aeronautics and Space Administration
NATO	North Atlantic Treaty Organization
NCA	National Climate Assessment
NCCG	National Climate Change Coordination Group
NGO	Non-Governmental Organisation
NIE	National Intelligence Estimate
NOAA	National Oceanic and Atmospheric Administration
NSS	National Security Strategy
ODUSD-ES	Office of the Deputy Under Secretary of Defense – Environmental Security
ODUSD-I&S	Office of the Deputy Under Secretary of Defense – Installation and Environment
OECD	Organisation for Economic Co-operation and Development
ORSAM	Ortadoğu Stratejik Araştırmalar Merkezi – Centre For Middle Eastern Strategic Studies
PAN	Partido Acción Nacional – National Action Party
PDCI	Partners for Democratic Change International
PECC	Programa Especial de Cambio Climático – Special Programme on Climate Change
PEACC	Plan Estatal de Acción ante el Cambio Climático – State Level Plan for Climate Action
PEMEX	Petróleos Mexicanos – Mexican state-owned oil company
PIK	Potsdam Institut für Klimafolgenforschung – Potsdam Institute for Climate Impact Research
PKK	Partîya Karkerén Kurdîstan – Kurdistan Worker's Party
PRI	Partido Revolucionario Institucional – Institutional Revolutionary Party
PVEM	Partido Verde Ecologista de México – Ecologist Green Party of Mexico
QDR	Quadrennial Defense Review

REC	Regional Environmental Centre
RUSI	Royal United Services Institute
SAGARPA	Secretaría de Agricultura, Ganadería, Desarrollo Rural, Pesca y Alimentación – Mexican Secretariat of Agriculture, Livestock, Rural Development, Fisheries and Food
SAREM	Stratejik Araştırma ve Etüt Merkezi – Strategic Research and Exercise Centre
SEMARNAT	Secretaría de Medio Ambiente y Recursos Naturales – Secretariat of Environment and Natural Resources
SENER	Secretaría de Energía – Secretariat of Energy
SEGOB	Secretaría de Gobernación – Secretariat of State
SERDP	Strategic Environmental Research and Development Program
SPD	Sozialdemokratische Partei Deutschland – Social Democratic Party of Germany
SSCI	Social Sciences Citation Index
SWP	Stiftung Wissenschaft und Politik. Deutsches Institut für Internationale Politik und Sicherheit – German Institute for International and Security Affairs
TBMM	Türkiye Büyük Millet Meclisi – Turkish Parliament
TEMA	Türkiye Erozyonla Mücadele, Ağaçlandırma ve Doğal Varlıkları Koruma Vakfı – Turkish Foundation for Combating Soil Erosion, for Reforestation and the Protection of Natural Habitats
TIKDEK	Türkiye İklim Değişikliği Kongresi – Turkish Climate Change Conference
TMMOB	Türk Mühendis ve Mimar Odaları Birliği – Union of Chambers of Turkish Engineers and Architects
TÜBITAK	Türkiye Bilimsel ve Teknolojik Araştırma Kurumu – Scientific and Technological Research Council of Turkey
UAE	United Arab Emirates
UK	United Kingdom
UN	United Nations
UNAM	Universidad Nacional Autónoma de México – National Autonomous University of Mexico
UNCED	United Nations Conference on Environment and Development
UNDP	United Nations Development Programme
UNEP	United Nations Environmental Programme
UNFCCC	United Nations Framework Convention on Climate Change
UNGA	United Nations General Assembly
UNIDO	United Nations Industrial Development Organisation
UNSC	United Nations Security Council
US	United States
USCAP	United States Climate Action Partnership
USD	United States Dollar
VDA	Verband Deutscher Automobilhersteller – Association of German Automobile Manufacturers

WBGU	Wissenschaftlicher Beirat der Bundesregierung für Globale Umweltveränderungen – German Advisory Council on Global Change
WCP	World Climate Programme
WHO	World Health Organisation
WMO	World Meteorological Organisation
WWF	World Wide Fund for Nature (or World Wildlife Fund)

NOTE ON TRANSLATIONS

In order to improve readability, we have used translations of German, Spanish and Turkish documents throughout this text. All translations are ours unless stated otherwise.

1
INTRODUCTION

The climate–security nexus

Droughts that deprive people of food and water; floods that destroy homes; rising sea levels that make whole islands disappear; water scarcity that leads to violent conflicts and mass migration – climate change has long become an issue of security policies (see Brzoska 2012 for an overview). The 2015 United States (US) National Security Strategy lists '[c]onfronting climate change' as a major security threat, along with terrorism, violent conflict, the proliferation of mass destruction and health scares (The White House 2015: 12). The 2003 European Security Strategy (ESS) noted that 'competition for natural resources – notably water –, which will be aggravated by global warming over the next decades, is likely to create further turbulence and migratory movements in various regions' (European Council 2003: 3). Five years after its adoption, the European Council concluded in its review of the ESS that 'the security implications of climate change' have 'taken on a new urgency' (European Council 2003: 14). On the way to a revision of the ESS, the 2015 strategic review argues that 'climate change and resource scarcity … contribute to international conflicts and are expected to do even more in the future' (Carson 2011; European Council 2003: 7). On the member state level, the White Paper of the German Ministry of Defence sees climate change as exacerbating the fragility of states and societies in parts of Africa and Asia, even though climate change overall plays a less important role in this document (Bundesministerium der Verteidigung 2006: 21). And the United Kingdom's National Security Strategy warns that 'the physical effects of climate change are likely to become increasingly significant as a "risk multiplier", exacerbating existing tensions around the world' (HM Government 2010: 17).

The climate–security nexus is part of the wider context of broadening the concept of security, which has taken place since the 1980s. In an influential piece, Richard

Ullman (1983: 134) argued against a narrow military conception of security and saw 'a drastic deterioration of environmental quality' as a major threat. Since then, environmental security, and climate security with it, has become a standard reference point in security policies. Initially, non-governmental organisations (NGOs) – such as the World Watch Institute, the Climate Institute, the New Economics Foundation or Friends of the Earth – have been crucial in linking climate change to security in order to raise awareness and include the issue on the agenda of political leaders (Oels 2012a; Myers 1995). Eventually, this policy advocacy contributed to the adoption of the United Nations Framework Convention on Climate Change (UNFCCC), agreed in 1992 at the Rio Summit of the United Nations Conference on Environment and Development (UNCED). The 1997 Kyoto Protocol was the first in a series of attempts to commit states to binding targets for the reduction of greenhouse gas emissions that cause climate change.

As the scientific certainty of the anthropogenic effects on the global climate and the immense cost of adaptation measures turned out to be more robust, the urgent need to take measures to mitigate climate change (i.e. to tackle its causes) or to adapt to its potential consequences has become more widespread. Thus, since the turn of the millennium, the discussion about the possible security effects of climate change has again gained momentum (Brzoska and Oels 2011). Reports on the national level such as the influential Stern Report (Stern 2006) pushed governments to no longer defer policies to combat global warming and its effects. In 2007, even the United Nations Security Council (UNSC) debated the possible implications of climate change on international peace and security (UNSC 2007a), followed by a report of the Secretary-General (UNGA 2009b), various General Assembly resolutions (UNGA 2008; 2009a) and two further sessions of the UNSC on the issue in 2011 and 2013 (UNSC 2011a; 2013).

The puzzle of climate policies and securitisation

Given this strong and established link between climate change and security in distinct contexts, it is surprising that concrete measures to combat greenhouse gas emissions remain contested. It took more than seven years to bring together a sufficient number of states to ratify the Kyoto Protocol for it to take force. Even so, the US as the main emitter of greenhouse gases, after initially signing the Protocol, has never ratified it, while Canada withdrew as a party to the agreement in 2011 when it became clear that it was unable to meet its emission reduction obligations. A series of UNFCCC conferences, most famously in Copenhagen in 2009, has failed to produce an effective successor to the Protocol, and its extension in 2011 weakened its force, not least because even fewer member states agreed to it. Meanwhile, individual states have pursued very different climate policies. While some, notably the EU member states, have stuck to setting binding targets for emission reductions, others have preferred incentives for voluntary behavioural changes of private actors, have focused on adaptive strategies to be prepared for the inevitable, or have continued to privilege economic and energy security interests.

As a consequence, one of the central analyses of a widened security agenda has claimed that climate change has not been effectively represented as a security issue on the global level (Buzan et al. 1998: 74, 84, 92). While there have been a number of attempts to securitise climate change, the argument is that these attempts have not been sufficiently accepted to speak of a successful securitisation of climate change. While we take issue with this analysis, as we will discuss in greater detail below, we nonetheless need to recognise that on the present record, the climate–security nexus, while widespread, remains contested and has not translated into policies that are widely seen as necessary and appropriate on a global level. Instead, we see a great deal of variation in the way that climate security is debated and in the way that states react to climate change.

At first glance, economic interests seem to play a major role in explaining this variation – at least state actors tend to cite such interests, such as safeguarding development, energy supplies or employment, in their defence of policies that do not aim at reducing greenhouse gas emissions. A closer look, however, shows that the picture is much murkier. How come that Morocco and Mexico are among the top twenty in the Climate Change Performance Index, whereas other emerging economies such as Brazil and Turkey receive a rating of 'very poor' (Germanwatch and CAN 2015: 8–9)? Likewise, France and the UK are among the forerunners in their climate policies, whereas Canada and Australia find themselves in bottom place with Kazakhstan and Saudi Arabia (ibid.).

The argument we unfold in this book is that the discursive framing of the climate–security issue varies significantly between and within countries. There is thus not only one way to construct climate change as a security issue; there are many different ways of doing so, and these different climate security discourses matter in the legitimisation of specific policies. As such, our normative assessment of whether linking climate change and security is a good (for instance, because it places climate change on the agenda and accelerates political decisions) or a bad thing (for instance, because it enables the military to expand its policy reach and thereby neglect climate policy) depends on the exact ways in which the securitisation of climate change unfolds. How this happens is in turn a consequence of a combination of structural factors such as the historical development of political institutions and the agency of those we will call 'discursive entrepreneurs' who are able to shape climate security discourses at particular junctures, and whose framing of climate security thus significantly influences the development of the debate.

While the starting point of this book is thus the empirical puzzle of the multiplicity of climate–security linkages, we use this case to also make a theoretical contribution to the debate about securitisation. In the so-called Copenhagen School of security studies, security does not carry any objective, substantive meaning. Instead, what counts as security depends on the successful representation of something or someone as an existential threat to a referent object (such as the state in traditional military security or the individual in human security) to legitimise extraordinary measures (Buzan et al. 1998: 24). 'Successful' in this context means that individual securitising moves (the individual speech acts that represent the existential threat) are accepted by their audience and extraordinary measures thus seen as legitimate, even if they do not necessarily have to be implemented (Buzan *et al.* 1998: 25). Many researchers before us have used the issue of climate change to demonstrate the shortcomings of this definition, as we will elaborate below. They have criticised its narrowness, being modelled on the logic of military security; its imprecise definition of extraordinary measures and the audience; and its neglect of routine policies that nonetheless amount to security policies (see, among others, Floyd 2010; Trombetta 2008; Detraz and Betsill 2009; Corry 2012; McDonald 2013). We build on their work to develop a six-fold matrix of securitisation along two dimensions: the level of the referent object (whether climate change is seen to threaten states or other territories, individuals, or the planet as a whole), and the construction of security as an existential threat (as in the original Copenhagen School formulation) or as risk (which, as we will argue, follows a much more diffuse logic). This matrix allows us to trace securitisations in much more detail than the literature has so far done. Furthermore, it allows us to clarify the relationship between security, threat and risk, which the security studies literature has not yet been able to settle satisfactorily, and make these categories available for empirical analyses. Last but not least, our distinction of different climate security discourses and their policy influences also allows us to engage with the normative debate about securitisation, which Wæver (1995) saw as a problematic development in its constraining impact on the political debate, while others have pointed to the potentially positive effects of securitisation in terms of agenda-setting and policy legitimisation (e.g. Elbe 2009; Floyd 2010).

A comparative design

Our study is based on the comparison of climate security debates in four countries: the USA, Germany, Mexico and Turkey. Our choice of a comparative analysis of national debates is driven by our empirical puzzle of diverging policies despite similar economic standing, our hunch that these may be result of different predominant ways to frame climate security in these debates, and our aim to trace the development of securitisation in detail. We are not analysing the global climate change debate and its link to security, not least because this is an issue that the literature has covered extensively (Oels 2011; Detraz and Betsill 2009; Corry 2012). Our comparative approach may run the risk of methodological nationalism, reinforcing the boundaries of states when in fact, climate change debates are transnational to some degree, and pushed forward by transnational actors from international NGOs to expert panels as part of an epistemic community. Yet climate policies ultimately have to be adopted in national contexts, and political debates about climate change, while certainly also taking place on a global elite level, therefore largely take place within national contexts. International and transnational actors clearly influence these debates, but we take care of this by highlighting such linkages – and analysing whether they are successful or not. We thus will show how the EU has been influential in enforcing climate policies in

Turkey in the absence of an effective securitisation, whereas the UK-based Royal United Services Institute (RUSI) unsuccessfully tried to securitise climate change in Mexico. All in all, our comparative setup allows us to draw out the distinctive development of the securitisation of climate change in our four cases, and demonstrate how this has affected national climate policies.

We have chosen our case studies on the basis of our research aim of showing the development and impact of divergent climate security discourses. To do so, we selected two country pairs. Each pair has a similar level of economic development but differs significantly in their climate policies. According to 2010 estimates, Germany and the US had a per capita income of 35,700 USD and 47,200 USD, and ranked 10 and 4 respectively in the Human Development Index (HDI). In contrast, Mexico had an estimated income of 12,900 USD per capita, Turkey of 12,300 USD. The two countries ranked 56 (Mexico) and 83 (Turkey) in the HDI. Each pair is also similar in their emission levels. In 1998, the US emitted 20.35 tons of carbon per capita per year and Germany 10.63, whereas the figures for Mexico and Turkey are significantly lower at 1.1 and 0.9 tons of carbon (World Bank 2013a). While these figures provide only a snapshot and are not the latest available, they are indicative of the countries' performance during our entire period of analysis from the 1990s to 2014, which roughly covers the period from the early linkages of climate change and security from Rio onwards, through the peak of global securitisation in 2006/7, until the completion of empirical data gathering in the framework of our project.

While the US and Germany are thus very similar in their developmental stage, as are Mexico and Turkey, the picture is very different when we look at their ranking in the Climate Performance Index. Whereas Germany and Mexico are in the top ten in the years 2008–2013 (Germany averages at number 6, Mexico at number 10), Turkey and the US share a rather embarrassing rank 52 (Germanwatch and CAN 2015). Even considering that such rankings have to be taken with a pinch of salt, the status of Turkey and the US as laggards when it comes to climate change policies is undisputed in the literature, whereas both Germany and Mexico are widely seen as relative vanguards, whatever the imperfections of their climate policies may be. Different past impacts of climate change do not explain this variation in policies either. While Germany ranks number 22 in Germanwatch's Climate Risk Index 1994–2013 (Germanwatch 2014), the US is at number 26. According to these figures, Mexico indeed has been more affected than Turkey (ranks 38 and 97 respectively), but both have been significantly less affected than either Germany or the US. The Vulnerability Index of the Gain Index that measures the present and projected impact of climate change shows a similar picture concerning the differences within the same country category. However, since this index does also account for the ability to adapt to climate change, the two industrialised countries are less vulnerable than the two emerging economies. Germany and the US rank 6 and 10 (lower numbers indicate less vulnerability) and Mexico and Turkey 49 and 37 (ND-Gain 2015). Hence, the difference in vulnerability cannot explain the difference in climate policies either, especially between the US and Germany. Again, the methodology underpinning these statistics may be questionable, but they can serve as a useful indication of the problematic relationship between affectedness and policy.

At the end of Chapter 2, we will discuss our methodology in greater detail. Suffice it to say at this point that we argue that climate change and security, both because of historical developments and structural constraints on the one hand, and because of the agency of specific discursive entrepreneurs on the other, have been linked very differently in our four cases, and that this has enabled policymakers to legitimise and pursue different policies. In order to show the development of climate security debates, we have traced securitising moves and their acceptance or rejection through an analysis of parliamentary debates, government papers and NGO and think tank reports, supplemented by newspaper reporting and interviews, where the latter were particularly important in reconstructing the policy networks in which particular climate security representations were propagated, taken up or rejected. Our country cases show a significant degree of securitisation of climate change in Germany and the US, but in very different forms. While in the US climate change was quickly linked to territorial state security concerns, conceptions of individual risk and security and even references to planetary security prevailed in the German case. In Mexico, the securitisation was moderately successful with a clear focus on individual security. Yet other politicising argumentations also played an important role, and thus climate change remained largely an environmental issue. Moreover, the existence of other security issues such as organised crime overshadowed the climate threat and hindered an even more successful securitisation, especially on the territorial level. In contrast, the securitisation of climate change was largely unsuccessful in Turkey, with only very few attempts to link climate change to security and virtually no impact on policies. Developmental and energy security concerns have clearly overridden climate security as major issue in the Turkish debate.

The contribution of a comparative study of climate security discourses

Differentiating securitisation

The contribution of our study is thus the development of a conceptual matrix of securitising climate change and its application in detailed case studies. Their comparison allows us to discuss the conditions under which specific securitisations prevail, and to discuss their political and normative consequences. We thus address a number of shortcomings in the existing literature on climate security.

Rooted in earlier debates on environmental security (Ullmann 1983; Mathews 1989; Buzan 1983: 117–119, 2007), the initial literature on the security implications of climate change amounted to a securitising move in itself. Homer-Dixon (1994; 1999) and Myers (1995; 2002) linked environmental changes to a rise in violent conflicts through water shortages and migration. While the possibility of such a conflictive development clearly exists, the quasi-automatic linkage between climate change and conflict underestimates the human capacity to deal with resource scarcity cooperatively, or to adjust to changing environmental conditions. Consequently, recent literature has questioned these neo-Malthusian arguments (Hartmann 2010; Nordas and Gleditsch 2007; Reuveny 2007; Salehyan 2008; Gleditsch 2012; Buhaug 2010; Buhaug et al. 2014). These largely quantitative works do not dispute that in some cases, droughts have increased violent conflict either directly or indirectly through increased migration, but demonstrate that there are also counter-cases so that the correlation between climate change and conflict is at best disputed. For our purposes, this debate is only relevant in as much as the climate-change–conflict link is a common argument used in climate security discussions. Our research does not directly engage with the consequences of climate change. However, our analyses of climate security discourses do allow us to draw conclusions about the possibility that governments pursue policies that are more or less likely to tackle such consequences in a peaceful way, or whether the prevailing discourses tend to legitimise military interventions and exclusionary policies that could aggravate violent conflict.

Our main point of departure in the existing literature is the debate about the securitisation of climate change. As we have already noted, Buzan et al. (1998) claimed in their core work that environmental securitisation had not been successful, as there had been no identifiable emergency measures taken in this field. Yet especially in the field of climate change, other authors such as Parsons (2010), Trombetta (2008), Brzoska (2009) and Brauch (2009b) clearly identify securitisation processes. They all take issue with the reduction of security to emergency politics in the form of extraordinary measures built on the image of war and resulting from friend–enemy decisions in what they see as an understanding of security in line with the work of Carl Schmitt (Williams 2003; McDonald 2008; Huysmans 2008; van Munster 2005). Consequently, they argue, following Balzacq (2011), Guzzini (2011) and above all Stritzel (2007; 2011), that we need to contextualise securitisation – that what the Copenhagen School considers the inherent 'grammar' of securitising moves is merely one form of securitisation prevalent in the military sector and in Western contexts. Because of their narrow definition of securitisation, these authors claim, Buzan et al. look at climate change discourses through a lens that prevents them from seeing securitisation.

In the debate about climate security, such a contextualisation of climate change has led to the proposition of a variety of forms of securitisation. Detraz and Betsill (2009), for instance, differentiate between an 'environmental security' and an 'environmental conflict' discourse. They develop the environmental conflict discourse based on Homer-Dixon's work on resource scarcity (see for example Homer-Dixon 1994) and see such a discourse referring to the emergence of violent conflict resulting from a degradation of natural resources, threatening primarily the security of states. In contrast, the concept of 'environmental security' is closer to the concept of human security. Thus, the referent object is the individual, and the direct impact of climate change is on the daily lives of people rather than on state security and violent conflict.

McDonald (2013) has added to this the notion of 'international' and 'ecological security' discourses. He sees the international security discourse as an extension of what Detraz and Betsill (2009) have called environmental conflict discourse. It is rooted in traditional understandings of military security, but instead of the nation state as the main referent object, climate change in this representation threatens the stability of the international system as a whole. A more radical extension of Detraz and Betsill's framework is the 'ecological security discourse'. Taking up arguments by Barnett (2001), Pirages (2005) and Dalby (2009), (McDonald 2013: 48) sees the 'biosphere' as the main referent object of this discourse. While individual human beings, at the centre of the environmental security discourse, are part of the biosphere, they are no longer the single focus of the threat. Instead, the ecological security discourse conceptualises them as part of nature, the balance of which climate change brings into disarray. Indeed, humans in this rendering of climate change are not only the referent object, but also the threat itself, as in the era of the 'Anthropocene', they are the cause of the existential threat to nature.

These works have refined our understanding of securitisation largely by differentiating between various referent objects of security. As such, they are still relatively close to the original Copenhagen School formulation, and they remain on the level of a largely theoretical discussion that develops ideal types of discourse inductively from the existing literature. Apart from providing an in-depth empirical analysis, on the theoretical side our framework suggests a more systematic way of distinguishing climate security discourses. In doing so, we draw on Detraz and Betsill (2009) as well as McDonald (2013), but we build our categories of climate security discourse more deductively by developing two dimensions. One of these includes different levels of referent objects. The other addresses a second area of literature on climate security that the literature reviewed so far largely ignores, or at least does not draw on systematically. This is the literature on risk.

Introducing risk

One of the long-standing criticisms of the Copenhagen School by Bigo (2002) and others associated with the so-called Paris School, or what Balzacq (2011: 22) more appropriately calls the 'sociological' approach to securitisation, is that Buzan et al. fail to see the emergence of security framing through day-to-day bureaucratic practices and routines, as well as diffuse forms of power in decentralised networks, including private actors such as the insurance industry. This has led to a burgeoning literature on the increasing relevance of risk in security practices (van Munster 2005; Aradau and van Munster 2007; Hameiri 2008), as bureaucratic planners and insurance brokers are more likely to frame their security concerns as risks. Such work has put forward analyses of 'assemblages' of a variety of interconnected discursive and material forces engaged in the production of security (e.g. Aradau and van Munster 2007) and 'resilience' as a strategy of individuals and societies to prepare for the worst in situations of risk (e.g. Coaffee and Wood 2006).

The literature does not agree on a single definition of risk. However, there are a number of features common to most conceptualisations. Risk poses a rather long-term potential threat that is characterised by a radical uncertainty and leads to a more diffuse sense of unease (Goede 2008; Bigo 2002; Corry 2012). Security threats are existential, direct and urgent (violent resource conflicts, the drowning of whole islands or the destruction of ecosystems), whereas risk often seems manageable and invites the calculation 'of the incalculable', to use Beck's famous phrase (Beck 2002: 41). It is only potentially an existential threat, and if it is invoked as such (e.g. in the future risk of increased probability of violent conflicts, disaster intensity or ecosystem destruction), it essentially corresponds to security in the sense of the Copenhagen School. Furthermore, security threats tend to be identifiable or even personifiable (as, for example, a specific country, group of people or certain practices), whereas risk is often a lot more diffuse, with a diffuse referent object (e.g. certain risk-groups, risk-areas, potentially risky behaviour). Risk policies thus are focused on precaution, and risk-reduction programmes aim to increase the resilience of the referent object (Corry 2012: 245). Security threats are uninsurable because they lead to destruction, whereas risk is typically the object of insurance (Stripple 2012: 190; Aradau 2004: 266). If, as in the war on terror, the potential threat is so destructive that the risk can no longer be insured, a security logic sets in. Such a logic calls for emergency measures to prevent the threat from materialising under any circumstances (Aradau and van Munster 2007). A risk-based approach, in contrast, tries to mitigate the possible consequences of climate change or other threats (for instance, through increasing resilience) and to tackle their constitutive causes, following Beck's conceptualisation of risk as the unforeseen consequence of human action (Beck 2000).

It is immediately evident that risk may be an appropriate way of framing the threat posed by climate change. Most prominently, Corry (2012) has done so in distinguishing between two different logics of security, which he identifies as 'securitisation' and 'riskification'. In line with our discussion so far, he links security to direct harm and defence against threats with exceptional measures. He sets this against risk as taking into account the 'conditions of possibility' for harm, and the implementation of precautionary measures to increase 'governance capacity' (Corry 2012: 248). While we largely agree with this characterisation of risk and security, we see risk as a variation of security rather than a category separate from it. The fact that risk is normally subsumed under security considerations, as well as the historical development of the security-risk debate summarised above, speaks in favour of this position. In our analytical framework, we will therefore distinguish not between securitisation and riskification, but between riskification and threatification, and see both as variations of securitisation that form the two poles of a continuum, on which risk and threat (or security, in traditional terms) can intersect. This takes up the argument, put forward for instance by Methmann and Rothe (2012) in their treatment of 'the logic of apocalypse', that risk arguments in climate security discourses actually include references to existential threats to bolster their argumentative force.

Enlarging the scope of security to include risk implies a relaxation of the criteria that allow us to recognise securitisation. The original Copenhagen School formulation relies on a strict distinction between normal politics and securitisation. Employing the grammar of securitisation – thus invoking an existential threat to justify extraordinary measures – is an attempt to move a debate out of the realm of 'normal' politics. It is depoliticising because if the audience accepts the representation of an existential threat as such, there can be no political debate or choice: urgent measures need to be taken. The literature that emphasises the different forms of and the contribution of bureaucratic routines to securitisation has provided us with important insights into the different logics of securitisation, as they seem particularly pertinent to an analysis of climate change debates and policies. Yet it has largely ignored the problem that such a widening of the scope of security runs counter to the attempt of Buzan et al. to separate analytically the realms of politics and security. Our own analytical framework will therefore include politicisation as a third process besides threatification and riskification as the two possibilities of securitisation. While we thus agree with the need to discuss the different logics of politics and security, at the same time we will not return to the dichotomy of Buzan et al., but rather conceptualise the space between politics and security as yet another continuum. Consequently, we can see political arguments having both a politicising and a securitising effect.

Assessing normative implications

In contrast to the analytical implications of broadening the concept of securitisation, the literature has discussed the normative consequences extensively. In fact, criticism of the negative view of securitisation in the Copenhagen School has sparked a debate about the ambiguity of securitisation. Elbe (2006; 2009) has contributed pioneering work to this debate, highlighting the ambiguous effects of the securitisation of AIDS in both placing the issue on the agenda and opening it up to militarisation. In the context of climate change, Floyd has made similar claims, and has tried to develop the idea of a 'just securitisation theory' by elaborating the conditions under which securitisation can be seen as normatively positive through a deduction from general ethical principles (Floyd 2011). The problem with her approach is that it ties 'just' securitisation to the 'objective' existence of an existential threat. The whole point of the Copenhagen School, in contrast, was to say that the nature of such a threat is at least in part dependent on its discursive representation. Moreover, her further criteria of the moral legitimacy of the referent object and the appropriateness of security measures rely on standards that can only be determined outside her framework. In an earlier piece, Floyd (2007b) makes such an evaluation dependent on the assessment of alternative representations and asks rhetorically: 'would the US environment and by extension the American people be better off after a process of desecuritisation of the environment?' (Floyd 2007b: 347).

We engage in this debate by following McDonald (2013) who, as we do, argues in favour of differentiating between various securitisations of climate change and assessing their political implications against normative standards from a particular standpoint. Apart from securitisation not only closing down the political debate but potentially also placing new issues on the political agenda, it therefore becomes necessary to discuss securitisations normatively on their own merit in terms of the consequences that they have for policy (Floyd 2007a). Securitisation is therefore not good or bad in and of itself, but it has ambivalent effects on the political debate. We can assess its implications normatively, but only against standards that will always come from a particular ethical standpoint. Developing this argument in Chapter 2, we will thus also have to make clear where our standpoint is in relation to combatting climate change, and acknowledge that other points of view may be possible.

Providing empirical analysis

Apart from these broader theoretical insights, we also see a major contribution of our work, as we have already argued, in a detailed, systematic and comparative analysis of climate securitisation processes. Even though the concept of securitisation implies such an empirical analysis, Buzan and Wæver as the main contributors of the Copenhagen School have stuck to theoretical discussions or analysed securitisations on a very abstract, global level. As a detailed analysis of securitisation moves is not possible on such a scale, they resort in their main empirical work *Regions and Powers* (Buzan and Wæver 2003) to using actual security measures as a proxy indicator for successful securitisation. They do so even if the actual implementation of such measures is not a prerequisite for securitisation according to their own argumentation (Buzan *et al.* 1998: 25). We thus suggest that more detailed empirical studies of security discourses are necessary, not least because it is only in such analyses set in specific contexts that we can properly discuss the conditions for and political effects of securitisation and thus add an empirical basis to the debates summarised above.

In the field of climate security, a few empirical studies do exist. Above all, Floyd has based her theoretical and normative reflections on an extensive analysis of environmental security discourses and policy in the US (Floyd 2010), which includes climate change as a major issue. We will draw on her work when providing our own analysis of the US case, as we will naturally draw on other secondary literature that discusses our other cases. Yet so far, this literature is highly uneven with a heavy focus on the US, and it lacks a systematic comparative dimension. It is only through comparison, however, that we can highlight the specific conditions and implications of securitisation, or point to similarities across national boundaries.

Most other empirical work on climate security discourses has focused on the global level. Trombetta (2008) traces such discourses within the United Nations (UN) and the European Union (EU), but her work is also representative of other pieces in that its actual empirical basis is rather cursory, and the analysis does not go into much detail when it comes to individual securitising moves and their development. We have deliberately excluded the global level as our empirical focus. Our interest is the reconstruction of political debates as they still predominantly unfold within states. If our analysis were to show that global actors were able to influence these debates, we would consider this an important finding, and perhaps climate security debates are increasingly intermeshed. As we shall see, there certainly is some influence of global actors, and the UNFCCC or the International Panel on Climate Change serve as frequent points of reference, as do international NGOs or organisations such as the World Bank. Yet our analysis will also show that national debates have evolved in very different ways, and that purposive attempts to influence them from outside have not always been successful.

The structure of the book

To prepare such an analysis, Chapter 2 will expand our own theoretical and methodological approach, based on the review of the literature we have just provided. We outline our distinction between politicisation on the one hand and threatification and riskification as two sides of securitisation on the other. We then develop a six-fold categorisation of climate security discourses along the dimensions of referent object and securitisation form before outlining how we trace these discourses and their development in our four cases. We conclude this chapter with a reflection on the possibilities of normatively assessing securitisations. The chapters that follow present our case studies, beginning in Chapter 3 with the US, followed by Germany (Chapter 4), Mexico (Chapter 5) and Turkey (Chapter 6). Each of these chapters will begin with a general overview of the development of climate policies in the respective case. We then record the different climate security discourses that we have found before establishing which of these has been dominant. This is followed by an outline of the main actors involved in the securitisation of climate change and how they have influenced each other, a discussion of the policies legitimised by these securitisations, and an analysis of the contextual factors in which securitising actors – our 'discursive entrepreneurs' – operate. These empirical findings will then allow us to draw comparative conclusions on the emergence of particular forms of climate securitisation in Chapter 7, and to assess the political implications of climate security discourses across cases. In Chapter 8, we will then return to the themes identified in this introduction and reflect on the merits and limitations of our work.

2
ANALYSING CLIMATE SECURITY DISCOURSES[1]

How do we analyse the climate security discourses in our four case studies? In this chapter, we outline our theoretical and methodological framework, and elaborate on the arguments that we have summarised in Chapter 1. At the heart of our approach is a two-dimensional conceptual matrix, which allows us to identify different forms of climate securitisation. On one dimension, the matrix distinguishes between threatification and riskification as two forms of securitisation. We develop this distinction, and relate securitisation to politicisation, in the first section of this chapter. On the other dimension, the matrix differentiates between three different levels of referent objects. Here, we systematise the existing literature, leading to our conceptual scheme with six climate security categories in the second section. We then discuss a number of potential conditions that may influence the development of climate security debates. In particular, we identify possible structural factors and define and discuss our conception of discursive entrepreneurs. In the last section of this chapter, we locate our normative standpoint and discuss the problem of normatively assessing climate securitisation.

Securitisation as threatification and riskification

As we have outlined in the introductory chapter, the Copenhagen School's conceptualisation of security may be too narrow if applied to non-traditional security sectors such as the environment. In particular, scholars have pointed to the increased importance of risk as a security category and have questioned the neat boundary between normal politics and security in the Copenhagen School's dichotomous treatment of the two (Bigo 2008; Trombetta 2011; Oels and von Lucke 2015; Corry 2012). But how exactly does this change the field of security? What is the relationship between risk and security? Do the languages of risk and security differ in their effects on political decision-making? These questions are not new to the literature, but they are still somewhat marginal to the debate and in our view have not been answered comprehensively and consistently enough (see Buzan and Hansen 2009: 217). In the following, we argue in favour of a re-conceptualisation of politics, security and risk, which sees risk as a sub-category of security and re-labels the Copenhagen School's concept of securitisation as 'threatification', and thus only as a sub-set of different forms of securitisation. While we acknowledge that risk also invokes threats, threatification increases the urgency and immediate existentiality of those threats. It therefore produces the extreme threats of the Copenhagen School's narrow securitisation process, which we summarise under the label of Danger. Politics, Danger and Risk thus become the poles of a triangle in which political (in a broad sense) debates unfold. Issues can be 'threatified' by articulating them in ways that move them towards the Danger pole, or 'riskified' by coming closer to the Risk pole. They can also be 'politicised' by increasing their political relevance without reference to a threat, or 'desecuritised' and thus 're-politicised' by weakening their invocation of security in either form.

Our argument centres on the idea that invocations of risk or danger are intimately related in that they both invoke threats in order to legitimise policies. Yet as we have just noted and as we elaborate below, threats of risk are less urgent and thus seem weaker than those of danger, even if they are also potentially existential. This allows us to develop a variety of different securitisations, and to argue that rather than distinct categories, we are dealing with spectrums of articulations. Yet we insist that both riskification and threatification (which in practice we hardly ever see in their ideal-type form) change the nature of politics by transforming the rules of the debate and legitimising policies that would otherwise not have been considered legitimate. Politically, perhaps the most interesting question that arises concerns the effects of articulations that combine risk and danger, such as in the invocation of an apocalypse in climate security debates (Methmann and Rothe 2012). Because of the parallel invocation of danger and risk, the political impact of such an articulation may be particularly strong as it legitimises extraordinary measures to counter the immediate threats, while it also strives to prolong these measures into the infinite future to cope with the remaining risks.

In developing this framework of politics, risk and danger, our first argumentative step is to locate risk and danger in the same discursive formation of security. While we acknowledge the differences between riskification and threatification (see below), we still think that there are substantial arguments weighing in favour of treating them as closely related.

First, as we have already argued in the introduction, the specific conceptualisation of risk that we are interested in developed within security debates. As such, risk emerged in security strategies and as a reference point of security policy pamphlets and speeches from about the turn of the millennium. It is thus no surprise that there is a significant academic debate about risk that unfolds in security journals such as *Security Dialogue* (C.A.S.E. Collective 2006; Goede 2008; Guzzini 2011; Huysmans 2011; Lobo-Guerrero 2007; Methmann and Rothe 2012). Whatever its origins, risk is therefore part of a broader institutionalised discursive setting that runs with the label 'security' (see Buzan and Hansen 2009: 217). Treating the two as completely separate concepts runs counter to this historical emergence.

Yet there are also less formal and more substantive reasons for our choice of seeing the two as closely related. The core feature of articulations of both danger and risk is that they invoke a certain threat. As we have already seen, in the traditional understanding of security, the existential threats invoked are more imminent and concrete than in risk, but nonetheless, neither danger nor risk make sense without this invocation of a certain degree of threat. We thus suggest treating articulations of risk and danger as two different instances of securitisation. Given the many different concepts that crowd the field already, it may not make sense to introduce yet another one. Yet we need a label for what we see as a distinct form of securitisation, and threatification leading to danger captures the core aspect of the Copenhagen School's 'grammar' of security, the invocation of an existential threat.

A basic and widespread distinction between riskification and threatification thus relies on the level of threat concretisation. The threats invoked in risk are more diffuse than the existential threat of threatification as a narrow form of securitisation in at least three respects. First, the threats themselves are more diffuse. They do not emanate from a clearly identifiable enemy such as the United States or the Soviet Union; they are difficult to grasp and locate. In relation to climate change, the threats of risk are also characterised by structural changes rather than a static Other. Thus, a familiar strategy of moving risk into the realm of danger is the personification of threat – attaching a face to migration or terrorism makes threats more concrete and thus changes the dynamic of securitisation (Gaufman 2015). Second, the referent object of risk is more diffuse than the referent object of danger. While risk articulations tend to also propose a referent object (a risk for individuals, a risk for the nation, a risk for coastal regions), it is much more difficult to identify such a referent clearly. Thus, even if a risk articulation constructs a specific referent object (such as coastal land or the people inhabiting small islands), this does not mean that the threat does not apply to others as well. Not least because of the diffuse nature of the threat, its referent object is also more diffuse. Third, the threat of risk is more diffuse in relation to its time horizon. Articulations of danger present threats as imminent in the sense that they may extinguish the referent object at any time. In risk articulations, the threat is more distant in the future and, because of its processual character, does not have a clear time limit. This does not mean that there is no urgency: even if, or perhaps rather because we do not know about the future, we need to prepare now.

These aspects of the diffuse character of threat in risk articulations are related to a different relationship between the referent object and the threat. Articulations of danger represent the threat as independent of the referent object: we have to face the security threat and defend ourselves. In risk terms, following Beck, referent object and threat cannot be neatly separated. We are implicated in producing the threat. As Wæver (Wæver 2004: 63), referring to Niklas Luhmann, notes, 'more and more dangers are the product of our own actions, and fewer and fewer attributable to forces completely external to ourselves – thus threats become risks'. While Wæver thus underscores our point, we differ from him in that we would still see the articulation of risk as an invocation of threat – however, a different form of threat than in danger. The implication of the referent object is also evident in that we have to take risks. Ultimately, this also means that we may be able to influence the severity of the threat through our own behaviour.

As a consequence, the extraordinary measures legitimised through threatification and riskification differ as well. Security measures in a 'danger mode' are, in principle, designed to eliminate the existential threat that poses the danger. They may not actually be able to eliminate the threat, but they should move it out of the danger zone. Risk measures, in contrast, presume that the threat will affect us to some degree whatever we do, and they try to minimise the effect so that it becomes bearable and not existential. They are therefore much more calculating in their approach, and it is for these calculations that a different kind of technical expertise is needed in comparison to the security strategist. This does not imply that risk measures are less extraordinary – the resilience measures limiting the impact of climate change or terrorism through policies of surveillance and preparedness are as radical in their legitimisation as the security measures of war or building walls and fences.

Articulations of danger and risk often use specific concepts and words, which are therefore typical for these discourses. Some of them we have collated in Table 2.1. We do not intend this to be a coding scheme. Nonetheless, use of these terms can often be a first indication of the type of climate security discourse we find.

How do danger and risk, and the associated strategies of threatification and riskification, relate to politics? By invoking threats, articulations of risk and danger both provide politics with the need to do something to avoid or counter the threat. If, following the Copenhagen School, we understand politics in a Habermasian sense to be the sphere of deliberation, the invocation of threat thus tries to move an issue beyond free deliberation and constrain the policy options available, focusing on and no longer questioning the threat put forward.

We accept that this is an idealised notion of politics and that it is difficult to imagine political debates without some invocations of risk and danger. Yet it is important to remember that the problem lies not with individual moves but with

TABLE 2.1 Important keywords distinguishing between the danger and risk dimension

Danger	Risk
Threat, security, short term, immediately, urgent, existential, extraordinary, danger, direct, certain, clear-cut, clear, inevitable, emergency, emergency measures, survival, defence, destruction, eradicate	Long term, risk, risk management, resilience, probability, risk groups, risk areas, uncertainty, contingency, statistics, diffuse, unclear, indirect, scenario planning, precautionary principle, precaution, risk reduction, preparedness, manageable

Source: Revised from von Lucke et al. 2014b: 863.

the widespread acceptance of securitisation. It is this acceptance, or what we may call hegemony, of security that closes off the debate. In other words: Yes, political debates are always also characterised by threatifying and riskifying moves, but these are only really an issue when they are no longer contested and if policies are being pushed through on their back that would otherwise not have seemed legitimate.

We also acknowledge that securitisation may be necessary to place an issue on the political agenda. As such, the invocation of threat may not be a closing but an opening move; it broadens rather than constrains the political debate. Without such an invocation of threat, the issue may simply not be debated at all (Floyd 2013; Trombetta 2011). The solution to this old problem of the securitisation debate is that its classic formulation stresses only one element of securitisation (the invocation of threat) and not the process of legitimising policies. Thus, following Roe (2008a) and Balzacq (2011), we may distinguish between different phases of securitisation. The placing of an issue on the political agenda is a first phase that is compatible with or even a prerequisite for our understanding of politics. This becomes more problematic in the light of deliberation if the nature of the threat can no longer be debated (i.e. if it has become an unquestionable truth). In a final stage, securitisation leads to the adoption of policies that would have otherwise not been legitimate. Arguments against these policies are ridiculed, marginalised or even penalised. It is in this sense that we can speak of emergency measures, although based on our reasoning, we prefer the label 'extraordinary measures'.

In relation to climate change, such extraordinary measures can be adaptation and mitigation strategies. They may combat either danger or risk – it depends. If adaptation means calculating how far we can go to increase the resilience of populations knowing the threat will materialise, it is a response to risk. If adaptation means preparing to defend us against the threat and keep it out, for instance by changing military strategies to guard against migration flows or spillover of water conflicts, it is combatting danger. If mitigation strategies are designed to eliminate the threat at all cost, they are strategies of danger – it is such strategies of climate emergency overriding all other concerns that the Copenhagen School found wanting in their analysis of environmental security on a global level. If mitigation, however, is to decrease the effects of the threat by calculated measures (such as emissions trading regimes), it is rather a risk strategy. In any of these cases, the measures taken would not have been legitimate, or at least not have come about in the same timeframe or on the same scale, without an effective discourse of securitisation. After all, even an emissions trading scheme constrains the freedom of private as well as public actors and as such needs to be legitimised as a measure that marginalises other concerns.

The preceding discussion has highlighted that we do not see politics, danger and risk as distinct categories. Instead, they are ideal types that operate as poles in a space of three continua. The 'sphere of danger' cannot easily be separated from either risk or politics other than for hermeneutic purposes. Instead, political articulations move issues in this space through politicisation or securitisation in the forms of threatification or riskification. As we have argued, some degree of threatification is indeed necessary to do politics at all; others move an issue slowly beyond deliberation until political debate is no longer possible. Yet hardly ever do we have a situation in which the entire 'audience' accepts a threat and the policies legitimised. Even at the height of the Cold War (the foil against which Wæver developed the concept of securitisation), there was contestation. In fact, this is an inherent problem of any empirical application of securitisation – it is very difficult to establish when an issue is securitised, and Buzan and Wæver's trick in *Regions and Powers* (2003) to take security measures as indications of successful securitisation runs against the whole gist of their theoretical framework, in the centre of which are discursive processes, and in which the actual taking of emergency measures is not a necessary requirement for successful securitisation.

Thus, we propose that the analytical and normative importance of the framework of securitisation is to observe gradual moves on the continuum between politics on the one hand and risk and danger as two variations of threat invocation on the other. In addition, there is also a continuum between risk and danger. Just as in the differentiation between security and politics, these are not separate categories. An issue may be moved from risk to danger, or from danger to risk. In addition, we expect most threats to be framed in some combination of the languages of risk and danger. To once more take the example of the Cold War, securitisations of the East or West always had an element of risk, even if the language of danger prevailed.

Our discussion so far has distinguished between politics, risk and danger but has emphasised that these are ideal types, and that we would expect to find most articulations located in a field somewhere between these poles. We have argued that articulations can move issues from politics to danger or risk and vice versa, but also from risk to danger and back. At the same time, we have argued that there is a point at which issues can no longer be seen as being debated in a deliberate form of politics because they have moved too far down the stages of threatification, while some degree of threatification may be necessary for placing issues on the political agenda in the first instance. Thus, as will become apparent in some of our empirical cases, and in particular the Mexican case, it is to a certain degree possible to politicise and securitise issues at the same time to generate attention and to legitimise policies. Only if the process moves too far in the direction of danger or risk does the debate get successively closed down and politicisation and securitsation cease to be compatible.

Drawing on these arguments, we arrive at a map of the politics/risk/danger space, which we depict in Figure 2.1. The figure shows a triangle formed by the three ideal types of politics, risk and danger. We distinguish movement along the axes of this triangle as securitisation 1 (threatification as a move from politics towards danger), securitisation 2 (riskification as a move from politics towards risk), and a danger–risk oscillation between the two poles of security. For sake of simplicity, Figure 2.1 does not include politicisation as the reverse move on the first two axes. This does not mean that such forms of desecuritisation in terms of de-riskification and de-threatification do not exist, although as we are primarily interested in climate security discourses, our main focus in this book is on the articulations that move issues in the other direction. At first sight, the figure also

Analysing climate security discourses   19

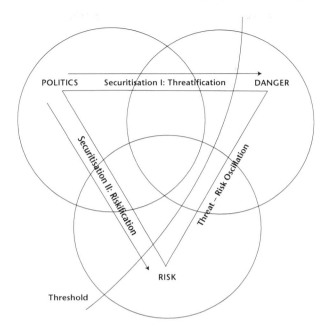

FIGURE 2.1 The space of politics and security

seems to exclude the agenda-setting function of securitisation that contributes to politicisation in the first instance. Yet as soon as there are securitising moves that try to place an issue on the political agenda, we witness a weak form of politicisation. On the continuum between politics and security, politicisation and securitisation thus are not incompatible, and may even reinforce each other, until they reach a threshold beyond which security pushes politics out.

We have drawn same-size circles around each of these poles to indicate these tentative borders where issues leave one realm and move into another. Importantly, these circles overlap to emphasise that we need to think of these borders not as fixed but as zones of transition, and that articulations will often mix risk and danger. Our 'threshold' is an indication of where issues become successfully securitised and are moved out of the sphere of politics in a narrow, deliberative understanding. Again, we want to understand this border as a tentative rather than a hard one. In both articulations of risk and danger, there is a moment when extraordinary measures cannot be questioned any more without the question being ridiculed. It is that moment that marks the border. It is important to emphasise that 'extraordinary' in our understanding does not necessarily mean militaristic or undemocratic but merely a policy that attaches a certain urgency to the issue and would have not been legitimate without a securitisation that changed reality through the successful articulation of danger or risk. In empirical terms, we cannot determine this border in an absolute way. Yet this does not mean that it does not exist – issues will at some point have been moved out of the political debate, however gradually. Thus, despite our widening of the notion of securitisation, we would still want to maintain that our two forms of securitisations change the nature of political decision-making. In contrast to the Copenhagen School, we would see this as a gradual movement, but in line with the Copenhagen School, we would argue that there is a moment when an issue has indeed left the normal political debate.

A two-dimensional matrix

The distinction between two forms of securitisation is only one dimension along which we can distinguish climate security discourses. As we have already outlined in the Introduction, the literature has put forward a number of different referent objects which distinguish different forms of climate securitisation (Barnett 2001; Dalby 1992b; 2002; Pirages 1991; 2005). Among these are environmental security and environmental conflict in Detraz and Betsill (2009), or national, human, international and ecological security in McDonald (2013).

Our second dimension thus follows a core distinction of climate security discourses that builds on the existing literature. Systematising the existing classifications, we suggest that the main distinguishing criterion is the level of the referent object. In the environmental conflict discourse, Detraz and Betsill conceptualise the state as the main referent object, although articulations of this discourse may also refer to other group entities. What is at stake here is the defence of a particular territorial order. In that sense, McDonald's international security discourse is merely an extension of this discourse, as McDonald himself notes (2013: 44, 47–48). In contrast, the environmental security discourse, due to its links with human security, focuses on the individual or on a global society of individuals as referent objects, and thus is in line with McDonald's human security discourse. Finally, in the ecological security discourse with its cosmological and holistic outlook, it is the planetary ecosystem or the biosphere as a whole that is threatened. Thus, we conceptualise this dimension as consisting of three levels on which referent objects are situated: territorial, individual, and planetary.

The two dimensions developed in the previous section lead us to a typology of six climate security discourses summarised in Table 2.2, in which we also provide an illustrative example of a typical speech act.

Drawing on the literature on framing (Benford and Snow 2000), we argue that articulations in each of these six discourses have to address two constitutive questions. First, a diagnostic one that gives a distinct description of the problem at stake and the threat involved; and second, a prognostic one that proposes a specific solution, i.e. a measure to counter the threat. Therefore these discourses can be expected to have very different impacts on political processes and the resulting policies (Stripple 2012: 189). Taken together, our framework allows systematic empirical comparisons of climate security discourses to distinguish different securitisations of climate change in political debates between and across countries, to trace these in political processes and to assess their policy implications.

Let us now elaborate on each discourse in more detail.

TABLE 2.2 A typology of climate security discourses

Level of referent object	Logic of securitisation	
	Threatification	*Riskification*
Territorial Speech act example	Territorial danger Climate change as triggering and increasing violent conflict that endangers state security	Territorial risk Climate change as long-term risk for states located in risk areas
Individual Speech act example	Individual danger Climate change as endangering daily food and water supplies	Individual risk Climate change as increasing the risk of periodic flooding
Planetary Speech act example	Planetary danger Climate change as destroying the ecosystem	Planetary risk Climate change as creating ecological imbalances with unforeseeable consequences

Source: Adapted from von Lucke et al. 2014b: 864.

Territorial danger

Territorial danger resembles the 'neo-Malthusian' (Hartmann 2010: 234) climate-conflict discourse (Homer-Dixon 1991; 1994; Ross 2004; Cudworth and Hobden 2010). At the diagnostic level it focuses on national security conceptions (Nordas and Gleditsch 2007: 635) with the state or a geographical region as the referent object. Concretely, it proposes the possibility of violent conflict in the face of limited and degrading resources due to climatic changes. On the territorial level, the actual threat is neither climate change as such nor its direct physical effects, but rather the indirect socio-economic effects on social orders. Concerning the prognostic level, this discourse focuses on often extraordinary short term actions to counter these socio-economic problems and often focuses on immediate adaptation measures in the military sector instead of long-term mitigation efforts. The actual measures can be political as well as military interventions in countries and regions that face climate-induced conflicts or instability, in order to reinstate statehood and prevent conflicts from spiralling out of control and becoming a threat to industrialised countries, for example through large-scale migration movements or terrorism. Articulations of this discourse are widespread among actors that focus on security and defence policy, and particularly in the United States.

Territorial risk

At the diagnostic level, the territorial risk discourse focuses on the probability of climate-induced conflicts or instability in certain risk areas as identified by statistical risk assessments and scenario planning schemes, requiring contingency planning for events that seem unlikely but may entail catastrophic consequences (Briggs 2012:

1054, 1056). Just as in the territorial danger discourse, adaptation measures and military actors play a decisive role at the prognostic level. Yet here the focus lies more on transforming the referent object and on a general readiness of the respective actors and the enhancement of resilience to climate change effects in case the risk turns into reality. Because constructing climate change in terms of risk entails longer time horizons than the direct identification of threats, this discourse leaves more time for the implementation of counter-measures – for example resilience building – and acknowledges the possibility of preventing the worst outcomes, i.e. of lowering the risk to a tolerable level for certain states if appropriate actions are taken (Smith and Vivekananda 2007: 8, 38). We find this discourse particularly widespread in military planning documents, where it is often used to substantiate and complement territorial danger arguments with a long-term dimension or in cases where planners have incomplete information about the threat.

Individual danger

The individual danger discourse builds on the concept of human security and prioritises the individual or human communities not tied to particular states (Trombetta 2008). This discourse is similar to what Detriz and Betsill (2009: 306) have called 'environmental security', McDonald (2013: 49) 'human security' and Adger (2006; see also Eakin and Luers 2006; Vogel and O'Brien 2004) 'human vulnerability'. On the diagnostic level, it highlights the vulnerability of individuals and groups to a changing environment, and the direct implications for the everyday life of human beings of factors such as decreasing crop yields, water scarcity, disasters and the spread of vector-borne diseases. In the prognostic dimension, articulations of individual danger emphasise strategies aimed at the reduction or, better, complete elimination of the direct threat or vulnerability of individuals to climatic effects, for instance through adaptation measures by increasing development aid, providing technical support in building dams or organising the relocation of threatened populations (O'Brien et al. 2007: 78–79). We find that this discourse is relatively widespread in reports and debates of the United Nations General Assembly (UNGA 2009a; 2009b) and Security Council (UNSC 2007a; 2011a) and is often preferred over national security conceptions by developing countries because of the rather favourable image associated with human security. Furthermore, articulations from NGOs or other actors in the development sector often invoke individual danger.

Individual risk

The individual risk discourse does not directly identify specific individuals or communities as referent objects a priori, but relies on risk assessment to generate statistically certain groups that are seen to be especially at risk (Elbe 2009). It thus focuses on the probability of a diverse set of climatic effects in certain risk areas for particular risk groups, and accepts a general level of uncertainty concerning the scope and regional impact of these effects. The prognostic focus lies on long-term preventive strategies to mitigate climate change (Detraz and Betsill 2009: 308; Trombetta 2008: 594) and on increasing the coping capacity and resilience of individuals and communities. In contrast to the individual danger discourse, the focus is more on the referent object itself and on reducing the 'contextual' vulnerability of communities, which includes strengthening the society or community as a whole, thus increasing its general resilience to possibly harmful impacts (Vogel and O'Brien 2004: 78–79). Another strategy is the provision of insurance schemes for populations/individuals and areas that are at risk of being hit by adverse climatic effects (Stripple 2012: 189). All these strategies do not aim at entirely eliminating the threats but rather at reducing the risk to a tolerable level. In the insurance industry as well as in IPCC documents, climate change insurance schemes already play an important role (Stripple 2012: 190; Jagers et al. 2004; Höppe 2008). In general, we find this discourse in similar arenas to those of the individual danger discourse, yet as discussed, it constitutes a less direct approach to the problems and interferes less with the normal political handling of the problem.

Planetary danger

The planetary danger discourse is at least partly a critical response to linking national security with the environment in the territorial security discourse (Deudney 1990) and new conceptions of environmental security – also labelled complex ecology – as put forward by Cudworth and Hobden (2010), Pirages (2013), Barnett (2001) or Dalby (1992a; 1992b; 2009; 2013). At the diagnostic level it focuses on the embeddedness of human beings in the global ecosystem and the symbiotic nature of this co-existence (Cudworth and Hobden 2010: 8), as well as on the strong interdependencies of human activity with the environment – in positive (conservation, mitigation measures) as well as negative (economic activity that destroys, over-uses or pollutes the environment, e.g. the global climatic system) ways. Consequently, it considers the health of the environment (Bertell 2001) and an intact biodiversity as important goods as such, i.e. as threatened referent object. The actual threats at the planetary level are dangerously high CO_2 levels, as well as human activity or certain practices that lead to changes in the atmosphere. On the prognostic level this discourse proposes concrete, immediate and relatively drastic measures to stop human activity that has the potential to harm the planetary security, such as global greenhouse gas (GHG) production. Tangible examples could be a global GHG moratorium or tax to secure the conservation of the ecosystem and atmospheric stability, as well as concrete initiatives to conserve certain ecosystems, species or regions (Brauch 2009a; 2009b). The planetary security discourse is often used by environmental activists (Greenpeace n.d.) and discussed at climate summits and in IPCC reports.

Planetary risk

In the planetary risk discourse, the diagnostic level highlights long-term risks for the well-being of the global ecosystem that are statistically identified. Following the older limits-to-growth debate (Meadows and Meadows 1972; UN World Commission on Environment and Development 1987), articulations of this discourse identify unsustainable economic activity, as well as a growth-centred and (fossil) resource-based capitalist system as core problems putting the whole planet at risk. At the prognostic level, the restructuration of risk-creating activities on a planetary scale is being highlighted, such as an adaptation of the capitalist economic system, a move to more sustainable ways of economic activity, hence the enhancement of planetary resilience and a move to the precautionary principle. The goal is to prevent possibly devastating and not exactly known consequences of climate change from becoming concrete threats. Because of the conceptualisation in terms of risk, the measures do not have to be as extreme and immediate as in the planetary danger discourse; likewise the goal is not a complete eradication of the threat, but management of the risk to keep it at a tolerable level. Concrete measures could be the fostering of energy efficiency or renewable (green) energy sources, for example through tax-based incentive schemes. This discourse is discussed predominantly by scientists and environmental activists and organisations as a normative blueprint, for instance by the IPCC (2012).

The development of climate security discourses

Analysing climate security discourses and charting their development over time is an essential part of our comparative endeavour. Yet our objective is also to link such discourses to policy, and to understand the factors that influence the success or failure of securitising moves (i.e. the degree of success), as well the prevalence of specific security discourses. This requires some further theoretical reflection.

First, we need to distinguish between discourse and policy. This is not as straightforward as it may sound. In fact, one of the problems of using discourse for the explanation of policy is that policy is part of and not separate from discourse (Diez 2001: 13). Authors from the Paris School have thus rightfully reminded securitisation researchers that policies can themselves securitise and are not simply the effect of securitisation (Salter 2011: 118). Nonetheless, we may distinguish between different types of securitisation that take place at different stages and in different institutional realms of the securitisation process.

Climate security discourses and policy

A first relevant distinction in this respect is the difference between a broader societal security discourse and the security discourse within formal political institutions such as parliaments or governments. Security discourses will always transcend these institutional boundaries. Yet at the same time, the prevalence of climate security discourses within them may be different. The fact that researchers such as Elbe (2006; 2009) and Floyd (2007b; 2013) have pointed to the politicising functions of securitisation as agenda-setting supports this argument. Their idea, underpinning our main research interest, is that securitising moves predominantly come from civil society actors pressuring formal political actors to take up their claims and pursue climate policies. We can thus speak of a first kind of policy impact that changes the way in which parliamentarians and government officials debate policies. Such debates may then have a reinforcing impact on securitisation. As our case studies show, this is the path securitisation has taken in Germany and the US, whereas the failure of securitising moves, especially in Turkey, is at least in part a consequence of lacking a civil society structure that would have been able to carry out successful climate securitisation. In contrast, the German case showcases discourse coalitions across sectors and how symbiotic the relationship between governmental and non-governmental actors can be. Yet it is important to remember that securitisation can work the other way round. In fact, in the Copenhagen School politicians are among the most influential securitising actors because of their position in society, which is one of the 'felicity conditions' for successful securitisation in Buzan et al. (1998: 31). Securitisation would then move from the policy world to society – although the fact that this is the main model of securitisation in the original Copenhagen School formulation further demonstrates its base in the military sector, where such a pathway is more likely than in an area such as climate change, which has not traditionally been on the policy agenda. Yet our Mexican case study shows that parliamentary debates may well play an important role in advancing individual risk discourses and thus securitise climate change – without, however, calling for military involvement.

A second distinction is then between the actual policy measures and the broader policy debate. This is of course what Buzan et al. and most of the securitisation literature focuses upon: the legitimisation of extraordinary means. Such means normally have a kind of force that goes beyond the illocutionary or perlocutionary forces of the speech act (Austin 1975). Above all, they either use physical or legal force to make actors do what they otherwise would not have done, to paraphrase Dahl's famous formulation of relational power (Dahl 1957: 203). 'Policy impact' in this second, narrower sense thus does not only transform the policy debate but changes such measures as such. To reiterate, this does not mean that such measures are not discursive in and of themselves, and thus they constitute securitising moves, too, and may further reinforce or undermine securitisation. Nonetheless, they differ from climate security articulations in the form of speech acts because of the force that is inherent in them.

Climate security articulations and discursive entrepreneurs

Discourses have a 'dual quality', a phrase that Wiener (2007; 2008: 37–58) coined in a similar way for norms. They are both 'structuring and constructed' (Wiener 2008: 38). Thus, we consider discourses both as a structure and as an ensemble of individual articulations, which, following Laclau and Mouffe (1985), we define as the drawing together of different discursive elements such as specific threats, referent objects and emergency policies in the classic Copenhagen School formulation of securitisation. In security discourses, articulations come in the form of securitising moves – following from our earlier discussion these can be speech acts but also other forms of actions, including policies.

Such securitising moves are performed by actors in specific institutional and discursive positions and contexts. The institutions and discourses that they operate in, and which have shaped them, constitute their position, with specific worldviews, norms and interests. At the same time, actors perform in a historically and culturally specific context of institutions and discourses that make some articulations more acceptable than others. In order to be successful, securitising moves thus have to be 'translatable' into such a context (Guzzini 2011; Stritzel 2011; Diez 2001: 26). Neither this nor the fact that actors speak from a particular, historically developed position means that institutions and discourses determine articulations. In reproducing discourse, articulations always also transform discourse – meaning is never fixed, but it also cannot be simply changed overnight, at least not under normal conditions (Diez 1999: 607). Securitising moves, by invoking threat and arguing for extraordinary measures, claim such extraordinary conditions. Yet because they are only claims, a large part of the audience must either have already accepted or be able to make sense of them within the discursive panorama available at the time. By audience, we do not mean an isolated audience that exists outside of the securitising discourses that address it. Rather we concur with several extensions of the Copenhagen School that there are different forms of audience (e.g. the public or the parliament) and different forms or degrees of audience consent (acceptance of the threat construction or acceptance of the extraordinary counter-measures) (Roe 2008a; Karafoulidis 2012; Léonard and Kaunert 2011). Yet, to account for the success of securitisation, instead of trying to identify the exact audience and searching for its consent, we focus on whether the debate within the national publics of our case studies has been transformed by the security framing, or whether securitisation has led to the effective legitimisation of concrete policies. We can thus be agnostic about the audience of a specific speech act and centre our attention on the changing nature of the political debate on an aggregate level.

Our research shows that some actors are much more influential with their securitising moves than other actors. We call them discursive entrepreneurs. In doing so, we draw on a large set of literature that has used similar terms. Most famously, Finnemore and Sikkink (1998) have coined the term 'norm entrepreneurs' for actors who push specific norms in the early stages of the emergence of a norm. These norm entrepreneurs 'attempt to convince a critical mass of states (norm leaders) to embrace new norms' (Finnemore and Sikkink 1998: 895). There are many similarities between such attempts and securitising moves: the articulation of events in a way that 'dramatizes them' (Finnemore and Sikkink 1998: 897); the need to convince others, which on the one hand relies on translation, yet on the other hand may sometimes require 'activists … to be explicitly "inappropriate"' (ibid.). As we have done in our elaboration of diagnostic and prognostic aspects of climate discourses, Finnemore and Sikkink also link their concept to the framing literature and see norm entrepreneurs as framing a particular issue through 'reinterpretation or renaming' (ibid.).

Nonetheless, we prefer the concept of discursive entrepreneurs for our purposes. We do so partly because we are not interested in the propagation of particular norms as such, but in the construction of particular representations that become dominant in the form of securitisation to legitimise particular policies. Our actors do not necessarily propagate merely a particular norm; they want their audience to see a particular issue in a different way – as a threat – and to take measures against that threat. Furthermore, we want to emphasise the discursively constructed positions from which these entrepreneurs speak, and which do not play a major role in the framework of Finnemore and Sikkink.

Léonard and Kaunert (2011: 68), following Kingdon (1984), liken securitising actors to 'policy entrepreneurs' who, 'having been waiting for a policy window to open ... seize the opportunity offered ... to propose, lobby for, and sell a specific policy proposal'. This, too, focuses too much on the creative agency of these actors, which misses the enabling and constraining context they work in, as well as on the actual policy promotion, which underestimates the diagnostic element of climate security discourses. We always need to de-centre such actors to account for the position from which they speak (Diez et al. 2011; Bode 2012; 2014).

Thus, we speak of 'discursive entrepreneurs' who articulate climate security from particular institutional and discursive positions to transform ('securitise') the climate change discourse and to advocate specific policy responses as extraordinary measures (Holzscheiter 2005: 742). At this point it is important to stress that some actors who articulate climate security do not only seek to transform climate policy but directly target security policy, e.g. they want the security sector to incorporate climate change as a threat. Others have termed this phenomenon the 'climatization' of the security sector (Oels 2012a). Such discursive entrepreneurs can be 'catalysts for change as they draw on and articulate the ideas of discursive communities' in which they are embedded (Schmidt 2008: 310). This concept of discursive entrepreneurs has been well captured by Langenohl (2008: 70) in relation to the reshaping of organisational orders. He defines them as actors who try 'publicly to legitimize or de-legitimize a certain institutional order ... but in attempting this they must refer to generalized understandings ... in society at large'.

As we will see, in our case studies individuals have played a particularly important role as discursive entrepreneurs (see also Bode 2012; 2014). Yet as the work of Holzscheiter illustrates, collective actors may also perform this role. In her case, these are NGOs, and these are important as securitising actors in the field of climate change as well. Beyond that, we encounter think tanks, which sometimes operate in a semi-official function advising governments, as well as research institutions and military actors operating in an advisory capacity. On the one hand, they form the civil society from which securitising moves regarding climate change often emerge. On the other hand, we should not see them as opposed to 'the state' (Tepe 2012, following Gramsci's notion of the 'integral state') – as pointed out above, discourses often transcend these borders. Furthermore, many of these actors are funded or even founded by the state or other political actors in the narrow sense.

Felicity conditions of successful securitisation

What makes securitising moves, and above all those of discursive entrepreneurs, successful? The literature, following Austin (1975), discusses this under the heading of the 'felicity conditions' of securitising moves. Buzan et al. (1998: 32–33) note internal and external factors. Internally, the degree to which the securitising move corresponds to the 'grammar' of securitisation is crucial. As we have extended this grammar, however, we would rather see this criterion simply as one of being consistent. More important for our purpose, the Copenhagen School authors list the 'social capital of the enunciator' and the degree to which a threat is 'generally held to be threatening' as core external conditions (Buzan *et al.* 1998: 33).

What Buzan et al. refer to as 'social capital', we have described as the institutional position of discursive entrepreneurs. In the original securitisation formulation, such actors 'must be in a position of authority, although this should not be defined as official authority' (ibid.). As the literature has pointed out, it is unfortunate that Buzan et al. nonetheless in their work focus on actors with such official authority. As our case studies will show, in climate security actors who have crossed the border between official politics and political advocacy, or those who have a strong scientific reputation yet are also able to 'sell' their research to a wider audience, are particularly influential. 'Authority' thus, following Bourdieu (1986), includes official position as much as social capital generated from 'personal and social relations', symbolic capital in the form of 'appreciation, esteem, status, prestige, legitimacy' as well as the person's habitus (as a way of acting in public) and cultural capital acquired through socialisation (Bode 2012: 54–56).

The slightly tautological formulation that securitising moves are more likely to be successful if the audience already accepts the threats they invoke, we resolve as an issue of translatability. Stritzel (2011) sees securitising moves themselves as acts of translation that transport issues because in different discursive contexts, different constructions of meaning may prevail. Thus we cannot assume, for instance, that even European societies share concepts such as 'state' and 'nation' (Wæver 1996; Balzacq *et al.* 2015; Wæver 2002). Securitising moves therefore always encounter a specific context, which we assume to be above all a national context if they are articulated in order to change national policies. The art of the discursive entrepreneur in climate security discourses is then to perform such a translation so that the threat and referent object on the diagnostic, and the extraordinary policy measure on the prognostic side of the articulation are acceptable to at least a large segment of the public. However, this art is necessarily constrained by the boundaries set by the prevailing meanings in societal discourse. The discursive entrepreneur may thus be as creative as possible – certain articulations of climate change may simply not be translatable into specific national contexts. We may see the context in which securitising actors operate thus as 'interactive' (Balzacq 2005: 179). Contexts are neither completely constraining, as they leave room for the securitising actor to change them, nor are they entirely unimportant, as they do set limits to what can be said at a given moment in time.

Analysing securitisation

Following these theoretical considerations, our first task in the empirical chapters to follow is to reconstruct climate security discourses in our four case studies, their status in the overall debate and their development over time. We have done so by using Table 2.2 as a guide to analysing a variety of documents. These included civil society reports on climate change, parliamentary debates, government statements, other speeches by politicians that the public debate often refers to, as well as newspaper articles to test and expand our findings. Each chapter will provide more details on the sources used and may deviate from this structure to a certain extent, as there are some variations in the national context that we had to take into account.

In order to establish a sense of which discourses prevailed in certain documents (for example think tank or NGO reports and parliamentary debates), we used the frequency of articulations as well as their position in the documents (for instance, do they appear in the title, executive summary, conclusion or merely somewhere in the middle of the text?) and the intensity of the articulation as an indicator (for instance articulations may use alarmist and dramatic vocabulary or more cautious and neutral terms in either of our six discourses). To the extent that policy measures had been taken, we used them as well to conclude that the specific securitising moves that had legitimised them must have been successful. While this follows Buzan et al. (1998; 2003), we want to emphasise once more that the actual implementation of extraordinary measures (that we understand in a broader sense), while clearly indicating successful securitisation, is not a necessary condition for the latter. While it may seem problematic to come to assessments about dominant discourses in the absence of such measures, we found that most often it was quite clear which discourses were the most widespread ones, even without having to resort to a formal quantitative analysis by counting signal words. In our empirical chapters we will make these findings as plausible as possible.

To reconstruct the broader debate, linkages between actors, the motivation to use securitising articulations, and to assess the relative importance of certain discursive entrepreneurs, we conducted semi-structured interviews in each country. The interviews took place between April and June 2014 in Mexico and the US (complemented with some interviews in London in November 2014) and between April and September 2014 in Germany and Turkey, complemented with some additional selective interviews in 2015. In each country we conducted about twenty interviews. We talked to representatives of the most influential actors in the climate security debates (NGOs, think tanks, scientists) as well as to government officials. We identified our interview partners based on the secondary literature followed by a snowball systems once we were in the countries. Each interview lasted between 30 and 90 minutes, and if requested we conducted them on the basis of anonymity. As the interviews were not part of our formal discourse analysis but were supposed to generate additional background insights, we did not record them but produced detailed interview logs to register the information.

In combination with interviews we conducted in our cases, these documents allowed us also to identify the main actors pursuing securitising moves, and thus our discursive entrepreneurs. In our chapters, we reconstruct the history and standing of these entrepreneurs in order to understand how they were able to influence climate security debates in such a decisive way. Likewise, we locate them and the broader discourses they articulated in the wider institutional and discursive context of the case at the respective point in time to show the translatability of their articulations. To visualise their embeddedness in a broader network, we performed a network analysis for each chapter, mapping references of climate security articulations to each other, to demonstrate the position of actors. In this network citation analysis we proceeded as follows. Based on our own research, we first assembled a list of the most relevant actors and documents for the climate security debate in each country (plus some additional actors that were important for the global debate). On average, we included sixty actors in each case and roughly the same number of documents. However, since we focused on the most relevant documents, some actors contributed several documents to the analysis while others contributed none. Although this procedure certainly creates a bias and may overestimate the influence of certain actors, we think it is justified because it mirrors their importance for the debate. Second, we counted which actors were mentioned by whom and how often. We differentiated between different forms of citation, for example in the acknowledgements, in the text, in the recommendations and in the bibliography. In this step, we also grouped some actors together, for instance different UN organisations were grouped under 'UN'. Furthermore, if one document was authored by several actors, each author received an 'out degree' entry if this document cited someone else or an 'in degree' entry if the document itself was cited. Third, we analysed the resulting data with the network analysis program Visone to produce a graph that visualises who cited whom and how often (indicated by the size of the nodes – arranged in the 'stress minimisation' mode – and direction and size of the links between them). For reasons of clarity, we only included the most relevant actors in these graphs and deleted those that only played a marginal role. Due to the small sample size and several further methodological problems, we are aware of the limited validity of this network analysis alone. Yet it suffices for our purposes, i.e. a visualisation that complements our more thorough qualitative analysis of the country cases.

On the basis of these combined data sources, the chapters that follow tell the distinctive stories of the securitisation of climate change in our four cases. Comparing them in the last chapter allows us to underline commonalities as well as idiosyncratic features of each case, as well as to re-address some of the normative issues involved in securitising climate change.

On the normative implications of securitising climate change

The Copenhagen School's normative assessment of securitisation focuses on the closures to the political debate and thus on the constraints to deliberation. This is a central yet formal normative concern, but there may of course be other normative concerns. Discursive entrepreneurs in particular will perhaps even be willing to achieve closure of the debate because of substantive normative concerns about climate change. Furthermore, as we have discussed above, not all forms of securitisation in all their stages are 'bad'. The first stage of securitisation – leading to opening up the political agenda – clearly is not, and whether we regard the other stages as 'bad' depends on a weighing-up of different normative concerns and an assessment of the quality of the measures taken. While we thus agree that securitisation may well be 'just' (Floyd 2011), we think that such assessments will always have to be made in specific historical and cultural contexts.

Given the debates about the ethics of securitisation (e.g. Elbe 2006; Browning and McDonald 2013; Floyd 2007b), our differentiation of different climate security discourses raises the question of whether some forms of securitisation may be normatively preferable to others. In particular, the question arises whether the articulation of risk may avoid some of the problems of the articulation of danger in terms of closing down the political debate, as the Copenhagen School argues, and whether the individual and the planet as a whole are more defensible as a referent object of security than a particular territorial order because they are less exclusionary. Furthermore, we suggest that we may also assess securitisations of climate change according to their justification of military means and their utility in tackling the causes of climate change. These criteria are interlinked and relate to Floyd's suggestion that what she calls 'just' securitisations need to allow for measures that are 'appropriate to the threat in question' (Floyd 2011: 428). On the one hand, this argument builds on the understanding that there can be such a thing as 'positive' securitisation if it promotes particular values and enables appropriate policy responses that would otherwise be marginalised (Roe 2008b: 779). On the other hand, it returns to the original purpose of the widening of the concept of security, which was to wrestle security out of the hands of the military (Buzan and Hansen 2009: 187–188).

Security versus risk

Some authors suggest that a risk-based securitisation may be less problematic because it does not necessarily lead to the exceptional and undemocratic emergency measures foreseen by the Copenhagen School (Corry 2012: 255). Others argue that even within a risk-based approach – if aimed at radical uncertain, incalculable but possibly catastrophic risks – undemocratic and exceptional precautionary policies can be legitimised (Aradau and van Munster 2007). A third strand, based on the Paris School of securitisation, puts forward the idea of routine and hidden securitisations through riskification that also have their perils (Bigo 2008; Huysmans

2004). There are indeed significant differences between danger- and risk-centred discourses at the diagnostic and prognostic level. On the one hand, a risk-oriented argumentation leaves the referent object and threat more diffuse, broadens the time horizon and favours long-term and precautionary measures. If a risk-based securitisation leads to more preventive measures, aimed at the root causes of the problem, and thus predominantly mitigation measures, they can be regarded as positive for the ultimate goal of stabilising the global climate. Moreover, due to less dramatic language and proposed measures, risk-based securitisations may be more compatible with the parallel and 'normal' politicisation of the same issue.

Yet, following Corry (2012) and Oels (2013), one has to bear in mind that the goal of such measures is not to eradicate the risk completely but to manage and govern it, and to contain it at a *tolerable level*. While this is presumably more in line with the 'normal' that is democratic politics, it raises the important normative question: tolerable for whom? The most serious climatic effects will first, and almost exclusively, hit poor populations in developing countries, whereas industrialised countries might even experience some advantages of warmer temperatures (Parry *et al.* 2007). Keeping the risk at a tolerable level for industrialised countries – which clearly dominate the climate security debates – can thus very well mean to do only as much in terms of mitigation and adaptation as to avoid what the worst forecasts predict. This could mean, for instance, keeping violent conflicts at bay through the deployment of development aid and peacekeeping forces, without doing a lot in terms of mitigation. What constitutes a question of long-term and possibly tolerable risk for some countries (wealthy industrialised countries and their inhabitants) might very well be a question of survival for others (people in developing countries and most extremely those living in small island states). Indeed, as our research on climate security debates in the US and Germany show, it is mostly the developing countries that are seen as endangered – a risk which can be kept at bay through minor adaptation interventions. However, this is slowly beginning to change in the light of experiences such as hurricanes Katrina or Sandy that have demonstrated the vulnerability of even advanced industrialised societies.

A further criticism more in line with the so-called Paris School suggests that the resulting policy changes in a risk-based discourse will be less observable and subject to public scrutiny than the public speech acts of invoking existential threats to legitimise extraordinary measures. Even if one assumes that measures taken in such a framework are lower in their immediate impact, over time they can have adverse effects and alter the ways and possibilities for governing climate change (Oels 2011). Risk-centred securitisation has already led to changes in how climate change is seen in military circles, has altered procedures and played down other options (Briggs 2012). Securitising climate change along the presented risk-based discourses therefore can lead to a less extreme but permanent or indefinite state of emergency.

Adding to that, a risk-based approach entails the danger that the groups or areas that are diagnosed to be especially at risk become stigmatised and in the end dangerous themselves (Methmann and Oels 2013): 'risk-based categories can generate further stigma for individuals who are deemed to be members of those risk groups. To be "at risk" is effectively to be at odds with, or even a danger to, the welfare of the population' (Elbe 2009: 140). Eventually, riskification may be no less harmless than a threatification – at least not as a general rule – and does not vaccinate against normatively negative effects.

Good and bad referent objects

If we move to the different referent objects or levels of securitisation, are some normatively preferable to others? On the *territorial* level, we agree with other scholars (e.g. Detraz and Betsill 2009) that the securitisation of climate change in terms of conflicts between groups or states and national security conceptions is hugely problematic. On the positive side, this discourse helps to raise attention and is conducive to forging coalitions between actors that would otherwise not have approached the topic seriously, as UN Security Council meetings (UNSC 2007a; 2011a) exemplify, and our analysis of the US debate in particular will show (see also Richert 2011; 2012; Fletcher 2009). However, such an argumentation distracts attention from the core issues – slowing down climate change through decisive mitigation efforts – to rather ad-hoc adaptation measures and interferences in at-risk countries that could in the end take the form of military intervention (Wagner 2008; Hartmann 2010). As a consequence, military and defence actors are increasingly involved in climate politics, and adopt concepts from the climate sector into military planning (Brzoska and Oels 2011: 51–67). Actors prepare themselves to cope with climate change's secondary effects instead of preventing global warming from happening in the first place (Oels 2013: 13). But again, this assessment does not necessarily hold for all times and contexts. In some cases the benefits of putting climate change on the agenda through a territorial securitisation might outweigh the costs and even open the door for subsequent mitigation measures.

On the *individual level*, Detraz and Betsill (2009) argue that these pitfalls of the territorial discourse can be avoided, making the individual discourse more appropriate for climate security debates. Indeed, on the positive side, individual-level securitisation focuses on the ones most affected and vulnerable to climate change and avoids national security conceptions that draw on a traditional, militarised and state-centred security logic. Nonetheless, there is the danger that a focus on individuals lead to the 'vulnerable becoming dangerous' themselves (Methmann and Oels 2013). In line with this argument, securitising actors may use the seemingly less dangerous individual discourse quite easily to make a more problematic territorial argument. If poor populations in unstable developing states are hit first and hardest by climate change, i.e. threatened in their human security, it is not difficult to extend this argument to destabilised, weak or failing states, large-scale migration movements, terrorism and widespread conflict. This in turn could transform into national security concerns for industrialised states (see e.g. CNA 2007; WBGU 2007b: 2, 5). Examples from our empirical research – particularly in the US case – strongly support this argument. Moreover, a concentration on the vulnerability of individuals can have the somewhat ironic effect that less is done to mitigate climate change, because the individuals at risk mostly do not live in the biggest polluter states but in poor developing countries. To lower the immediate risk adaptation measures – which can be integrated into ongoing development aid programmes without having to change too much in Western economies – seem more compelling than mitigation efforts – a practice which again can be confirmed in our empirical cases.

Planetary level discourses seem to be the least problematic. They highlight the interdependency of the entire human existence with its surrounding ecosystem, and call for decisive measures to reduce greenhouse gases, and for the restructuring of risk-creating activities, i.e. more sustainable economic activity. However, such an approach at the same time does not seem to lead to a very successful policy output, and concurrently has difficulties generating the same amount of attention as other arguments that present a clear and local referent object. Moreover, it might be too close to the prevailing environmental framing of climate change in the past and thus be dismissed as naive and unworldly. Although being extended to a second period, the only legally binding agreement, the Kyoto protocol, accounts for about 15 per cent of worldwide GHGs and merely aims at a reduction of about 18 per cent until 2020; and even with these conservative goals, its success is rather doubtful (Harmeling *et al.* 2012). Furthermore, the constantly failing negotiations about the inclusion of the US and other major emitters like China, India, Canada, Australia or Brazil into a new global agreement from 2020 on exemplifies the difficulties with such a planetary approach. Eventually, a securitisation along this discourse might be too weak in its political effect, and thus be normatively problematic if we employ a consequentialist ethics (Floyd 2007b; 2013).

Although in the risk dimension the time-horizon widens and mitigation is an important option, a focus on managing the risks and keeping them at tolerable levels can also have the effect of doing less than needed. And because of the already stated problems, the planetary discourse has difficulties gaining widespread approval and therefore does not lead to substantial efforts either. Eventually it may be true that the securitisation of climate change focused on territorial security has so far prevented rather than furthered its primary goal: the radical reduction of GHG emissions. Yet, even where we find the prevalence of such climate security discourses, the normative assessment is more complex. Thus, securitisation may have helped to get the topic on the agenda, form new coalitions and to quick-start important attempts at climate legislation (Fletcher 2009: 808; Kueter 2012: 36; Mildner and Richert 2010: 12; Richert 2012; 2011). Its normative utility in general might be described as an inverted U-curve that if carefully applied has its benefits, yet if taken too far can have hugely problematic consequences. On this basis, securitisation, in its variety of forms, is a strategy to be carefully employed by political actors. In climate security, it has been vital for making climate change a credible topic to be addressed, but it may be counter-productive if further securitisation moves are not scrutinised carefully. We will return to these issues both in our case studies and in the conclusion of this book.

Note

1 Parts of this chapter draw on F. von Lucke, Z. Wellmann and T. Diez (2014) 'What's at Stake in Securitising Climate Change? Towards a Differentiated Approach', Special Issue: Rethinking Climate Change, Conflict and Security, *Geopolitics* 19(4): 857–884. Reproduced with permission of Taylor and Francis.

3

THE UNITED STATES

Climate change as danger to the state

Introduction

Our first empirical case, the United States (US), is generally seen as an obstacle to an international treaty on the reduction of GHG emissions. Until 2006, the US was the single biggest emitter of GHGs, contributing about 20 per cent of global emissions (Donner and Faltin 2007: 4; *New York Times* 2007). Although China has now exceeded US emissions, the US still has one of the largest per capita emissions count, with an average of about 19 metric tons per annum in the last two decades (World Bank 2013a), and its energy and resource consumption counts as one of the highest worldwide (Falkner 2005: 591). Most importantly, it is by a wide margin the single largest contributor of historical emissions, with 339,174 MT or 28.8 per cent between 1850 and 2007. China ranks second with 105,915 MT or 9.0 per cent, and our other industrialised country case, Germany, ranks fourth with 81,194.5 MT or 6.9 per cent (*Guardian* 2011). The high emissions output and the slow adoption of meaningful federal climate legislation or international commitments have led to the US ranking in the lower regions of most international climate policy tables. The Climate Performance Index (CPI), for instance, lists the country on average on the 50th rank between 2008 and 2015 – close to Turkey, but at the opposite end of the scale from Germany and Mexico (Germanwatch and CAN 2015).

Yet as we show in this chapter, this does not mean that there have been no climate change policies, or that climate change has not been securitised in the US. Instead, we argue, the main problem in the US is the prevalence of the territorial danger discourse, at least since the 2000s. This has legitimised a focus on military adaptation measures, leading to what some have called the 'climatisation' of the security sector (Oels 2012a). Our focus in this chapter is on the national level. Many individual states have passed and implemented more far-reaching mitigation policies, but while these are important, they cannot substitute for a lack of such a policy for the country as a whole.

As our analysis shows, a few discursive entrepreneurs whose personal background drove them to seek connections with the military have heavily influenced the debate in the US. They were successful not least because of the standing and credibility of the military among large parts of the US public. At the same time, this public, and particularly political actors, have viewed environmentalist NGOs with suspicion. The difficulties of Al Gore as a discursive entrepreneur around the turn of the millennium have led to further discrediting of environmental activists, at least in the short run.

This chapter is based on the analysis of over fifty core publications of relevant climate change actors among think tanks, in civil society and government institutions and in 270 parliamentary debates on climate change containing securitising articulations between 1989 and 2014. We narrowed down our empirical base to debates containing securitising articulations because the number of general debates on climate change would have run into several thousand. To further substantiate the findings, we conducted over twenty mainly semi-structured and informal interviews with think tanks, NGOs and state representatives in the country, and additionally performed a network citation analysis.

In the following, we analyse the dominant climate security discourses, the main actors and the political consequences of the securitisation of climate change in the US in detail. But to situate this analysis in the broader context, we first elaborate on the development of the general climate debate.

The climate debate in the United States: the fallen forerunner

From the late 1960s, due to a thriving environmental movement that had its origins in emerging scientific fields such as ecology, the environment became an important policy concern in the US. The country became a forerunner in environmental issues, with a vibrant scientific and environmental advocacy community and quite progressive laws (Falkner 2005: 585, 590; Vig and Kraft 1984: 8–9; Kraft 2013: 111). For example, the Clean Air Act of 1963 – which later became a particularly important policy instrument in relation to climate change – was adopted at that time, and the Environmental Protection Agency (EPA) was founded in 1970, and became a role model for similar institutions in many other countries (Harris 2001: 5). US environmental organisations such as the Sierra Club, the National Audubon Society, the Environmental Defense Fund, or the World Resources Institute have been forerunners in their field and later also became influential in the climate debate (Park 2000: 77). Inter alia, because of the pressure from the scientific community (Pielke Jr 2000a: 14–17), the US was highly involved and exerted considerable leadership at various international conferences (e.g. Stockholm 1972) and agreements on environmental issues such as whaling or the ozone layer (Falkner 2005: 590; Harrison 2000: 89).

While climate change had been a matter of debate amongst US scientists since the late 1950s (Park 2000: 79), the first tangible policy action was the National Climate Program established in 1978, which was supposed to facilitate research on human-induced climate processes (Pielke Jr 2000a: 12). The country's status as a progressive player in environmental matters still applied to a certain extent at the beginning of international climate negotiations in the late 1980s until the mid-1990s, and the US was one of the most influential actors in the early days of the climate regime (Donner and Faltin 2007: 5; Harris 2000a: 16). Although Republican president Ronald Reagan (1981–1989) was not an environmentalist and tried to reduce federal environmental regulation (Vig 2013: 88–90), he was not able to significantly dismantle the policies of earlier decades (Harris 2001: 5). His successors, the Republican George H. W. Bush (1989–1993), and even more so the Democrat Bill Clinton (1993–2001) were fairly sympathetic to environmental issues (Vig 2013: 90–94) – although often under pressure from a Congress controlled by the more environmentally-friendly Democrats (Harris 2002: 150). Moreover, the American public was becoming increasingly aware of climate change after the summer of 1988 proved to be one of the hottest in US history and NASA scientist James Hansen proclaimed that they had detected a serious greenhouse effect (Leiserowitz 2005: 1435; Park 2000: 80; Grundmann and Scott 2014: 222).

It was also in the 1980s that climate change became more important in Congress, particularly due the efforts of the Democrats Albert Gore and Timothy Wirth and the Republican John Chafee, who called several debates on the issue (Pielke Jr 2000a: 16; Park 2000: 80; Bryner 2000: 112). In 1987, the Global Climate Change Protection Act increased the budget for research on climate matters, advised the EPA to prepare a national climate policy and directed the secretary of state to coordinate international policy (US Congress 1988). The creation of the Committee on Earth and Environmental Sciences in 1990 further institutionalised the political handling of climate change. Finally, due to a presidential initiative of 1989 and the Congressional Global Change Research Act (GCRA) of 1990, the US Global Change Research Program was established, which was supposed to develop and coordinate research on climate change but also to support policy development (USGCRP 2015; Pielke Jr 2000b: 134–136). However, despite the progressive domestic policies and the high level of involvement of the US in the international negotiations, at the UN Conference on Environment and Development 1992 in Rio, the United States nonetheless opposed a too strict and binding climate convention. In the end this contributed to the creation of the UNFCCC that foresees only voluntary commitments to reduce emissions (Harris 2001: 8; 2000a: 17; Vig 2013: 91).

This involved but rather conservative stance towards the international climate regime changed somewhat with the election of Bill Clinton and Vice-President Albert 'Al' Gore, who was known as an environmentalist (Harris 2001: 11; 2000b: 38–43; Falkner 2005: 592; Vig 2013: 91). Moreover, since the late 1980s, a first environmental and climate security debate had emerged, which saw its peak during the Clinton/Gore administration and contributed to increased attention for climate issues (see also Park 2000: 82). In the wake of this heightened attention to environmental issues, the US began to take climate change more seriously, acknowledged the findings of the IPCC, and in 1993 published a Climate Action Plan that foresaw significant though voluntary emission reductions (Brunner and Klein 1999). Beyond that, the US agreed to binding emission reductions in 1996 and signed the Kyoto Protocol in 1998, yet not without demanding that developing countries make a contribution as well (Harris 2000a: 17). Inter alia, because this condition was not met and due to increased opposition in the Senate, where the Republicans had held a majority since 1994 (Kraft 2013: 112) – epitomised by notorious Byrd-Hagel resolution (National Center for Public and Policy Research 1997) – the protocol was never ratified. In 2001, the Bush Jr administration eventually withdrew its signature (Müller 2003: 10). These developments exemplify the changing domestic political landscape of the late 1990s, when support for strong environmental regulation was increasingly fading and attitudes more sceptical of climate change gained momentum (Grundmann and Scott 2014: 222).

Under the presidency of George W. Bush (2001–2009), this trend consolidated (Harris 2002: 153; Vig 2013: 94). Both Congress – especially the traditionally more anti-environmental Republicans, for instance Senator James Inhofe (Harris 2001: 20; US Senate 2003b: S13489) – and an influential non-governmental lobby, particularly from the business community, were increasingly rallying against environmental and climate policies, especially if these involved international, legally binding agreements (Falkner 2005: 590; Leiserowitz 2005: 1435; McCright and Dunlap 2011: 158). The opponents of climate legislation also included outright climate-sceptical organisations such as the George C. Marshall Institute, the Competitive Enterprise Institute, the Heritage Foundation, and the Cato Institute (Rosenberg *et al.* 2010: 312). They were backed up by strong economic players, such as Koch Industries, that funded numerous anti-climate initiatives (Greenpeace USA 2011) but also by influential public figures such as novelist Michael Crichton (Wilson 2005), and succeeded in discouraging strong legislative action at the federal level (Fletcher 2009: 806). In comparison, climate sceptics were much more influential in the US than for example in Germany or Mexico (Grundmann and Scott 2014: 226–227). Many members of the Bush administration, including the president himself, on various occasions expressed their doubts that humans influenced the climate in any relevant way, and hence saw no pressing need to cut emissions (Barnett 2004). Consequently, climate policies remained few, non-binding and focused on technical solutions (Donner and Faltin 2007: 5; Yamin and Depledge 2004: 45–48; Eckersley 2007: 315–319).

At the same time, climate change turned into a field of political polarisation along party lines, which made it even more difficult to reach federal agreements (McCright and Dunlap 2011: 158–159; Guber and Bosso 2013: 62–64). During his second term in office (2005–2009), George W. Bush at least acknowledged the existence of anthropologically induced climate change (Clarke 2005) and agreed to more – though non-binding – agreements at the international level (Fletcher 2009: 805; Donner and Faltin 2007: 15; Mildner and Richert 2010: 31). Moreover,

Democrats gained a majority in Congress again in 2006 and increased pressure on the Bush administration (Kraft 2013: 112). Around this time the atmosphere in the business community began to change as well, and in 2007 several companies called for a legally binding framework (Guber and Bosso 2013: 55) and together with environmental organisations founded the US Climate Action Partnership that called for emission cuts (USCAP 2013). In addition, some states took a more climate friendly stance, particularly California (Donner and Faltin 2007: 11–14; C2ES 2012; Mildner and Richert 2010: 30–32). These developments were embedded in a second climate security debate, which began to develop from 2003 onwards and had its peak between 2007 and 2010 (Mildner and Richert 2010: 12; Brzoska 2012: 172; Fletcher 2009: 808, see the next section). Towards the end of his second term, George W. Bush in 2008 even committed to cut US emissions to 20 per cent below 1990 levels by 2025 (Bush 2008).

With the election of the Democrat Barack Obama as President in 2009, climate issues returned to the top of the political agenda (Vig 2013: 98–102), and at least the rhetoric towards them changed: '[T]the United States will once again engage vigorously in these negotiations, and help lead the world toward a new era of global cooperation on climate change' (Obama 2008). A shift in public opinion towards recognising the threats posed by climate change, and a more favourable stance of business actors supported this development. While the political divide between Democrats and Republicans persisted (McCright and Dunlap 2011: 155), the Democrats had gained a majority in both chambers of Congress. In addition, Obama appointed several well-known climate experts to important posts in his administration, such as Todd Stern as Special Envoy for Climate Change, Carol Browner as head of the White House Office of Energy and Climate Change Policy and Lisa Jackson as head of the EPA (US Department of State 2009; Mildner and Richert 2010: 18).

However, the picture changed again after the failed UNFCCC negotiations in Copenhagen in late 2009 and the Democrats' defeat in the Senate in the mid-term elections of 2010, and later in the House of Representatives (Mildner et al. 2012: 3; Leggett and Lattanzio 2009). During 2009 and 2010, several attempts to pass a federal climate law did not succeed in Congress. Thus, the Obama administration stopped pushing for such legislation and instead focused on influencing the domestic climate field through technical regulations issued by the EPA and the departments of Transportation (DOT) and Energy (DOE). Yet steering through these regulations did not go without major criticism from the opposition and did not allow the pursuit of more important climate measures (Mildner and Richert 2010: 21).

Additionally, during the early 2010s the US saw a renewed oil and gas boom (IEA 2012: 2). This further hindered Obama's original plans of investing more in renewable energies. Meanwhile, public interest in climate matters declined. According to a 2012 poll, climate change was last on a list of important political issues (Pew Research Center 2012: 1). Nevertheless, the examples set by individual state level climate policies, international pressure, domestic advocacy efforts and increased media coverage of domestic natural disasters contributed to keeping climate change on the agenda (C2ES 2012; Scherwitz 2014; Brulle *et al.* 2012). In 2014, a new National Climate Assessment (NCA) highlighted the serious consequences of climate change for the US, and the think tank CNA published a widely noticed update to its 2007 report on climate change and security (CNA Military Advisory Board 2014). Moreover, in 2014 the US struck a bilateral deal with China over mutually reducing their emissions by 2025 and 2030 (Taylor and Branigan 2014) and in 2015 Obama announced a Clean Power Plan that aims to reduce US emissions by 32 per cent from 2005 levels by 2030 (The White House 2015b).

The securitisation of climate change

One can divide the climate security debate in the US into two separate phases: a first phase in the second half of the 1980s and in the 1990s overlapped with broader debates on environmental security; a second phase starting in the mid-2000s focused exclusively on climate change.

Phase 1: environmental and climate security

The first precursors of the climate security debate in the US can be found as early as 1960 when a range of environmental problems, including climate change, had been identified by certain expert communities as possible threats, often linked to discussions about the atmospheric repercussions of nuclear weapons testing and later the 'nuclear winter hypothesis' (Dalby 2009: 37–39). Environmental security concerns (including resource scarcity and global warming) began to generate more attention on a political level in the 1970s when they were linked to 'Malthusian' discussions about overpopulation (Ehrlich 1968), the limits to growth (Meadows and Meadows 1972) and especially the 1973 oil crisis and general debates on resource scarcity (Dalby 2009: 14; Brown 1977: 7; Hartmann 2010: 234). Based on these discussions and worrying projections of the US National Academy of Sciences about climate change (National Academy of Sciences 1975; 1977), in the late 1970s the first calls to include environmental problems and climate change as 'national security' issues appeared, for instance by Lester R. Brown of the Worldwatch Institute (Brown 1977; see also Floyd 2010: 67). The focus of these early climate security arguments was particularly on sea level rise and food security, and falls into our 'planetary and individual' category (Brown 1977: 19–23).

This being said, the actual beginning of the first environmental and climate security debate on a broader scale in the US was in the late 1980s and early 1990s and gained particular strength under the Clinton–Gore administration from 1993 on (Allenby 2000: 10; Matthew 2013: 346, 351–352). While the environmental security argument had been around for some time, it had been overshadowed by the all-encompassing Soviet threat. The end of the Cold War left more room for the discussion of non-traditional security issues (Dalby 2002: 16–17; Allenby 2001: 45; Dabelko *et al.* 1995: 4). It also left the US security establishment without a clear enemy and therefore led it to focus on 'new discourses of danger' (Doran 2000: 59; Harris 2002: 150–151; Floyd 2010: 65, 69, 119). Moreover, the academic discussions about 'new security threats' and connections between population growth, environmental problems and conflict had intensified (see Chapter 2 of this book) (Myers 1989; Mathews 1989; Homer-Dixon 1994; Kaplan 1994). In particular, the 1994 article 'The Coming Anarchy' by Robert Kaplan and the ideas of Thomas Homer-Dixon (1994) – who was even invited to Washington, D.C. to brief Vice-President Gore – were picked up by political practitioners in the US to either justify military spending or to advance their environmental agenda (Floyd 2010: 73–75; Dalby 2009: 27; 2002: xix, 6). The eager adoption of environmental problems as national security issues, however, also met criticism, and scholars such as Daniel Deudney pointed to the opposing logics of environmentalism on the one side and war, militarisation and nationalism on the other (Deudney 1990: 214; Levy 1995).

Despite these criticisms, the environmental security argument thrived and within this debate climate change gradually became one of the most important environmental security concerns, a process which was driven by scientists, civil society and political practitioners. Thus, at that time think tanks took up the issue, for instance the Woodrow Wilson Center with its Environmental Change and Security program (Woodrow Wilson Center 2015). The first program report (Dabelko *et al.* 1995) contained several articles by renowned environmental security scholars of that time, such as Geoffrey D. Dabelko, who is one of the discursive entrepreneurs who have significantly driven the climate security debate in the US. Moreover, the military sector itself also began to be more interested in environmental security matters, as indicated for instance by publications of the Strategic Studies Institute of the Army War College (Butts 1993). Further important actors that pointed to climate change as a threat were the Union of Concerned Scientists and the National Academy of Sciences, which were both quoted in Congressional debates on climate change and security (US Senate 1992b: S7511).

Among active politicians, Gore, then a Democrat senator, was one of the first to explicitly use climate security arguments (Harris 2002: 151; US Senate 1989a: S5252). In our analysis of Congressional debates between 1989 and 2014, we found a first peak of climate security articulations in the 101st (1989–1990) and 102nd (1991–1992) Congress, where members frequently evoked climate change as security threat. While references to US national security do appear (US Senate 1989a: S5252), the focus in general is more international and pictures climate change as an *individual* or *planetary* danger to argue for the need to establish an international climate regime:

> Potential climate change presents such a serious threat to human well-being throughout the world, that the United States should undertake urgent action to support and encourage negotiations necessary to bring about a framework convention for international cooperation on limiting the emission of greenhouse gases ...
>
> *(US Senate 1990a)*

Interestingly, such statements often conflated climate change with the destruction of the ozone layer (US Senate 1989a: S5252) – a pattern that was also quite common in Germany at this stage (see Chapter 4). After ozone security arguments had led to the adoption of the successful Montreal Protocol in 1989 (Trombetta 2011: 143–145) and after the IPCC (1988) and UNFCCC (1992) had been established and influential scientific actors from the US such as NASA and the National Academy of Sciences had presented more evidence, the focus shifted towards climate change understood as global warming.

Fewer climate security debates in Congress took place between 1993 and 1996 but those that did kept arguing on the individual and planetary level, often in a rather cautious and risk-focused way (US House of Representatives 1994b: H4984; 1995: H9942). Throughout the 105th (1997–1998) until the 107th Congress (2001–2002), climate security argumentations appeared more frequently, especially in relation to the Kyoto Protocol (US House of Representatives 1998a: H3577). In contrast to later phases, they continued to focus on individual and planetary risk (US House of Representatives 1998b: H6224; US Senate 1999a: S2330; 1999b: S9744). Some actors who have repeatedly linked the environment and climate change to security in these early debates in Congress – particularly Albert Gore, Joe Lieberman and John Kerry (US Senate 1989a: S5252; 1992a: S6275; 1992b: S7511) – would later reappear as important discursive and legislative entrepreneurs in the second phase of the climate security debate in the 2000s.

What about the success in terms of transforming the climate debate and legitimising concrete policies? One of the first attempts to legitimise climate legislation with security articulations came from Senator John Chafee, when he introduced the eventually failed Stratospheric Ozone and Climate Protection Act and spoke of a 'massive threat that is posed by uncontrolled global climate change' (US Senate 1989b: S13293). This was followed by the House Concurrent Resolution 248 sponsored by Representative Benjamin Gilman, which expressed the sense of the Congress with respect to the link between environment and national security and was passed by the House but never adopted by the Senate (US House of Representatives 1990). A further far-reaching and eventually successful decision was the establishment of the US Global Change Research Program in 1990 (US Government 1990). In the Congressional debates, the urgent necessity of such a programme was partly legitimised by articulations focusing on planetary danger. Representative Christopher H. Smith for instance highlighted that the 'devastating effects which a rise of only a few degrees of temperature could have on our planet', and demanded 'that we take steps now to prevent such manmade changes on our global environment' (US House of Representatives 1989: E3575). When Clinton and Gore assumed office in 1993, they increased research funding particularly for the socio-economic dimensions, including the security implications, of climate change (Floyd 2010: 78–79). Moreover, they appointed some strong proponents of an environmental security agenda to high-ranking positions in the government, including Timothy Wirth at the State Department and Sherri Goodman as Deputy Under-Secretary of Defense for

Environmental Security (Harris 2001: 151; Interview 2014z; Matthew 2013: 353) – both became important discursive entrepreneurs within and outside their government function. Having ratified the UNFCC, in 1996 at the third Conference of the Parties to the Convention (COP-3) in Kyoto, Wirth committed the US to binding emission regulations, which made the Kyoto Protocol possible. Climate security argumentations in Congress played an important role in generating support for these treaties (US Senate 1990a; 1997; US House of Representatives 1994a).

Despite its focus on the planetary and individual level, this early climate security debate also had an impact on US foreign and security policy. Although not as dominant as in the later climate security debate of the 2000s, territorial danger arguments and references to US national security did appear in these earlier debates (US Senate 1989a: S5252; US House of Representatives 1990: H7684). Thus, although not being an environmentalist, Reagan, under pressure from NGOs and a Democrat majority in Congress, was one of the first to acknowledge environmental degradation and resource scarcity as important security problems for the US (Harris 2002: 150). George H. Bush, who already had proclaimed more action on climate change during his campaign (Pielke Jr 2000a: 21), for the first time explicitly mentioned climate change in the NSS in 1991, although with a rather low priority (The White House 1991: 2, 22). The first NSS (1994) under the Clinton–Gore administration went a step further and depicted climate change as 'environmental risk[s] serious enough to jeopardize international stability' (The White House 1994: 15). Climate change thus became a serious threat to US and global stability (Harris 2002: 151; Below 2007: 709; Richert 2009a: 10). Further practical outcomes were the establishment of various programmes and initiatives at the intersections between the environment and security (Floyd 2010: 102, 106). The Strategic Environmental Research and Development Program (SERDP), which had been promoted by Gore, adopted in 1990 and further extended in 1994, allowed the use of intelligence capabilities to monitor the environment (DOD 2015; US Senate 1990b: S12406; The White House 1994). Moreover, in 1993 the Clinton–Gore administration established the US Department of Defense's (DOD) Office of the Deputy Under-Secretary of Defense – Environmental Security (ODUSD–ES) and appointed Sherri Goodman as its head. This office was supposed to oversee the environmental impact of the DOD's activities, dealt with various environmental security topics and cooperated with the EPA (EPA 1994; US Senate 1991). In addition, the US Central Command (CENTCOM) under General Anthony Zinni also dealt with questions of environmental security and cooperated with the ODUSD-ES. Finally, the administration established a State Failure Task Force and asked it to inquire whether environmental changes posed a threat in this respect, and promoted environmental security through the DOS (Matthew 2013: 355–356).

Similar to the general climate debate, the climate security debate became less prominent at the end of the 1990s. One important reason was the increasing influence of climate sceptics who campaigned against any binding commitments to tackle climate change and its security-relevant effects (Leiserowitz 2005: 1435;

Rosenberg et al. 2010: 312; Fletcher 2009: 804–805). Moreover, the planetary and individual climate risk arguments that had dominated the debate throughout the 1990s mostly portrayed climate change as a rather distant long-term and global risk, of relevance primarily to distant places and peoples – a portrayal that made it difficult to mobilise greater support from the American public or in political circles (Leiserowitz 2005: 1438–1440).

After the election of George W. Bush as president in 2001, climate issues, and even more so climate security arguments, ceased to play an important role (Harris 2002: 153). The terror attacks of 11 September 2001 and the ensuing 'war on terror', as well as the war in Iraq eventually led to an almost exclusive focus on these issues within the US security sector – a new 'discourse of danger', so to speak – leaving no room for 'soft' security issues such as climate change (Floyd 2010: 122). Consequently, the two NSS under George W. Bush (2002 and 2006) no longer directly linked the environment and climate change to security (The White House 2002; 2006). Bush's first administration actively reversed the steps of the Clinton administration to combat climate change and to link it to security concerns (Harris 2002: 153; Matthew 2013: 356). This included cuts in funding, the renaming of institutions, reversing executive orders and the replacement of important personnel. For example, Bush called for an opening of protected areas for resource exploitation, backtracked on his previous pledge to cut the CO_2 emissions of electricity plants, and withdrew US support of the Kyoto Protocol (Harris 2002: 153). The ODUSD-ES became the Office of the Deputy Under Secretary of Defense – Installation and Environment (ODUSD–I&E). Environmentalist actors appointed by Clinton and Gore such as Goodman left office (Floyd 2010: 128, 142). Nevertheless, influential nongovernmental actors and opposition politicians continued to articulate their concerns about climate matters and their dissatisfaction with Bush's moves, which eventually contributed to the emergence of the second climate security debate (Harris 2002: 155–156; Interview 2014z).

Phase 2: the rise of territorial danger

The first sign of the beginning of the second and this time more exclusively climate-focused security debate appeared in October 2003 with a study commissioned by the DOD's influential defence adviser Andrew Marshall, who was renowned for his unorthodox thinking and often referred to as 'Yoda' of the Pentagon. After hearing of new scientific findings about abrupt climatic changes in the past (National Research Council 2002), Marshall hired Peter Schwartz, former head of planning for Shell Oil, and Doug Randall of the think tank Global Business Network to explore the implications of abrupt climate change for US national security (Fincham 2014). The report employs rather alarming phraseology and states that 'climate change ... should be elevated beyond a scientific debate to a U.S. national security concern' (Schwartz and Randall 2003: 3). Its publication during Bush's first term in office diametrically contradicted the administration's official stance on climate change. Allegedly because of its provocative content, the administration suppressed the study for four months before it was leaked to the press (Townsend and Harris 2004). The study generated considerable public attention, especially because in 2004 the major Hollywood movie *The Day After Tomorrow* depicted similar dramatic and abrupt effects of climate change. However, despite its disturbing language and drastic scenarios, or maybe because of them, the report only had a short-lived and limited impact on the political climate debate (Interview 2014p). Thus, while in 2003 two attempts at legislation were introduced that sought to increase research on abrupt climate change – the Abrupt Climate Change Research Act of 2003 and the Climate Stewardship Act – both eventually failed to gain a majority (US Senate 2003b; 2003a).

Nonetheless, the study paved the way for a whole series of think tank publications on climate security, which appeared after 2007 and which, in contrast to the earlier debate during which mostly scientific reports and politicians drove the securitisation, significantly dominated the second climate security debate. The most influential report came from the Military Advisory Board (MAB) of the security-oriented semi-governmental think tank CNA (2007), now run by Goodman. Further influential studies were published by the Center for Strategic and International Studies (CSIS), the Center for a New American Security CNAS, co-founded in January 2007 by former CNA President Kurt Campbell (Campbell *et al.* 2007), the Council on Foreign Relations (CFR) (Busby 2007) and many more.

Beginning in the year 2003 and growing in number and intensity until 2007, Congressional initiatives on climate security also became more widespread. Furthermore, the first changes in the structure of the administration likewise foreshadowed the renewed importance of climate security issues. These included the creation of the Deputy Directorate for Energy and Environmental Security in the Office of Intelligence and Counterintelligence within the DOE in 2007, reflecting the discursive linkage of climate with energy security and the economic opportunities of a 'green economy' (Fletcher 2009: 809–810). Carol Dumaine, who had previously been working for the CIA and had a strong interest in environmental security matters, became head of this directorate. Moreover, important discursive entrepreneurs from the first climate security debate emerged again, above all former vice-president Al Gore. Together with the IPCC he received the Nobel Peace Prize for his commitment to combatting climate change – in particular his 2006 movie *An Inconvenient Truth* had a big impact on the public and media debate on climate change in the US (Grundmann and Scott 2014: 229; Guber and Bosso 2013: 54). In 2007, in his widely publicised acceptance speech, he clearly tried to securitise climate change using a planetary danger argumentation (Gore 2007):

> We, the human species, are confronting a planetary emergency – a threat to the survival of our civilization that is gathering ominous and destructive potential even as we gather here. … We must quickly mobilize our civilization with the urgency and resolve that has previously been seen only when nations mobilized for war.

However, despite Gore's focus on the planetary level, and contrary to the first climate security debate, the second debate increasingly framed climate change as a territorial danger issue. This discourse became particularly prominent after 2007 and contributed to a lessening of Gore's influence because he was not a military security expert. While the individual level kept playing a role (though mostly to support territorial arguments), the planetary level progressively lost in importance. The focus on US national security began to transform the image of climate change from being a distant, global and abstract environmental concern to an issue with immediate security consequences for the US. Thus the opposition now put pressure on Bush to put climate change back onto the political agenda (Brzoska 2012: 172) and succeeded in raising considerable awareness of the topic among the general public as well as in political and military circles (Mildner and Richert 2010: 12; Fletcher 2009: 810–811). This second climate security debate in the US reached its peak between the end of 2007, when the fourth assessment report of the IPCC, including security-related impacts of climate change, was published, and 2010 (Fletcher 2009: 808; C2ES 2007/2008b; Interview 2014q; Becker 2007).

After several political setbacks at the international and domestic level, however, from 2010 on the climate security argument gradually faded away and funding for climate reports decreased (Interview 2014u; 2014t). But the debate never disappeared completely and continued to exert influence until the end of our study period in 2014 when the influential 3rd National Climate Assessment (Melillo *et al.* 2014) was published and CNA delivered a much-noticed update to its 2007 report (CNA Military Advisory Board 2014). The climate security debate has also influenced a whole series of political discussions, programmes, policies and planning schemes, which we will discuss in more detail below.

A closer look at climate security discourses

In the course of the second climate security debate starting in 2003, the discourse of *territorial danger* becomes more and more influential. While individual and planetary risk articulations still played an important role in Congressional debates between 2003 and 2006 (US Senate 2003b: S13500; US House of Representatives 2005: H4291), the territorial danger discourse became dominant in 2007. It appeared in many Congressional debates on climate change (US Senate 2008a: S4868; US House of Representatives 2009b: H8481), and runs through all twenty-eight relevant think tank reports on climate security that we analysed. In our analysis of these reports, we estimated the dominance of each discourse based on its frequency, position in the document and strength of the internal argumentation. The most common articulation presents US national security as threatened by the direct physical and indirect socio-economic and political effects of climate change. The influential 2007 CNA report thus argues: 'Projected climate change poses a serious threat to America's national security. ... These conditions have the potential to disrupt our way of life and to force changes in the way we keep ourselves safe and secure' (CNA 2007: 6; see also Rogers and Gulledge 2010: 7). Climate change is depicted as a 'threat multiplier' (CNA 2007: 6) that could worsen problems in a number of societal sectors and eventually even lead to nuclear war (Campbell *et al.* 2007: 78).

Among the most common threats articulated in these reports are socio-economic and political problems such as instability and conflict exacerbated by climate change in already fragile countries around the world (mostly in Africa) (CNA 2007: 13, 20; Rogers and Gulledge 2010: 16). These may create further instability, endanger current US military operations, necessitate new interventions (McGrady *et al.* 2010: 3), or even lead to the spread of terrorist ideologies (CNA 2007: 13, 17, 31). Climate change 'acts as an accelerant of instability, which may lead to violence. These disruptions will burden civilian and military institutions around the world, including the U.S. military' (Foley and Holland 2012c: 12). Mass migration could lead to conflict and destabilisation (CNA 2007: 18; Werz and Conley 2012: 1; Campbell *et al.* 2007: 9):

> This increased migration will very likely affect global security, which makes it imperative for the United States and other nations to begin formulating responses to climate migration now. ... In some cases, climate migration hot spots overlap with already volatile and unstable regions, where substantial migration could easily give rise to border conflicts and national security concerns.
>
> *(Werz and Manlove 2009: 1–2)*

Alongside such indirect threats, there are also direct dangers to US military installations and training procedures as well as to US combat operations arising from climate change (Carmen *et al.* 2010: 1; Foley 2012). As Foley (2012: 3) argues: 'Climate change poses costly threats to our domestic installations and potentially destabilizing threats to our international installations that hold strategic importance to the U.S. military'. Finally, particularly at the beginning of this phase, many reports constructed US energy security as threatened by climate change and connected it to national security conceptions (CNA 2007: 41; Campbell *et al.* 2007: 65, 96; C2ES 2009: 2). However, later reports refrained from referring to energy security too openly because instead of leading to improved climate or security policy, it rather facilitated discussions about energy independence and to renewed calls for domestic oil explorations, which was not what most think tanks wanted to accomplish (Interview 2014p).

Second to territorial danger are articulations of *individual danger*. Often the reports contain a discussion of the academic debate on 'new security threats' and try to acknowledge broader conceptions of security: 'Environmental threats blur traditional notion of national security: secure states do not automatically mean secure peoples and climate change is proving that' (Foley and Holland 2012a: 1). Extreme weather events, droughts, famines and disease that particularly affect people in developing countries are core threats in these articulations (Albright *et al.* 2006: 7; Campbell *et al.* 2007: 56; Busby 2007: 9). Towards the end of our study period, reports also focus on endangered individuals in the United States with a focus on the increased frequency and intensity of storms and hurricanes (CNA Military Advisory Board 2014: 27; Foley and Holland 2012b: 33, 43). To exemplify this point, they often refer to devastating storms such as Katrina (2005) and Sandy (2012): 'However, Hurricane Katrina demonstrated all too well the possibility that an extreme weather event could kill and endanger large numbers of people, cause civil disorder, and damage critical infrastructure in other parts of the country' (Busby 2007: 5). However, most reports link individual danger to territorial danger claims. Hence, the individual security discourse is normally only part of a chain of argument that in the end focuses on territorial security considerations. The CNA report, for instance, warns that a 'health emergency involving large numbers of casualties and deaths from disease can quickly expand into a major regional or global security challenge that may require military support, ranging from distribution of vaccines to full-scale stability operations' (CNA 2007: 15).

The *planetary level* that used to be a focal point throughout the first climate security debate no longer features prominently, and only nine of the twenty-five reports include it at all. It is never the core narrative of the reports and mainly used to support articulations of other discourses, for example of individual danger: 'Coastal hurricanes and sea-level rise are threats to coastal communities and *ecosystems*' (Foley and Holland 2012b: 43, emphasis added). This shift from the 1990s is part of an attempt to emancipate climate change arguments from the environmentalist discourse, which was deemed ineffective (Interview 2014z; see also the section below on 'Political impact').

The risk dimension is less important in the US climate security debate. Although many of the analysed reports tap into climate risk discourses (mostly on the territorial level), these articulations often play only a supporting role. By pointing to the potentially catastrophic impact of climate risks, they effectively make a security-based argument:

> Adm. Bowman concludes that regardless of the probability of the occurrence, the projected weather-driven global events could be dire and could adversely affect our national security and military options significantly. He therefore argues that the prudent course is to begin planning, as we have in submarine operations, to develop a similar defense in depth hat would reduce national security risks even if this is a low probability event, given the potential magnitude of the consequences.
>
> *(CNA 2007: 41)*

Thus, risk vocabulary is quite common in relation to military planning. Concepts such as 'risk management' (CNA 2007: 10), 'black swan events' (i.e. highly unlikely events with possibly devastating consequences) (CNA and Oxfam 2011: 13); and 'contingency planning' (Carmen *et al.* 2010: 3) appear on a regular basis. A common argument is that the military is much better equipped to handle the long-term risks of climate change because its planning intervals are longer than those of political actors (Campbell *et al.* 2007: 14). Moreover, the military is supposed to be used to planning with incomplete risk-based information, as this quote by General Gordon R. Sullivan, a co-author of the 2007 CNA report, exemplifies: 'If you wait until you have 100 per cent certainty, something bad is going to happen on the battlefield' (CNA 2007: 10). This sentence later even found its way into Congressional debates (US Senate 2008d: S5191). Nevertheless, the predominant logic of the second climate security debate always remained focused on danger and operated with even more concrete threat scenarios than articulations in the first phase (Interview 2014p). In a sense, the security discourses incorporated risk concepts from the scientific debate into a danger narrative. But this absence of a strong risk discourse may be due to our empirical focus on security think tanks and political actors. We might have found more risk articulations in the scientific, business and insurance sector. However, actors from those sectors remained marginal to the broader debate, as the secondary literature, our own research and expert interviews all indicate.

As the main counter-measures, most reports include classical mitigation measures such as cutting emissions, increasing energy efficiency, emission trading schemes and multilateral cooperation (Campbell *et al.* 2007: 19, 89, 109; CNA 2007: 23, 45-46). They urge Congress to allocate more money to climate research programmes and to develop climate legislation (Busby 2007: 17–18). Yet the focus of many reports is on adaptation to the security effects of climate change and increasing the resilience of the US and its military to climate change (CNA 2007: 46). Consequently, they often directly address the DOD (Rogers and Gulledge 2010: 9), the intelligence sector (CNA 2007: 23, 45) and the Armed Forces (Carmen *et al.* 2010). This is not surprising, given the fact that most reports focus on dangers to US national security and the US military, for which the immediate solution is not long-term mitigation but short-term adaptation. Thus, most reports recommend integrating climate threats into the planning schemes of the security, military and intelligence sector, above all into the Quadrennial Defense Review (QDR), the National Security Strategies (NSS) and into the National Intelligence Estimates (NIE) (CNA 2007: 46; Carmen *et al.* 2010: 6). More concretely, they call for institutional reforms in those sectors to develop new military capabilities that match the dangers of climate change (CNA 2007: 20, 29, 39). This entails adjusting military bases, providing new climate-resilient equipment and enhancing training for interventions in crisis regions around the world where the situation could worsen due to climate change (McGrady *et al.* 2010: 35; Campbell *et al.* 2007: 108; CNA 2007: 16, 25, 40).

Following the connection between territorial and individual danger arguments, the reports also recommend better cooperation between military, civilian and development as well as climate actors (e.g. USAID) (CNA 2007: 45; CNA and Oxfam 2011: 3; Carmen *et al.* 2010: 12; Werz and Manlove 2009: 5). A CNA report (McGrady *et al.* 2010: 3) for instance argues that the 'presence of armed conflict may make disaster response or humanitarian assistance operations more complex, requiring military or other forces to stabilize the situation before aid can be delivered'. Moreover, several reports call for a much closer cooperation between climate science and the defence sector, and argue for an investment 'in a community of climate-security translators' (Rogers and Gulledge 2010: 11).

Finally, due to the increasing focus on the domestic effects of climate change on US citizens, some of the reports also recommend improving the disaster management capabilities in the US and especially address the Department of Homeland Security (DHS) and the Federal Emergency Management Agency (FEMA) (Werz and Conley 2012: 9–10, 35; CNA 2007: 7; Foley and Holland 2012b). On the one hand, this shift in focus can be attributed to several severe storms that hit the US between 2005 and 2012, events that the media and the public increasingly connected to climate change. On the other hand it was also a strategic choice, as it had become clear that the American public attached only limited importance to a problem that only lay in the distant future and would affect distant parts of the planet (Leiserowitz 2005: 1437; Interview 2014z).

Discursive entrepreneurs

The first thing that meets the eye when analysing influential actors in US climate security debates since the turn of the millennium is the relative absence of environmental NGOs (see also Grundmann and Scott 2014: 227, 231). Instead, security think tanks dominate the debate. There are several reasons for their great influence in the US. First, these think tanks often employ experienced and high-ranking former political or military personnel. In the US – more often than for instance in Germany – it is common to switch between think tank and government positions, allowing networks to extend across these borders. Second, because of the heavy workload of the active political personnel, they often do not have the time to develop policy concepts to deal with problems of the more distant future, such as climate change (Interview 2014z). Think tanks provide such 'thinking' and often even ready-to-use talking points and policy drafts for government actors (Interview 2014p; 2014y). Third, think tanks tend to have good connections to the media and other non-governmental actors and thus are able to provide cover and backup for government actors who go public with a new and possibly provocative view, such as climate change as a national security issue (Interview 2014y).

The starting point for security think tanks to take up climate security was the gridlock in the general debate on climate change during the George W. Bush presidency (Interview 2014z; 2014p; 2014u). Actors such as Sherri Goodman, Kurt Campbell and Geoffrey D. Dabelko, who had already participated in the first environmental security debate of the 1990s and who had useful connections to political and military circles, saw the need for a reframing of climate change (Interview 2014z). We have already introduced Goodman. Campbell, who knew Goodman personally, had served in the Navy and several security-related government positions before becoming one of the most influential individuals in the climate security debate. He worked for several of the most relevant think tanks in the debate (CNAS, CFR and CSIS). He co-founded CNAS in 2007, and was one of the lead authors of the CSIS/CNAS 2007 report on climate security. Dabelko is an influential academic and director of Environmental Studies at the George V. Voinovich School of Leadership and Public Affairs at Ohio University, as well as being affiliated to the Woodrow Wilson Environmental Change and Security Program.

These individuals realised that starving polar bears and climatic effects in distant places would not convince broader parts of the public and the political establishment of the importance of climate change and of robust counter-measures. Indeed, a 2005 study on the risk perceptions of the American public showed that although the majority viewed climate change as a risk, the predominant image was that of environmental problems in distant places that did not directly affect the US (Leiserowitz 2005: 1440). At the same time, our discursive entrepreneurs felt that climate change could actually affect the US military's capacities, which coincided with the perception of the US Navy itself (US Navy 2009; Interview 2014x). In addition, several influential foundations such as the Energy Foundation, the Rockefeller Foundation, the Skoll Global Threats Fund and the Carnegie Foundation, who likewise saw a chance to reframe the climate debate using security arguments (Interview 2014z), had significantly increased their funding for climate security research.

Part of the strategy that these discursive entrepreneurs employed was to approach the issue by assembling high-ranking retired military officers and various security think tanks to talk and write about the connections between climate change and security (Interview 2014z; 2014u). This was immensely important in underscoring the significance of climate change because the military has an exceptionally good reputation among broad sections of the US public (Gallup 2014) and in political circles (Interview 2014z; US Senate 2007b: S13502) – especially if compared with Germany. The public and most politicians perceived the military as politically neutral and pragmatic, and not caught up in the political and ideological turf wars that dominated the climate debate in Congress at the time – 'trusted members of the security policy community, especially the military, can act to tilt policy discussions toward evidence-based conclusions' (Rogers and Gulledge 2010: 22). Engaging the military also the allowed the discursive entrepreneurs to address conservative and Republican audiences (Fletcher 2009: 808). On the other side, sections of the military, particularly the Navy, also had an interest in highlighting the security implications of climate change. They had already experienced the implications of extreme weather events and melting Arctic ice for their operations. Their engagement in humanitarian missions following such events around the world led to a concern that climate change could in the future increase their workload even further (Interview 2014ab; US Navy 2010: 5).

The most important actor in the climate security debate was the semi-governmental think tank can, which specialises in security and defence issues and has a long history of working for the DOD and military forces, especially the US Navy. Starting around 2006, Goodman – who, from her previous work for the DOD and the ODUSD-ES still had good personal relationships with people in the defence sector (Interview 2014z; 2014u) – assembled a Military Advisory Board (MAB) for the CNA that consisted of several high-ranking retired military officers (e.g. the former CENTCOM commander General Zinni). In 2007, the MAB, with financial support from the Rockefeller Foundation, published the most influential report to date on climate security, *National Security and the Threat of Climate Change* (CNA 2007). The aims of the report were to raise awareness of climate change in general, of the connection between climate change and security in particular, and to improve security policy by integrating climate security into military and intelligence planning, especially into the QDR and into the Intelligence Estimates (Interview 2014u).

In the same year, CSIS and CNAS delivered another widely publicised report, *The Age of Consequences: The Foreign Policy and National Security Implications of Global Climate Change* (Campbell et al. 2007). These two reports paved the way for a whole series of further reports and projects at the intersection of climate change and security between 2007 and 2012. Behind these reports were mostly further security-oriented think tanks. One of them was the American Security Project (ASP) (2012), the co-founder of which was John Kerry who would later, as secretary of state in the Obama administration, connect climate change to security concerns. Others included the Center for American Progress (CAP) (Werz and Conley 2012), the Center for Climate and Energy Solutions (C2ES, formerly the Pew Center on Global Climate Change) (Huebert et al. 2012), the Council on Foreign Relations (CFR) (Busby 2007) and the Operation Free, as well as the Truman National Security Project (2015), which are influential multimedia campaigns advocating the recognition of non-traditional security threats. In addition, think tanks with a broader remit such as the Brookings Foundation (Mignone 2007), the Woodrow Wilson Center (Woodrow Wilson Center 2009) and RAND (Treverton et al. 2012) also participated in the debate, although with a less exclusively security-oriented framing. Finally, the climate security debate also drew the attention of outright climate-sceptical organisations such as the George C. Marshall Institute, which questioned the relationship between climate change and security and accused the other think tanks of using the security argumentation for partisan politics (Kueter 2012). However, these sceptics remained a minority.

In 2010, the debate was further institutionalised with the foundation of the Center for Climate and Security (CCS) (Interview 2014q). The CCS acted as a research hub that collected all reports and government policies and documents at the climate security nexus (CCS 2015). Moreover, it became the most important convenor to bring together the different think tanks and governmental actors working on climate security. It organised informal periodic meetings in Washington, D.C. between important people working on these issues and drafted reports and policies for members of Congress (Interview 2014p; 2014y). The good relations between most involved think tanks deteriorated somewhat after several initiatives on federal climate legislation had failed in 2010, and the interest in climate matters declined among the public. Thus, accumulating funds became more difficult, which led to more competition among think tanks (Interview 2014u).

So why were environmental organisations such as Greenpeace, the Nature Conservancy or the WWF absent from this story? After informal agreements with the security think tanks, they deliberately kept away from the climate security debate to avoid damaging the argument with their liberal and environmental image (Interview 2014w; 2014p). Lacking expertise in traditional security-related and military matters, they saw their participation as most likely being perceived as sheer 'branding' of environmental issues with security considerations. Thus, they calculated that this would have damaged the credibility of climate security articulations (Interview 2014p; 2014v; 2014r). They had also seen several legislative attempts fail in Congress, inter alia because they did not link climate change and security in a credible way (Interview 2014y; see also the next section).

A further peculiarity of the US case, especially if compared to the German case, was the lesser involvement of scientists or research institutions in the second climate security debate. Given the high level of funding and worldwide impact of US climate research and the important role of scientific actors in the general debate on climate change and in the early environmental and climate security debate (Harris 2001: 24; Rosenberg et al. 2010; Pielke Jr 2000a; Bryner 2000: 111) this is quite remarkable. Regardless of the fact that most think tanks reports included their findings, climate scientists or research institutions did not directly participate in the second climate security debate, or at least did not receive much attention and were not successful with their framing. Nonetheless, there are a few exceptions and some actors and reports frequently appear in public and Congressional debates that connect climate change to security, especially between 2003 and 2006 when the planetary level had not yet been completely sidelined. Examples are reports of the NOAA (US Senate 2003b: S13497), the National Academy of Sciences (US House of Representatives 2005: H4290), and the National Climate Assessments of the Global Change Research Program (Melillo et al. 2014).

One of the reasons for the limited impact of scientific actors was that the think tanks' policy-oriented and catchy framing of climate security did not leave much room for more nuanced scientific argumentation. Thus, the think tanks acted as intermediaries and 'translated' complex scientific findings into the language of politics (see Rogers and Gulledge 2010; Interview 2014r). Furthermore, when the debate shifted towards territorial danger, expert knowledge from the security sector and the military became more important.

The polarised political debate on climate change also played its role. Conservative politicians and their constituency are much less likely to give credit to scientific findings about climate change (McCright and Dunlap 2011). Republicans often used the argument that 'they are not scientists' (Atkin 2014) and thus could not judge whether climate change is real or not, which exemplifies this anti-scientific sentiment. Moreover, arguments referring to scientific uncertainty had repeatedly been used by climate-sceptical actors in the past and thus proponents of the climate security framing avoided scientific arguments (Pielke Jr 2000a: 9; Rosenberg *et al.* 2010: 312). The problems of a scientific framing were increased by the US media's quest for 'balanced reporting', which led them to present climate-sceptical arguments as equal to mainstream climate science, thus leading large parts of the American public to believe that anthropogenic influences were still a matter of debate (Guber and Bosso 2013: 61). Especially amongst conservatives, climate science lost even more credibility and became associated with naive environmentalist framings, because 'old liberal bogeyman' Al Gore had extensively presented scientific findings. Gore comes from a well off and academic family and studied at prestigious schools and universities. At the beginning of his political career he was part of a group of young politicians who were responsible for the 'greening' of the Democrats in the course of the 1980s (Dionne 1989) and he later was highly involved in the early debates on climate change (Pielke Jr 2000a: 16). Hence, for many conservatives, Gore embodies the archetypical figure of a politician from Washington who is out of touch with the real world and therefore lobbies for luxury issues such as climate protection. Moreover, after the release of his climate advocacy movie in 2006, Gore's credibility was further diminished by accusations of environmental hypocrisy, e.g. that he lived in a big house, travelled around the world, and profited financially from his climate campaigns (Usborne 2009; Tapper 2007; Interview 2014u). Thus, while Gore had been an important discursive entrepreneur in the first climate security debate and kept exerting influence until around 2007, his influence increasingly began to fade and in fact turned into a disadvantage when the territorial danger discourse became stronger from the mid-2000s onwards.

Figure 3.1, the result of a network citation analysis (see Chapter 2) that we conducted between the fifty-three most relevant actors in the US's second climate security debate, illustrates the importance of security think tanks, especially CNA and CNAS. Moreover, the figure reveals that the efforts to construct climate change as security issue primarily targeted the defence sector (see the big nodes of DOD, Army, Joint Chiefs of Staff, Navy and Air Force) and not so much the environmental sector (smaller nodes of NOAA and EPA, but also of environmental NGOs such as Greenpeace or WWF). It also shows that Congress and the White House receive many mentions. Yet as our analysis has shown, these references are mostly related to security and defence policy. The quite large nodes of the UN (we combined all UN organisations under the UN label) and IPCC are due to the fact that most reports include an introductory section about climate science. Finally, the analysis reinforces the importance of individual discursive entrepreneurs such as Sherri Goodman, Kurt Campbell and Geoffrey Dabelko.

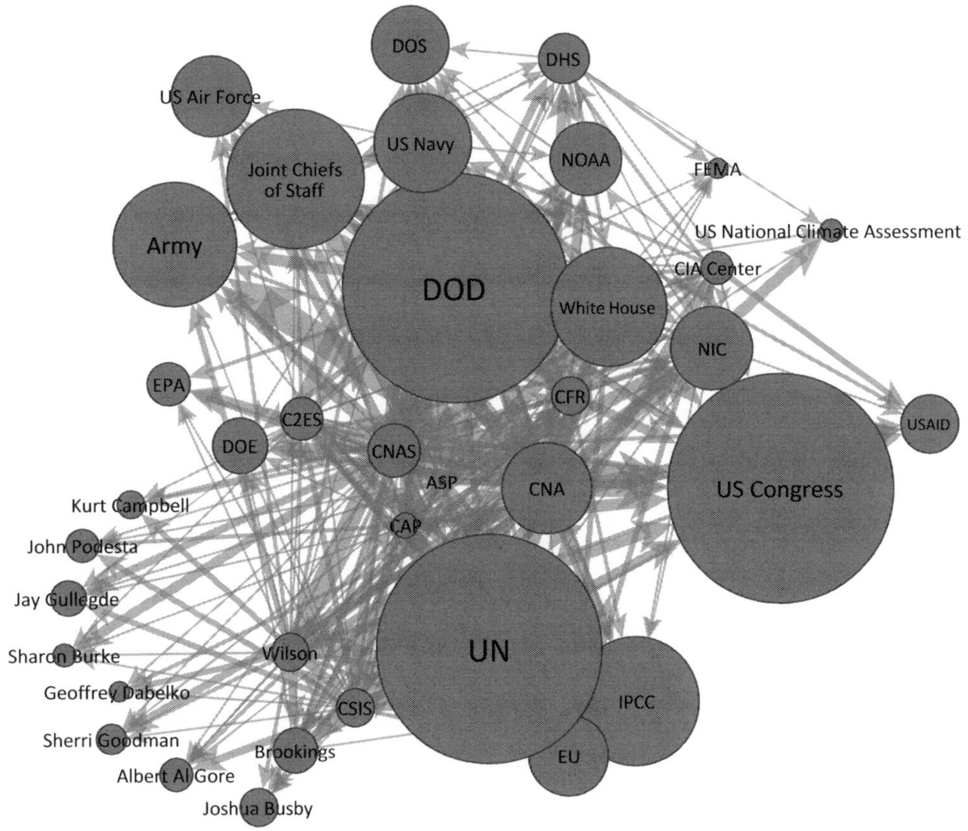

FIGURE 3.1 Network citation analysis (US case)

Political impact

We now turn to the political consequences of the climate security discourse in the US. As the overview at the beginning of this chapter has shown, the US has seen neither federal climate legislation nor a reversal of its position in international climate negotiations. However, to quote a think tank expert, 'the climate security debate has not scored a goal but has moved the ball a bit across the field' (Interview 2014u). First, it bridged the divide between conservatives and liberals and provided a platform from which politicians from the centrist, conservative and Republican spectrum were able to speak about climate change again without having to fear the wrath of their constituents or the environmentalist label (Interview 2014y; Fletcher 2009: 808, 811; Below 2007: 710; McCright and Dunlap 2011: 155; Eckersley 2007: 320). Second, following our argument of a first kind of policy impact, the climate security discourse gained increased attention for climate change among politicians and the public by elevating climate change to the realm of high politics. It thus contributed to an increase in climate legislation initiatives (see Fletcher 2009: 808; Eckersley 2007: 320). Although to date no federal legislation has been passed by Congress, several states have adopted progressive climate laws, and better awareness of the issue has increased compliance with climate regulations issued by the EPA and other parts of the administration (Interview 2014z; Brulle *et al.* 2012). Most importantly, however, the climate security debate has influenced policies in the security, defence and intelligence sectors (Interview 2014aa; 2014x; see also Oels and von Lucke 2015; Oels 2012b).

Let us first look at the resonance of the second climate security debate in Congress. Climate initiatives in Congress had steadily grown from only 75 in 2001/2 to 106 in 2005/6. They saw a further increase in numbers after the Republicans lost their majority in Congress in 2006 (Donner and Faltin 2007: 9), to 235 in the 110th Congress 2007/8 (C2ES 2008). Simultaneously, climate security articulations in Congress steadily increased.

The first major attempt to legitimise climate policy with reference to the security debate came from Democrat Joe Lieberman and Republican John McCain with the Climate Stewardship Act in 2003 that they introduced again in 2005 and 2007 as the Climate Stewardship and Innovation Act. In the corresponding Congressional debates, in 2003 Lieberman pointed to the threats climate change posed to the 'environment', the 'economy' and 'public health' (US Senate 2003b: S13485) and hence used the then still important planetary and individual argumentation. In 2007, when the territorial danger discourse acquired momentum, McCain also pointed to the threatened national security of the US (Talhelm 2007). These bills aimed at strengthening the research on abrupt climatic changes – a threat that became particularly prominent in the wake of the 2003 Pentagon study – reducing US emissions and introducing a cap-and-trade system, but eventually could not get a majority in Congress.

After 2007, various further attempts to adopt climate legislation (mostly coming from Democrats and moderate Republicans) tried to take advantage of the climate security framing and increasingly referred to the territorial danger discourse (C2ES 2007/2008a; US Senate 2008b: S4990). In 2007, the Global Warming Pollution Reduction Act introduced by Democrat Bernard Sanders stated that 'global warming poses a significant threat to the national security and economy of the United States, public health and welfare, and the global environment' (US Senate 2007a: S309IS). The Liebermann–Warner Climate Security Act, first introduced in 2007, and the corresponding debates highlighted the national security consequences of climate change and also referred to the 2003 study by the Pentagon (US Senate 2008c: S5017, 2008e: S5197). In connection to this bill, Republican Senator Elizabeth Dole for instance insisted: 'I understand this bill is viewed by most as an environmental bill – which it is – but it is also essential to our national security' (US Senate 2008b: S4989). The 2009 American Clean Energy and Security Act – because of its sponsors also termed the Waxman–Markey Bill – added a further dimension to the climate security debate. The argument was that clean energy sources, while contributing to mitigate climate change, would particularly strengthen energy independence, which in turn would enhance US national security (US House of Representatives 2009b: H8477).

All these bills marked important attempts to place climate change on the political agenda (Richert 2009a: 7; Brzoska 2012: 172) and their often bipartisan nature demonstrates that the ideological divide between Democrats as climate change 'believers' and Republicans as 'sceptics' has at least been weakened (Fletcher 2009: 807). Yet strong opposition to binding climate commitments in both parties still proved to be too high obstacles, compounded by the rise of the anti-government Tea Party movement and the onset of an economic crisis in 2008. Thus, while securitisation was successful in terms of our first mode of policy impact, it failed to create sufficient urgency to make policy changes possible, at least with respect to directly tackling climate change.

The resistance to climate policies rests to a considerable extent on the specific opportunity structure in Congress. Politicians must primarily answer to their local constituency and therefore are less bound to the overall party line. Hence, Senators from states with a strong focus on the coal, oil, gas and manufacturing sector (e.g. from Southern or Midwestern 'rustbelt' states) often opposed climate action no matter if they were Democrat or Republican (Interview 2014ab; Mildner and Richert 2010: 26; Guber and Bosso 2013: 69). In addition, in 2010 the Democrats lost their majority in the Senate. Furthermore, the use of national security language for climate bills did not convince all sceptics; some policy initiatives were thus regarded as cheap political tricks using the security label only to generate attention (Interview 2014y; 2014s; US Senate 2009: S10148; US House of Representatives 2009a: H5555). Most importantly however, the prevailing territorial climate danger discourse advanced by the influential think tank actors did not target climate laws and regulations in the first place but rather focused on the security, military and intelligence sector.

Consequently, while the legitimisation of a genuine, mitigation-centred climate policy through security articulations was not successful, from 2007 onwards, members of Congress had clearly taken up the climate security arguments from the thinks tanks that directly targeted the defence and intelligence sector and framed climate change now predominantly as an issue of territorial danger to national security and the US military. In a typical articulation, for instance, Republican Senator John Warner argued that 'there are also direct impacts on U.S. military systems, infrastructure and operations. Climate change will add stress to our weapons system, threaten U.S. bases throughout the world, and have a direct effect on military readiness' (US Senate 2008a: S4885).

Many speeches in Congress quote directly from the 2007 CNA and CSIS/CNAS reports. Republican Senator Elizabeth Dole, for example, summarised the findings of these reports:

> Additionally, last year 11 retired three-star and four-star admirals and generals issued a report, National Security and the Threat of Climate Change. They had four primary findings: (1) Projected climate change poses a serious threat to America's national security; (2) Climate change acts as a threat multiplier for instability in some of the most volatile regions of the world; (3) Projected climate change will add to tensions even in stable regions of the world; and (4) Climate change, national security and energy dependence are a related set of global challenges.
>
> *(US Senate 2008b: S4989)*

Phrases quoted (often without attribution) include:

- 'climate change as national security threat' (US Senate 2008a: S4868; CNA 2007: 6)
- 'the spread of terrorism and failed states due to climate change' (US Senate 2008a: S4885; CNA 2007: 1)
- 'climate change as threat multiplier' (US Senate 2007b: S13502; CNA 2007: 1)
- 'we are now in the age of consequences regarding the foreign policy and national security implications of global climate change' (US Senate 2008b: S4990; Campbell *et al.* 2007: 5)
- 'we can't wait for 100% certainty' (US Senate 2008d: S5191; CNA 2007: 10).

Sherri Goodman and other think tank experts testified to Congressional committees, which further reinforced the adoption of their concepts and terminology by political actors (Goodman 2014). The fact that the classification of climate change as national security issue came from retired military personnel and not from environmentalist politicians or activists greatly increased its credibility (Interview 2014s; 2014z), as this statement of Democrat senator Barbara Boxer exemplifies: 'This isn't from Al Gore. ... This is from our own retired admirals and generals: Projected global warming poses a serious threat to America's national security' (US Senate 2007b: S13502).

Thus, many debates in Congress particularly address the implications of climate change for the defence and intelligence sector and urge the corresponding institutions to include national security risks induced by climate change in their planning (US Senate 2008a: S4885; 2009). These calls directly correlate with the claims of many of the analysed think tank reports. In their recommendations most reports urge the DOD and the armed forces to bring climate change into their planning scenarios (Campbell *et al.* 2007: 20; CNA 2007: 46; Parthermore and Rogers 2010).

In a first attempt in 2007, the Global Climate Change Security Oversight Act asked the DOD to foster research into and readiness for the possible military consequences of climate change. While this had no direct consequences on policies, the National Defense Authorization Act 2008 succeeded in that it obligated the DOD to integrate climate change into the Quadrennial Defense Review, the most important and influential publicly available planning document of the DOD and the armed forces (C2ES 2008; see also Hartmann 2009). Thus, climate change appeared as an important security issue in the QDRs of 2010 and 2014 (DOD 2010: 84; 2014b: 8, 25).

The integration of climate change into the QDR has resulted in changes to a whole range of defence and security documents. Climate change had already appeared in the National Defense and Military Strategy of 2008 (DOD 2008: 5) and in 2011 its security implications were discussed in an extensive report of the DOD's Defense Science Board Task Force that underscored the important role of the DOD concerning climate change (DOD 2011: xv). Later, the DOD published two Climate Adaptation Roadmaps, one in 2012 (DOD 2012) and a second one in 2014, in which it called climate change a 'threat multiplier' and 'immediate risk' to national security' (DOD 2014a: foreword, 1). Additionally, it integrated climate scenarios into its Science, Infrastructure, Research, Development and Acquisition Plan and Strategic Sustainability Performance Plan 2014 (DOD 2014c). Finally, the United States Central Command (USCENTCOM) also took up climate change in one of its regional risk assessments (DOD 2014d).

Among the US armed forces the Navy was the most active on climate change. In 2009 it established a Task Force on Climate Change (US Navy 2009) and published its *Climate Change Roadmap* the following year (US Navy 2010). Furthermore, as recommended by think tank reports on climate security (Werz and Manlove 2009: 4–5), the DOD increased its cooperation with civilian and development actors such as the DHS and USAID (Hartmann 2010). This facilitated a further merging of defence and civilian approaches, and the rise of concepts such as 'networked security', 'integrated power', and 'sustainable security' (Werz and Manlove 2009: 5). In relation to this, the DOD began to highlight the importance of 'whole-of-government' or 'whole-of-community' approaches to tackle today's complex security threats and in particular climate change (DOD 2010: 70, 74, 87; 2014b: 22, 33; 2012: 6; Interview 2014aa). While this will affect the development and climate sector (as the demand for specific security related data will increase), it also 'climatised' (Brzoska and Oels 2011; Oels 2012a) the security and military sector itself. Thus, security and military experts began to adopt concepts from climate science and transformed the military to be fit to meet future climate challenges.

In addition to these concrete policy effects, the leadership of the DOD (Interview 2014aa), several high ranking military officials and members of the Obama administration, began to publicly acknowledge climate change as a serious security problem. In 2013, Navy admiral Samuel L. Locklear (chief of the US Pacific forces) even called it the 'biggest long-term security threat in the Pacific region' (Bender 2013). While Hillary Clinton as secretary of state (2009–2013) had not made climate change a priority, her successor John Kerry (since 2013) (Davenport 2014a; 2014b) and both secretaries of defense Leon Panetta (2011–2013) (Munoz 2012) and Chuck Hagel (2013–2015) (Davenport 2014c; Bendery 2014) were quite outspoken on the security implications of climate change. In May 2015, the White House published a report that summarised all national security implications of climate change as put forward in federal reports (The White House 2015a).

The US intelligence sector also picked up climate change and its security related effects. The Intelligence Authorization Act for Fiscal Year 2008 had tried to prompt the intelligence agencies to consider the national security and geopolitical implications of climate change, and the Intelligence Estimate (NIE) 2008 followed suit (Fingar 2008). The 2009 Annual Threat Assessments for the Senate Select Committee on Intelligence (Blair 2009) included climate change. In 2009 the CIA, then with Panetta at its head, even founded a Center for Climate Change and National Security (CIA 2009). Although it was disbanded as a stand-alone office in 2012, the CIA continued to monitor the security implications of climate change in different regional departments (Broder 2012; Interview 2014z).

Finally, as many think tanks had recommended, climate change and its various effects on individual US citizens also made it into several disaster management plans of the FEMA (2012) and into the National Infrastructure Protection Plans of the DHS (DHS 2013; see also Brzoska 2012: 174–175).

Overall, the securitisation of climate change had a particularly strong impact on the security, defence and intelligence sector in the US and refocused the debate on adaptation instead of mitigation measures. This shift from mitigation to adaptation is not the result of the climate security framing alone. It is also an effect of demands by actors in the development cooperation sector and developing countries to be supported in their efforts to cope with the climatic effects that already exist today (UNDP 2010; Stephens 2015). Nonetheless, the unique climate security framing in the US further reinforced and legitimised this trend. To evade difficult political discussions in a setting in which the anthropogenic causes of climate change are still disputed, many politicians and even some think tank reports and their military advisors focused on tackling security issues with adaptation measures. Yet, as some activists hope, the focus on such adaptation measures could become a door-opener for more extensive, mitigating climate measures in the future (Interview 2014z). For the time being however, the dominant territorial danger discourse in the US has redirected attention to adaptation and military planning.

Facilitating conditions and context for climate securitisation in the US

We now turn to the broader contextual conditions that have shaped the securitisation of climate change in the US. During the first phase from the late 1980s to the mid-1990s, when the planetary level still prevailed, environmental issues in general were quite important in the US, which was deeply involved in the early international climate negotiations. Moreover, the first climate security debate occurred at the end of the Cold War when new security concepts such as environmental security became increasingly popular not only in academia but also in political circles (Krause and Williams 1996; Dalby 1992b; Deudney 1990). The international climate security debate at that time also focused on the planetary and individual levels. This was in line with the rather cautious scientific language that always entailed margins of error and great uncertainty, thus facilitating a risk-centred and long-term argumentation. Climate change in this early phase of securitisation still seemed to be an important though still faraway environmental problem that would mostly concern distant places and that one would be able to handle with the appropriate risk management measures (Oels 2011: 21–22). Thus it is not surprising that the US climate security debate leaned towards planetary and individual risk, and articulations focused on bringing about effective international agreements and genuine climate protection measures.

However, even in these early days several concrete measures materialised, not only in the environmental sector but also in the defence and security sector, and climate change was integrated into central planning documents such as the NSS as early as 1991 (The White House 1991). As we have seen, these effects grew even stronger in the second phase, linked to the now predominant framing of climate change as a territorial danger. We argue that deeply embedded cultural and institutional characteristics have facilitated this development.

Going back to the struggle for independence against Great Britain and having stood on the right side of history in many of the wars of the twentieth century, in the eyes of the majority of US citizens the military has an exceptionally good reputation, as we have argued above. Although opposition to this sympathetic view of the military does exist, it is not as widespread as in other countries (Gallup 2014). Thus, bringing in the military into debates that touch on security questions is generally an accepted strategy and does not trigger great resistance or fears of militarisation, as it does for instance in Germany (Wagner 2008). Moreover, the US military itself has assumed a much more active role in the climate security debate – as well as in coping with climate change in general – than has the military in our other case studies, as we will see in the chapters to follow. Due to its international presence, the US military is often one of the first actors to deliver humanitarian aid to victims of natural disasters, such as the Indian Ocean tsunami of 2004 or cyclone Nargis that hit Myanmar (Burma) in 2008 (Interview 2014ac). In addition, both the Army Corps of Engineers (2015) and the National Guard are important actors in the domestic natural disaster management plans. The National Guard's involvement in the aftermath of hurricane Katrina in 2005 with the deployment of over 50,000 troops represents an important example (US National Guard 2015), although it also attracted criticism as excessive militarisation (Tierney et al. 2006; Giroux 2006; Masquelier 2006). On the basis of this experience, the military leadership became eager to address climate change (Interview 2014aa; 2014x; US Navy 2009). Furthermore, leaders still conceive of the US military as one the most important forces for global order. As such, they reckon that the United States military will be much more affected by climate change-induced instabilities and conflicts around the world than those of other countries (Interview 2014ac).

Closely connected to the high standing of the military in the US political debate is the predominance of the concept of national security. Coupled with a strong patriotic sentiment, questions of national security are one of the cornerstones of US national identity (Campbell 1992). Evoking security taps into this discourse.

The rising importance of the territorial danger discourse was facilitated by new scientific projections – especially the fourth IPCC report (2007b) – and observations by the Navy that lent themselves to illustrating the national security effects of climate change (US Navy 2009; 2010). By focusing on territorial danger, the orchestrating think tanks took advantage not only of the credibility of the military, but also of the political weight and de-polarising qualities that questions of national security can give to an issue in the US. As we have shown, using this narrative think tanks and politicians set themselves apart from a supposedly naive, left wing, liberal and environmentalist framing that previously had been associated with climate change.

This last point brings to the fore another distinguishing contextual factor of the US case: the extensive political polarisation of climate issues along party lines (see also Grundmann and Scott 2014: 233). This clash had not been as pronounced in the early days of the environmental and climate debate in the late 1980s and early 1990s. Yet since the Clinton administration's aggressive campaigning, especially by Al Gore, environmental and climate issues came to be seen as distinctly liberal and associated with the Democrats. This sparked an influential and mostly Republican countermovement of climate sceptics and deniers (Falkner 2005; McCright and Dunlap 2011), a trend that was consolidated under George W. Bush and led to a situation in which it became very difficult to talk publicly about climate change and its implications without triggering a major political headwind (Interview 2014ab). Thus, any framing of climate change as an environmental issue by traditional environmentalist organisations would only have reinforced the political divide, and, due to the US political system that often sees a divided Congress, would almost certainly have prevented any political action on climate change.

Conclusion

Our analysis of US climate security debates has shown that the construction of climate change as a security issue underwent a clear transformation. While the first phase of the 1980s and 1990s had a tendency to emphasise planetary and individual risk constructions, the second phase saw arguments that were focused on territorial danger. We tied this to the most important actors that led the second debate: these were mostly think tanks specialising in security and defence policy. On the one hand, they chose a different framing because they feared an increase in the security effects of climate change for the US military and wanted to improve defence policy. On the other hand, they also saw a strategic advantage in reframing the climate threat because it could both reinvigorate and bridge the polarised political debate on climate change and overcome the largely unsuccessful environmentalist framing of the issue. Within these think tanks, we highlighted the importance of specific individuals who acted as discursive entrepreneurs, enabled by their personal trajectories and networks. We also pointed out, however, that the success of these securitising moves relied on the reputation and credibility of the military and the importance of national security conceptions. As a consequence of the predominant territorial danger discourse, the political ramifications materialised particularly in the security and defence sector and tended to fall into the adaptation category. We will return to these findings and their assessment in our concluding chapter, in which we compare the US case with our other case studies.

4
GERMANY
Ambivalent forerunner in individual security

Introduction

Our second case, the development of climate security debates in Germany, could hardly be any more different from that of the US. While both are highly industrialised countries, their policies on climate change are at the opposite ends of the vanguard/laggard spectrum. Germany has been a consistent advocate of binding international climate agreements, passed various rounds of legislation to curb CO_2 emissions and reduced emissions to a considerably higher extent than many other countries. Accordingly, Germany occupies a high position in the Climate Change Performance Index (Germanwatch and CAN 2015). Germany decreased emissions by 26 per cent from 1990 to 2012, thus outperforming its Kyoto aims of 21 per cent reduction and contributing to an overall success of EU reduction targets (Werland 2012: 55). Its history of emission reduction policies reaches far back (Bruyn 2000: 212). For example, emission regulations for vehicles were introduced in 1983 (Jänicke 2009). Furthermore, an Enquete Commission, 'Preparation for the Protection of the Atmosphere', was set up in 1987, and an 'Interministerial Working Group on CO_2 Reduction' (*Interministerielle Arbeitsgruppe CO_2-Reduktion*) in 1990. Its aim was to reduce GHG emissions by 25 per cent until 2005 (Feindt 2002; Bayerisches Landesamt für Umwelt 2011: 2). In an effort to continue and improve its commitments beyond the period of the Kyoto Protocol, in 2007 the government set GHG reduction targets of 40 per cent by 2020, and 80–95 per cent until 2050 (compared to 1990) (BMUB 2014).

Underpinning this policy trajectory, discourses of individual risk and danger together with security framings on the planetary level have dominated the German debate from the beginning. Germany's Nazi past has undermined the reputation of the military and made it a lot more contested in public discourse than is the case in the US. Combined with a long-standing environmental concern even among conservative forces, an influential Green Party that has been an on-and-off member of coalition governments, a strong scientific community and an equally strong civil society sector, this has provided a context in which the territorial danger discourse has not flourished. Discursive entrepreneurs from environmental civil society actors have had a much easier task in these circumstances than those in the US or Turkey. Yet while they did not have to, and could not draw on the military as a consequence, they are also much less visible, as their articulations have been supported by a much more coherent and less conflictive, broader societal discourse (Schreurs 2003).

Why do we still call Germany an *ambivalent* forerunner? Despite having cut its carbon emissions significantly and having increased the share of renewables in the energy mix to 28 per cent by 2014 (Deutsche Welle 2015), Germany is unlikely to meet its own target of reducing CO_2 emissions by 40 per cent in 2020 compared to 1990 (Clean Energy Wire 2015). In fact, the decline in carbon emissions has slowed down significantly since the turn of the millennium, and emissions even rose between 2011 and 2013 (ibid.; Burck *et al.* 2012: 5). Even more contradictory, the steep decline in the early 1990s was in part due to outsourcing effects and the downfall of the heavy industries in the new eastern German states of the former German Democratic Republic after unification, and has therefore been labelled a 'wallfall profit' (DIW/SPRU 2001: 9). Meanwhile, the decision to withdraw from nuclear energy production has at least temporarily increased the importance of coal as an energy provider.

German industries have made more than ninety voluntary commitments concerning environmental and climate protection since the 1980s (Knebel *et al.* 1999: 62). However, in some cases, the declarations only served to prevent more resolute laws on energy or GHG taxation (Damm 1996: 25; Nordbeck 2002: 32). For example, Germany's influential car industry has lagged behind efforts to produce low-emission vehicles. This has led to the German blocking of EU initiatives to set lower fuel usage targets (Focus Online 2013; Bündnis 90/Die Grünen Bundestagsfraktion 2013). The German ambivalence produces not only struggles among different sectors but also concrete paradoxes on the government level. For example, the country's Ministry of Economy has increasingly been supporting research projects with a focus on the exploration of the melting Arctic in order to find new sources of fossil fuels (Panorama 2015). Last but not least, despite all its reduction efforts, Germany remains one of the biggest emitters of GHGs due to its carbon-intensive energy mix and high degree of industrialisation. Emissions per unit of GDP in 2012 were still above the EU-27 average (OECD 2012: 19). Thus, despite Germany clearly being committed to combatting climate change with a relatively strong level of securitisation on the individual and planetary level, it is important to bear in mind, as our story unfolds, that there are also strong ambiguities. Germany is not always the shining example that it often presents itself as.

This chapter is based on the analysis of over thirty-five core publications of relevant climate change actors in civil society and among think tanks and government institutions; and of sixty relevant parliamentary debates on climate change. To further substantiate the findings, we have conducted twenty-five mainly semi-structured and informal interviews with state representatives, environmental activists, scientists, think tanks and NGOs, and additionally conducted a network citation analysis as elaborated in Chapter 2.

We start by outlining the general environmental and climate change debates and policies in Germany, and in the following section identify two broader phases of climate change securitisation that are in turn marked by ups and downs. We analyse the climate security debate with a focus on the dominant climate security discourses and the dominant actors. This is followed by an overview of policies that have been legitimised or triggered by climate security discourses. We will then further explore the contextual conditions for the success of securitisation in Germany.

The general climate debate: Germany as an ambivalent forerunner

In the 1950s and 1960s, rapid construction and economic growth led to visible environmental pollution in Germany (OECD 1993). Germany belonged to the laggards of environmental protection, in contrast to the US (Weidner and Mez 2008; Krück et al. 1999: 8; WBGU 2001). Important impulses for German environmentalism thus came from the newly introduced American environmental policies and the 1972 United Nations Conference on the Human Environment in Stockholm. Reports such as the Club of Rome study on the *Limits to Growth* (Meadows and Meadows 1972; Mederake and Duwe 2014), also referred to as the 'Bible of the environmentalists' (Interview 2014ap; *Der Spiegel* 2012) and later the Brundtland report *Our Common Future* (United Nations 1987) heavily influenced international and German environmental and development debates, and introduced core concepts such as 'sustainable development'. The first UN International Climate Protection Conference in 1979 and the initiation of the World Climate Programme (WCP) by the World Meteorological Organisation (WMO) contributed to this momentum.

Thus, a significant part of German society became aware of 'the limits to growth' and demanded appropriate responses from the government (Roth and Rucht 2008; Feindt 2002). The environmental, anti-nuclear and peace movements in the 1970s and 1980s resulted in the creation of important actors such as Greenpeace Germany and the Green Party (1980), and led to further institutional and policy changes at the government level (Jensen 2009). Already during the chancellorship of Willy Brandt (SPD) and an SPD/FDP (social–liberal) coalition government (1969–1974), the policy field of 'environmental politics' was introduced and the government initiated an Immediate Programme for Environmental Protection (*Sofortprogramm Umweltschutz*) in 1970 and an Environmental Programme was started in 1971 (Jensen 2009). Helmut Schmidt, who succeeded Brandt as chancellor in 1974, downgraded the importance of environmental issues and environmental policy integration at the time of the oil crisis and a worldwide recession. The government was persuaded to give priority to consolidating the flagging economy (Beck et al. 2009: 14). Triggered by the oil crises of 1973–74 and

1978–79, the idea of saving energy and using alternative energy sources gained popularity (ibid.).

Pointing to the ambivalences of its policies, scholars have noted that 'Germany's stance toward climate protection appears to be characterised by extremes'. In the late 1970s and 1980s, the country converted from laggard to leader 'almost overnight' (Krück et al. 1998: 2). The concepts of 'ecological modernisation' and 'sustainable development' began to replace the 'limits to growth' paradigm and materialised in distinct policies (Arnold et al. 2012: 194; Eastin et al. 2011: 17). In 1978, the Federal Environmental Agency (Umweltbundesamt) organised an international experts' conference on climate issues and the government established a committee on climate research a year later (Weidner and Mez 2008: 362). Furthermore, the Federal Parliament (Bundestag) decided to set up a (West-) German climate programme in 1979, which eventually came into being in 1984 (WMO 1989; Arnold et al. 2012: 194).

The electoral success of the Green party in the 1983 elections contributed to the implementation of green policies by the government (Jänicke 2009). When Helmut Kohl (CDU) succeeded Helmut Schmidt (SPD) as a chancellor in 1983, directly after his election he implemented the policies against air pollution that he had previously promised. Such visible environmental issues kept drawing public attention to climate change (Beck et al. 2009: 14). Especially from 1986 until 1990, scientists increasingly also addressed other actors such as politicians (Weber 2008: 59–95), as we will further elaborate in the section below on securitisation. However, during the 1980s and 1990s the climate change discourse was not yet strongly connected to the notion of global warming as it is today. It also included scenarios on global cooling, and most importantly, the global greenhouse effect (Arnold et al. 2012: 189).

When the Chernobyl accident occurred in 1986, the nuclear discussion and climate debate provided good preconditions for ambitious environmental and climate policies (ibid.). The controversy over nuclear power constituted one of the origins of the debate on global warming (Beck et al. 2009: 15) and was perceived as a demonstration of the necessity to coordinate environmental policy at the federal level. The Federal Ministry for the Environment, Nature Conservation and Nuclear Safety (*Bundesministerium für Umwelt, Naturschutz, Bau und Reaktorsicherheit*, BMUB) was founded in the same year. At the same time, Germany also emerged as a leading exporter of pollution-reduction technology (Weidner and Mez 2008; Beck et al. 2009: 18). Awareness and sensibility concerning climate change rose among politicians, media and society and the majority of Germans stopped doubting its existence and was willing to accept ambitious reduction targets (Weingart et al. 2000; Beck 2004; Beck et al. 2009).

Between 1987 and 1994, Germany further developed its role as a leader in environmental protection, especially during the mandate of the environment minister Klaus Töpfer (1987–1994) who later became director of the United Nations Development Programme (1997–2006) and executive director of the Institute for Advanced Sustainability Studies (IASS) (IASS n.d.). Climate policy emerged as a separate policy field in 1987, when the Commission for Prevention for the Protection of the Atmosphere (1987–1995) was initiated (Krück et al. 1999: 1), that was widely acknowledged and had an unprecedented influence on the status of climate protection in Germany (Ganseforth 1996). After reunification in 1990, other issues such as social and economic concerns began to occupy the political agenda and environmental issues lost their political prominence (Jänicke 2009; Beck et al. 2009: 17). Forces of resistance to climate policies also persisted. In particular, the strong German automobile sector and heavy industries lobbied against too strict environmental legislation. Yet, the climate debate was continued by the work of the Commission and other actors. Germany continued with its innovative climate policymaking, but the picture is slightly more complex. The country has also been giving in to influential lobby groups such as the automobile industry (*Verband Deutscher Automobilhersteller*, VDA) and has blocked further CO_2 emission reduction policies on the European level (Focus Online 2013; Bündnis 90/Die Grünen Bundestagsfraktion 2013). Growing opposition during 1992 to the CO_2 and energy tax caused delays in policymaking, so that Germany was one of the last industrialised countries to submit a formal strategy of sustainable development in terms of Agenda 21 as agreed on in Rio (Damm 1996: 25; Jänicke 2009).

Yet at the same time, and in line with its image of a civilian power (Maull 1993; Risse 2004) Germany continued to support international efforts to combat climate change. Through distinct initiatives, German politicians gained attention and respect for their determination on climate action at international conferences over time. In 1992, at the time of the Rio Earth Summit, the German government brought together scientists from the German Advisory Council on Global Environmental Change (*Wissenschaftlicher Beirat der Bundesregierung für Globale Umweltveränderungen*, WBGU) to act as an independent expert advisory council. The WBGU later was to set a milestone in the securitisation of climate change nationally as well as internationally, as we will discuss below. A 1994 amendment to the German Constitution (*Grundgesetz*), through which the concept of environmental protection became a national objective (Jensen 2009) emphasised responsibility for future generations and obligated the state to 'preserve the natural resources' (Article 20a GG; Deutscher Bundestag 1949). The early 1990s also saw the founding of several important climate research institutions in the run-up to the Rio Earth Summit, such as the Wuppertal Institute for Climate, Environment and Energy (1991) and the Potsdam Institute for Climate Impact Research (PIK 2013a; Wuppertal Institute 2015c). The period of relative setbacks in climate protection and environmental policies that had begun after reunification continued when the Kohl government was re-elected in 1994 and Angela Merkel replaced Klaus Töpfer as environment minister (Beck et al. 2009: 16; Jänicke 2009). After all, the measures during the Kohl era count as early policies of ecological policy integration. But tackling climate change at that time was still regarded as a cost factor and job killer. Ecological and economic goals were polarised (Beck et al. 2009: 19).

Germany's role as a forerunner in climate policies gained further strength when in 1998 Social Democrats and Greens formed a new coalition government. It lasted for two election periods until 2005 and attempted to overcome the relative standstill in climate policymaking (Beck *et al.* 2009: 17) by embarking on a programme of 'ecological modernisation'. The step-by-step retreat and phasing out of nuclear energy, together with new climate policies, signified a big advance in Germany's environmental and energy policies (Egle *et al.* 2003). The programme included a Law on the Prioritisation of Renewable Energies (EEG) that aimed at doubling renewables' share in the energy mix, a programme to increase energy efficiency, and an ecological tax reform (*Ökosteuer*) that started in 1999. The Ökosteuer reform encompassed the introduction of new taxes such as the energy or fossil fuel tax (Jänicke 2001; DIW 2010). Furthermore, in the course of the Ecological Modernisation Programme, in 2000 a National Climate Protection Programme and Strategy for Sustainability was adopted by the Parliament in which it set an aim for a reduction of emissions of 25 per cent until 2012 on the basis of 1990 (Deutscher Bundestag 2000).

Generally, the Ecological Modernisation framework can be characterised by its strong focus on the potential of new technologies for solving environmental problems (Beck *et al.* 2009: 18; Jänicke and Jacob 2006). Through the logic of ecological modernisation, the problem of climate change was reframed: climate change to a certain extent ceased to be strongly perceived as a threatening global problem and became associated with economic opportunities for Germany that enabled it to transfer green technologies and innovations internationally (Beck *et al.* 2009: 19). The new laws and measures created the impression that the country's Kyoto aims of reducing GHG emissions by 12 per cent in the period from 1990 to 2008 were realistic. An agreement on the nuclear phase-out was reached in 2002. Because of its progressive environmental policies, the German environmental industry gained a leading position in the world market in 2003. While during the Kohl era action on climate change had been regarded as a cost factor and job killer, the 'Red–Green' coalition framed climate issues as a driving force for innovation and modernisation, and ecological and economic objectives that were previously polarised now became complementary (Beck *et al.* 2009: 19).

In 2005, a new grand coalition government of Christian and Social Democrats (CDU/CSU-SPD) was elected with Angela Merkel as the new chancellor. Merkel resolutely continued to support Germany's international role as a leader in climate protection and green policies (Jänicke 2009), set new demanding national climate change and energy goals, and actively supported international climate negotiations while also encouraging EU policies in this area (Weidner and Mez 2008: 356). The National Climate Protection Programme that had been introduced by the government of chancellor Schröder was updated in 2005. In the course of the programme, Germany committed itself to reduce GHG emissions by 21 per cent for the period 2008–2012. This time, a change in government did not lead to a change in policy direction, as international events and the securitisation of climate change helped to keep attention on climate change (Stern 2006; IPCC 2007a; Weidner and Mez 2008: 371), and at the same time also marked the first peaks in the ongoing second phase of climate change securitisation.

The securitisation of climate change

German policy on climate change has been heavily influenced by earlier environmental and climate-related debates (see Beck *et al.* 2009: 14; Weingart *et al.* 2002; Reusswig 2010: 80; Weber 2008). Mainly because of its institutional and political impact, we regard the time span from the beginnings of the environmental movement in the 1970s and 1980s until the mid-1990s as an early and separate period of climate change securitisation. As outlined earlier, in the 1970s and 1980s, the first debates on environmental security emerged. In the late 1980s and early 1990s, the foundation of the IPCC (1988), the Rio Earth Summit (1992) and the initiation of the UNFCCC (1992) marked the beginning of a new era of climate protection that at the same time had a different discursive framing that was centred increasingly around a global warming narrative and no longer on other alternative scenarios that had been developed earlier.

The earlier climate security discourses in Germany were, in line with the international agenda at that time, closely related to discourses on the depletion of the ozone layer (Litfin 1994; Arnold *et al.* 2012; WBGU 2001: 76), the *Limits to Growth* debate (Meadows and Meadows 1972; Eastin *et al.* 2011) and the invocation of a 'climate catastrophe'. While these debates were also noticed in the US, they were even more influential in the German case. Above all, they firmly established the idea that behavioural change is necessary if we want to save humankind from existential dangers. The overview of climate policies shows that securitisation of climate change worked as an agenda-setter in Germany from the mid-1980s onwards and led to advanced policies to combat carbon emissions. These were not unambiguous, yet the fact that a highly industrialised country with a strong economic focus on the car industry would embark on such a trajectory at all demonstrates the success of securitising moves.

In the context of the mid-1980s, we observed the first articulations of climate security. Most importantly, the Working Group on Energy of the German Physical Society (DPG) in December 1985 issued an influential call with the title 'A Warning of the Coming Climate Catastrophe' (DPG 1986). It called for measures to reduce fossil fuel energy consumption through an increase in energy efficiency while at the same time discussing its replacement with nuclear energy. After its publication in 1985, the narrative of 'climate catastrophe' was taken up by the popular news magazine *Der Spiegel* (*Der Spiegel* 1986) and other actors in media, science and politics with a strong impact on the public debate (Norck 2012: 26; Kirstein 2013; Beck 2004; Beck *et al.* 2009: 14; Weingart *et al.* 2000). The magazine's cover image of Cologne Cathedral drowning in floodwaters became the icon of the climate threat in Germany (Weingart *et al.* 2000: 261; Mauelshagen 2009: 218).

Only one year later, in 1987, the DPG in cooperation with the German Meteorological Society (DMG) published another call that was sent to 2,500 decisionmakers in politics, science, the media and the economy, with the less drastic title 'Warning of Global Anthropogenic Climate Change'. Despite the fact that the scientists had realised the need to formulate their concerns in less dramatic terms in order to prevent the media and other actors from further exaggerating the danger, their call for mitigation of climate change and government programmes to deal with the threat was repeated in a further document (DPG and DMG 1987). In both documents, scientists, among them physicist Peter Heinloth, called for measures to mitigate climate change through adjustments in the energy sector, including an increase in the use of nuclear power as a fossil-free energy carrier (Beck *et al.* 2009: 15; DPG 1986; DPG and DMG 1987).

From that point on, parliamentarians were to refer to the 'climate catastrophe' or 'climate death' in their speeches (Deutscher Bundestag 1993a: 12646; 1995d; 1995e). Member of Parliament Klaus-Dieter Feige of the Green party, for example, stated that: 'Considering the coming climate catastrophe, it is simply the choice between a tolerably secure human survival of human society as we know it, or drowning in chaos with unmanageable and unforeseeable consequences' (Deutscher Bundestag 1993a: 12646)…While such dramatisations were disputed by some experts, others regarded them as a necessary measure to raise awareness and motivate action (Weingart *et al.* 2000: 261). In the course of the debates, the notion of 'climate catastrophe' became characteristic of the German climate change discourse and is unique to German-speaking countries (Grundmann 2007; Grundmann and Scott 2014: 225). In both of their warnings of the potential catastrophe, the scientists, despite emission reductions and increases in energy efficiency, called for the creation of governmental research groups. The political reaction to the calls came immediately. Only one year after, the Bundestag set up an Enquete Commission for Preparation for the Protection of the Atmosphere (*Vorsorge zum Schutz der Erdatmosphäre*) for the period 1987–1990, that was continued for a second term as the Commission for the Protection of the Atmosphere (1990–1994) (Heyer and Liening 2004: 29). The fact that the Green Party was at the same time unsuccessfully pleading for the installation of a commission on long-term climate protection (Altenhof 2002: 139) and subsequently suffered heavy losses in the first post-unification parliamentary elections in 1990, in which it had campaigned with an emphasis on climate change, shows that climate change was not yet sufficiently established as an urgent issue (Kellerhoff 2010; Interview 2014m) and that unification concerns clearly overrode it on the public agenda (Jänicke 2009).

The Enquete Commission began its work in 1987. It included nine members of parliament and nine scientific experts, indicating the strong role of science in the German climate change debate from early on (Altenhof 2002). Notably, physicist Peter Heinloth, leading scientist of the DPG and DMG calls on climate catastrophe, was among other leading climate scientists a member of the commission (cf. DPG and DMG 1987; Deutscher Bundestag 1989; 1992; 1994; 1995a; 2013). Parliamentarian members of the commission were often experts and spokespersons on environmental politics for their respective parliamentary group (i.e. MdB Monica Ganseforth (SPD); MdB Michael Müller (SPD); MdB Peter Paziorek (CDU/CSU); MdB Christian Ruck (CDU/CSU)) and during the 1990s were among the main securitising actors in parliamentary debates (Deutscher Bundestag 1999b: 1086; 2009e: 599; 1993c: 14254).

The commission's task was to analyse knowledge about the condition of the atmosphere and propose national and international measures for its protection. Its reports emphasised the importance of the replacement of dangerous atmospheric gases, among other measures to mitigate climate change (Deutscher Bundestag 1989; 1994). The focus was not so much on the 'global warming' narrative and the 'effects' of climate change, but rather on the diminishing and endangered ozone layer (Deutscher Bundestag 1989; 1995a: 14). The mandate of the commission as a consequence of the emerging 'climate catastrophe' narrative and the successful framing of ozone depletion and climate change as security issues and future challenges that had a huge resonance and consequences for policies, represents a first successful instance of the securitisation of climate change (Ganseforth 1996). The Enquete Commission established climate politics as an autonomous sub-field of environmental politics. There were also improvements in climate science, and by the time the IPCC was established in 1988, the German climate research system had become one of the most advanced in the world (Bodansky 2001: 24; Krück et al. 1999). Germany emerged as a leading exporter of pollution-reduction technology (Weidner and Mez 2008; Beck et al. 2009: 18).

Apart from supporting climate change as an important topic on the national level, the strong influence of the DPG, DMG and Enquete Commissions in the debate of the second half of the 1980s also led to a support of nuclear energy in a heated public debate about nuclear disasters in the aftermath of the catastrophic Chernobyl nuclear accident of 1986 (Beck et al. 2009: 15; Jänicke 2009; Kirstein 2013). At least, the necessity to coordinate environmental policy at the federal level had – triggered by the accident – been recognised by decisionmakers. The controversy over the use of nuclear power in the face of a threatening climate change also constituted one of the fundamentals of the emerging debates on how to deal with global warming during the 1990s and early 2000s: 'Whoever wants climate change as a priority can for several decades not do without nuclear energy' (Deutscher Bundestag 1999c: 7259). The Federal CDU/CSU government of chancellor Kohl continued to promote the use of nuclear energy throughout its whole period in office: 'Nuclear energy has one of the biggest potentials to reduce CO_2 emissions in Germany sustainably. For this reason exactly, the Federal Government regards the use of nuclear energy as important for climate protection' (Deutscher Bundestag 1998b: II. 1.6.) A divide along party lines became visible, especially after a Red–Green government coalition was elected in September 1998 which then headed for the nuclear phase-out (Deutscher Bundestag 2012).

Not only concerning the use of nuclear energy but also with regard to the development of the climate security debate, both Enquete Commissions for the Protection of the Atmosphere had a lasting impact (Weingart et al. 2000: 269; Ganseforth 1996: 215; Deutscher Bundestag 1991; 1995b). Through the work of the commission, from 1987 onwards, the political attention to climate change increased continuously and reached its peak in 1995, the year of the first Conference of the Parties of the UNFCCC in Berlin (Weingart *et al.* 2000: 265). The impact of the reports and how they have been employed by members of the Parliament as a scientific and reliable reference to support their arguments is illustrated in the following statement:

> We have already heard a lot of dramatic announcements in the federal Parliament. This is why it seems that the three huge and voluminous reports of the Enquete Commission on the Protection of the Atmosphere do not concern or alert anyone very much any more. Though especially the third report reads as if it was a scenario for a horror film ... The consistent analysis is: There is only a short time left to save the Earth from descending into an uninhabitable state. If it were not 11.14 now, I would have said it is five to twelve.
> *(Deutscher Bundestag 1991: 3788)*

In the parliamentary debates of and shortly after the first phase of climate change securitisation, (1990–1994; 1994–1998) an individual danger framing of climate change was dominant, and was at times combined with arguments on the planetary level. Proposed measures centred around mitigation efforts, on how to employ nuclear energy in order to reduce CO_2 emissions, and on how to reconstruct eastern Germany in a sustainable manner. The dominance of the individual danger discourse in the Federal Parliament continued during the second phase from the turn of the millennium until 2014. However, occasionally we also encountered articulations of territorial danger in the early 2000s and increasingly during the term of 2005–2009. In line with the debates on environmental security that had also appeared in the US and on the international level during the 1990s (Homer-Dixon 1994), in the early 2000s securitisation still predominantly referred to the notions of 'environmental conflict' (*Umweltkonflikt*) and 'environmental security' (*Umweltsicherheit*) (cf. Eberwein and Chojnacki 2001; Carius and Lietzmann 1998). For example, the Institute for Development and Peace (*Institut für Entwicklung und Frieden*, INEF) in Düsseldorf issued a paper on 'Environment, Security and Conflict' (*Umwelt, Sicherheit und Konflikt*) in 2001 (Eberwein and Chojnacki 2001). The publication was co-authored by Dirk Messner, co-chairman of the already introduced WBGU, and director of the German Institute for Development Cooperation (DIE), an important actor in linking research on climate change, security and development policies in Germany (Debiel 2007; Adelphi 2011b; Biazoto 2010: 1; Auswärtiges Amt 2007; Faust and Messner 2004).

As a consequence of the early environmental security debates and the importance attached to environmental and climate protection during the 1980s and 1990s, new important discursive entrepreneurs emerged in Germany in the early 2000s. Most importantly, the think tank Adelphi, now a major securitising actor, was founded in 2001. Alexander Carius, one of the founders, had already in 1993 founded the think tank Ecologic (that later also played a role in linking climate change to conflict) and worked in various positions in government and research projects, among them at the Environmental Research Unit of the FU Berlin together with well-known environmental scientist Martin Jänicke, who later coined the concept of 'ecological modernisation' that became an important pillar of the Red–Green government programme (Adelphi n.d.a; Jänicke 2001). Through the expertise and networks of key individuals such as Carius, Adelphi had close links to governmental and research institutions and participated in important securitising moves.

A government-sponsored study on Climate Change, Environmental Stress and Conflict was issued in 2002 (Brauch 2002). The report was a product of the collaboration of the social science Working Group for Peace Research and European Security Policy (*AG Friedensforschung und Europäische Sicherheitspolitik*, AFES) and the think tanks Adelphi and Ecologic Institute for the German Environmental Ministry (BMU). It was presented at the 2001 UNFCCC Conference of Parties in Marrakesh and later published under the auspices of the BMU (Brauch 2002). At COP-7 in Marrakesh, however, the authors received a lot of blame for shifting the focus from mitigation to adaptation by employing the notions of conflict and security (Interview 2014as). After such unsuccessful single attempts to securitise climate change, the territorial danger dimension that had been addressed quickly receded into the background again.

The spread of securitising moves directly addressing climate change explicitly linked to global warming picked up from 2004 to 2005 in the run-up to the COP-15 meeting in Copenhagen 2009. The German public had high expectations that Copenhagen would constitute a turning point in the process of the international climate negotiations. Furthermore, popular culture and climate-related catastrophic events combined to have a strong impact on that public. The Hollywood blockbuster *The Day After Tomorrow* drew an enormous audience in Germany (*Der Spiegel* 2004) and even made an appearance in German parliamentary debates on climate change (Deutscher Bundestag 2007a; 2004a: 10244).

> If you go to the cinema this week, you will be confronted with the film *The Day After Tomorrow*. It is about climate change; however, it has only one scenario: 'abrupt climate change'. This is evidently not the most likely scenario, but it is possible.
>
> *(Deutscher Bundestag 2004a: 10244)*

Even ten years later, the film was discussed in a study of the Federal Armed Forces on climate change (Bundeswehr 2014: 4). During the mid-2000s, not only Hollywood, but real natural disasters such as hurricane Katrina (2005) drew attention to the catastrophic effects of climate change and demonstrated that these could hit not only unstable regions and societies, but also the industrialised world. The *Stern Review on the Economics of Climate Change* (2006) and the 2006 Nobel Peace Price for the IPCC and Al Gore for his movie *An Inconvenient Truth* (Weidner and Mez 2008: 371) further disseminated the perception of climate change as a threat. The Stern Report in particular turned out to be one of the most frequently cited documents in the German debate (GTZ 2008b; PIK 2007: 128; Greenpeace

2007; Deutscher Bundestag 2004f: 10244; 2007a: 9484; 2009c: 24255; 2008b: 17247; 2008a: 14268):

> I believe that we can rightfully call 2007 the most important year for international climate policy. Basically sparked by the Stern Report, climate change has not only been put on the covers of all international media, but also gained the attention of important sectors of society and thereby finally gained the attention that it deserves.
>
> *(Deutscher Bundestag 2008a: 12468)*

Mainly because it introduced a different framing that emphasised the probable huge economic danger posed by climate change, it served as a supplement of the individual climate security discourse. The report is mostly referred to as a relatively objective but strong argument for combatting climate change and global warming, as it provides an economic account of the costs and economic harm of climate change: 'It's not only since Nicholas Stern that it will cost us much, if we don't invest in climate protection' (Deutscher Bundestag 2014b). The report and its follow-up in 2014 at the same time pointed to the opportunities that climate change could provide. Instead of only securitising climate change, the German debates after Stern pictured climate change as an economic opportunity. Even eight years after its publication, the Stern Report remained an important reference point:

> Climate Protection is not a burden, but to the contrary, a big change for sustainable development and prosperity worldwide. This was confirmed by the 'New Climate Economy Report 2014', that updates the so called 'Stern Report'.
>
> *(Deutscher Bundestag 2014c: 2)*

The same logic was later also strongly represented by important key actors such as Ottmar Edenhofer, a German economist, co-chair of Working Group III of the IPCC, co-chairman and economic director of the Potsdam Institute of Climate Impact Research and director of the Mercator Research Institute on Global Commons and Climate Change (MCC) (PIK n.d.). Edenhofer on several occasions, among them the Munich Security Conference (2014) and the press conference on the release of the IPCC report in 2014, asserted that 'It does not cost the world to rescue the planet' (Mercator Stiftung 2014; Focus Online n.d.). In 2009, Edenhofer referred to Stern: 'Already the Stern Report in 2006 marked a turning point in the global debate. It convincingly demonstrated that investment in climate protection is sensible' (TU Berlin 2009). The Stern Report was with regard to its economic focus unique, corresponded to a need for objective calculations rather than alarmism in the debate, and thereby had a unique and complementary role, that was then also taken up by top level politicians such as chancellor Angela Merkel (*Die Welt* 2007a).

At the same time, securitising moves on the domestic level increased. In 2006, the think tank Adelphi conducted a project to produce a 'World Map of Environmental Conflicts' (Carius *et al.* 2007) for the WBGU, that only one year later was to publish its influential report on *Climate Change as a Security Risk*, which included outcomes of Adelphi's study (WBGU 2007d). Furthermore, in 2005 the NGO Germanwatch that had been founded in 2001 started publishing its annual Climate Change Risk Index and Climate Change Performance Index (Germanwatch and CAN 2015). In the insurance sector, several companies founded research institutions to analyse the security implications of climate change out of the realisation that 'insurance solutions can play a role in adaptation to climate change' (MCII n.d.), among them the Munich Climate Change Initiative (in 2005) by the world's largest re-insurer Munich Re. A number of civil society actors that later developed into powerful securitising actors and which until then had not focused on climate change as a security issue, now put the latter on their agenda (Interview 2014m; 2014j). These included the Mercator Foundation, the Protestant humanitarian emergency agency *Diakonie Katastrophenhilfe* (Interview 2014ag) and the German Institute for International and Security Affairs (SWP), that initiated a research project on climate change as a security threat for the period of 2009–2011 (SWP 2011).

Despite a change in government to a grand coalition made up of Christian and Social Democrats with the Green Party back in opposition after elections in 2005, climate security discourses, as in the US, Turkey and Mexico, reached their peak around 2007. In particular, the WBGU report on climate change and security (WBGU 2007b), published almost simultaneously with the Fourth Assessment Report of the IPCC, had a huge impact and became a major reference point of the debate from then on. The IPCC and WBGU reports as the two most influential studies were surrounded by a series of other publications and events that added to the debate (Greenpeace 2007; PIK 2007; GTZ 2008b). In the media, the climate security argument was more present than ever before (Norck 2012: 27; Weingart *et al.* 2000). The Federal government put climate change on top of the agenda of its double-presidency of the G8 and EU (Federal Foreign Office n.d.; Bundesregierung 2009; WBGU 2007a). Other events such as the 17th Forum on Global Issues in the Federal Foreign Office focused on climate security (Richert 2012; WBGU 2007b; Norck 2012; Auswärtiges Amt 2007). In contrast to the US case of climate change securitisation, in which the military and defence sector dominated, the German debate emphasised development and foreign policy, as we will elaborate on below.

In the course of this momentum, actors began to reorganise in networks, and as a result 2007 was also the year of the foundation of the Climate Alliance (*Klima-Allianz*), a platform that aims at coordinating the actions of climate-related NGOs (Interview 2014m). Similarly, the chief climate research organisations founded the German Climate Consortium (*Deutsches Klimakonsortium*, DKK) in 2008. In the context of this increased attention, the UN climate conference in Bali in December 2007 and the preparations for the 2009 Copenhagen Summit, the 'old' concept of climate catastrophe (*Klimakatastrophe*) reappeared in debates in the *Bundestag*, in civil society and in the insurance sector (cf. PIK 2007: 21; Heike Hänsel 2010; Jäger and Jäger 2010: 10; Allianz Umweltstiftung 2007; Germanwatch *et al.* 2013: 4), as this statement of MdB Hans Eichel (SPD), illustrates:

> Madam Chancellor, I appreciate that the climate issue will be a big issue of this conference. As bitter as the financial crisis is and as long as we will have to bear it, the climate catastrophe is a problem that is rooted much deeper. There has been thoughtlessness. To think that we cannot afford to react to the climate catastrophe because of the financial crisis is as wrong as anything can be.
>
> *(Deutscher Bundestag 2009a: 25623)*

Starting from the peak of the climate security debate in 2007, reports focused on the impact of climate change both on states and individuals. While organisations and think tanks such as the SWP, Ecologic, Adelphi and WBGU, apart from an individual danger framing also referred to the territorial danger dimension (Maas and Tänzler 2009; Kaim 2008; 2010; CLICO 2015; WBGU 2007b), humanitarian and environmental NGOs such as Greenpeace, WWF, Oxfam and Diakonie stuck mainly to framing their arguments in terms of planetary and individual danger. Reports also increasingly referred to 'climate migration' (*Klimamigration*) and 'climate refugees' (*Klimaflüchtlinge*) (WBGU 2007b: 124; Greenpeace 2007; Deutschlandfunk 2008; Brot für die Welt 2010; Angenendt 2011). However, while environmental migration, for example in the influential WBGU, study was discussed as an important risk factor, its political implications were not discussed apart from the proposal to create a stronger link to development policies (Deutscher Bundestag 2008d: II; WBGU 2007c: 3–12). In 2007, the Society for the German Language declared 'climate catastrophe' as 'Word of the Year' and argued that it represented concisely the 'dangerous developments that climate change induced' (*Die Welt* 2007b).

However, not only did NGOs increasingly produce publications on climate change as a threat after the mid-2000s, but so also did scientists and governmental organisations with a focus on climate change (Interview 2014ah). The Federal Ministry for Economic Development and Cooperation asked the official German development agency *Gesellschaft für Internationale Zusammenarbeit* (GIZ, formerly GTZ) to publish a report on climate change and security that was then issued by Adelphi (GTZ 2008a). Foreign minister Frank-Walter Steinmeier for the first time declared climate change to be an issue of national and international security at the International Munich Security Conference in 2007 (Federal Foreign Office 2008; Ederer 2007: 2; Steinmeier 2007). Minister of state in the Federal Foreign Office, Gernot Erler, in the framework of the G8 summit in Heiligendamm in June 2007, stated that 'we do not face a classic enemy, but we are in the process of rendering ourselves to be our own enemy' (Bundesregierung 2009). The influential, Parliament-funded German Institute for International and Security Affairs (SWP) set up a research programme on 'Climate Change as a Security Problem', which ran from 2009 to 2011 (Platzeck *et al.* 2008; Frank-Walter Steinmeier 2007; SWP 2011). And on the scientific level, also in 2007, the 'excellency cluster' CliSAP (Climate System Analysis and Prediction) was founded in cooperation with Hamburg University and the German Climate Computing Center (*Deutsche Klimarechenzentrum*, DKRZ) and now includes further cooperation partners such as the Helmholtz Centre in Geesthacht and the Max Planck Institute for Meteorology (CliSAP n.d.). CliSAP's anthology, *Climate Change, Human Security and Violent Conflict* (Scheffran *et al.* 2012) represented an important resource on climate security, with a distinct focus on human security.

After the failed Copenhagen summit in 2009, a discursive shift took place towards 'less alarmism and securitisation and more objectification' (Interview 2014n; 2014o; BAMF n.d.; Storch 2009). NGOs, think tanks and research organisations moved to provide technical advice and directly usable manuals to policymakers, such as the WWF's 'Study Model Germany – Thinking from the Target' (*Modell Deutschland – Vom Ziel her denken*). The report turned out to be an important blueprint for the German energy turn of 2012, which combined a renewed commitment to the withdrawal from nuclear power after the 2011 reactor meltdown in Fukushima with a focus on the increasing relevance of renewables in Germany's energy mix (Interview 2014o). In parliamentary debates between 2009 and 2013, the climate conferences in Copenhagen, Durban and Cancún dominated the agenda (Deutscher Bundestag 2010: 1–8; 2011b: 1–8; 2011a; 2009d), but securitisations and references to apocalyptic scenarios occurred with much lower frequency than between 2005 and 2009.

However, as a consequence of the securitisation attempts from 2005 to 2009, the climate change security discourse had by now been firmly integrated into policy planning. Even if German ministries only slowly began to coordinate their efforts, climate change had become an important pillar of development, foreign and energy policy, as we will discuss at greater length when we analyse the policy impact below.

A closer look at climate security discourses

As has already become clear, the individual and planetary level dominate the German climate security debate. This does not mean that there have been no articulations of territorial danger, as the BMU-funded study for COP-7 in Marrakesh and publications by the think tank Adelphi indicate. In contrast to the US, the articulation of territorial danger in Germany, however, does not so much invoke conflict as it highlights the threat to the sheer existence of states:

> Not least, the findings of the Enquete Commission on Protection of the Atmosphere show that such a trajectory would have catastrophic consequences for us all, including the developing countries. Some states such as Samoa or Bangladesh would perhaps even cease to exist.
>
> *(Deutscher Bundestag 1995b: 809)*

Towards the end of our study period, we note an increasing relevance of the territorial level, referring to distant climate security hotspots (WBGU 2007b; Bundeswehr 2012; 2014; Kaim 2008) but also to Germany itself as the referent object, especially with regard to the melting Arctic and environmental or climate refugees. Unsurprisingly, it is military and state actors or think tanks working at governmental level that articulate such threats (CLICO 2015; Bundeswehr 2014; Federal Foreign Office 2015). Yet, the predominant focus of the German climate change debate remains on threatened individuals in weak states in regions such as Africa, Latin America, Central and Southeast Asia or the Pacific (Germanwatch *et al.* 2013: 22; WBGU 2007b: 139–194; Bundeswehr 2012; Greenpeace 2007; GTZ 2008b; Adriazola *et al.* 2011; 2012; Maas and Tänzler 2009).

Furthermore, compared to the US case, the German debate draws a lot more on scientific data and the international debate, referring for instance to the Stern Report, the IPCC and the World Bank. In fact, German organisations and researchers work closely with these international bodies. Thus, for example, the World Bank report series 'Turn down the heat', published since 2012, is jointly produced by the German think tanks PIK and Climate Analytics (World Bank 2012c; 2013b; 2014).

A shift in discourses occurred with the decline of the climate security debate after the disappointing Copenhagen summit in 2009, when most scientific and civil society actors ceased to regard 'horror scenarios' as useful to achieve policy change (Interview 2015d; 2015c; Storch 2009). Typical of this prevalent German attitude is the following statement by Christoph Bals, political director of Germanwatch:

> We do not want to address the human reptile brain, but the cerebrum. If we address the reptile and invoke fear, the reaction will be a crude panic reaction, which may destroy more than it is going to help us.
>
> *(Interview 2015d)*

Instead, securitising actors from science and civil society as well as politics in Germany have been keen to promote a 'good global citizen' attitude (Interview 2014ap). This fits into a broader discourse of guilt in German political culture after World War II (Berger 2012; Maull 1993). In line with this construction of a restrained, peaceful and 'soft' German foreign and security policy as a 'civilian power', climate security articulations in Germany do normally not propose emergency measures involving the armed forces. One of the few public reports of the *Bundeswehr* on climate change, *Climate Consequences in Context: Implications for Security and Stability in the Near East and Africa*, prepared by the Foresight Analysis Section, is symptomatic of the taboo on military means in focusing on individual danger in distant areas, as the WBGU had already done in 2007. In the report, the *Bundeswehr* distances itself from any kind of military action (Bundeswehr 2012: 9, 133; 2012: 9) as the following quote illustrates:

Supporting the resilience of external actors is in the first place not a military task, but a challenge for the whole of society. For the armed forces, the task derived from this study is the support of an all-encompassing policy approach.

(Bundeswehr 2012: 9)

In a later study on Climate Change and Security in the Arctic after 2014, the armed forces emphasise the need to keep on monitoring climate change, which they continue to see not as a matter of conflict or territorial danger, even in the context of deteriorating relations with Russia:

For Germany as a monitoring nation in the Arctic Council, NATO member and leading export nation, environmental, economic and scientific policy dimensions of the region should be at the forefront. A relevant future challenge to security policy or the federal armed forces cannot be identified from today's perspective.

(Bundeswehr 2014: 1)

Ranging from civil society organisations to the Foreign Office and the armed forces, the focus is instead on the construction of individual danger, and in particular on the impact of water and food scarcity (Bundeswehr 2012: 101–104; Diakonisches Werk der EKD e.V. *et al.* 2008; CLICO 2015; Adelphi 2011a). Articulations propose mainly preventive measures, including further development and mitigation policies (Federal Foreign Office 2015), supporting the resilience of vulnerable regions (Bundeswehr 2012: 144), and the development of strategic early warning mechanisms (Bundeswehr 2012: 147; Adelphi 2011a) on the national as well as the European level. In line with this, the 2007 WBGU study emphasises that 'continuing climate change would increase the risk in the poorest developing countries that individuals due to the collapse of their natural livelihoods will be forced to leave their homes' (WBGU 2007c: 12). The central message of the study thus emphasises: 'Without decisive action, climate change will overstrain the coping capacity of numerous societies … and may induce environmental migration' (WBGU 2007b).

To the extent that territorial danger plays a role in these articulations, it 'beefs up' individual danger, in a reversal of the dominant discursive strategies in the US. Such securitising moves have, however, become more popular in the 2010s, as we have noted above. In a statement by the Federal Foreign Office, for instance, it says:

As a threat multiplier, climate change can exacerbate existing conflicts, for example over access to resources. Extreme weather events caused by climate change, such as tornadoes, drought and floods, and their impact (conflicts triggered by food and drinking water shortages and migration) have the potential to destabilise entire regions. Rising sea levels and the resulting loss of territory also harbour considerable potential for conflict.

(Federal Foreign Office 2015)

82 Germany

However, taken together, the German territorial discourse is still a lot more cautious than the American one. Civil society actors are quick to downplay potential dangers to Germany:

> In Europe migrants are perceived as a threat, because they all want or could come to Europe. In fact, this does not reflect reality. Most of the people that lose their homes due to environmental and climate catastrophe are not able to go somewhere completely different. They prefer their own cultural community to a new life in a faraway Europe.
> *(Wirsching cited in Wagner 2010)*

Another typical feature of the German debate is the relative strength of planetary danger discourses. Church and development organisations such as Misereor, *Diakonie Katastrophenhilfe*, or the Protestant development organisation Bread for the World (*Brot für die Welt/Evangelischer Entwicklungsdienst*, EED), in addition to environmental organisations such as the WWF, often employ such articulations of planetary danger, and link it to the individual level. They emphasise the responsibility of humankind for creation, i.e. the whole planet and not only specific states or individuals. At the same time, they stress the notion of climate justice (EED and Brot für die Welt 2009: 12), and in relation to this often invoke food security (Germanwatch 2013; Hirsch and Lottje 2009) and the increasing risk of individuals becoming climate refugees (Brot für die Welt 2010; DiakonischesWerk der EKD e.V. *et al.* 2008). The Catholic development organisation Misereor thus notes: 'Climate change affects us all, but not equally. Climate change is more than an environmental issue; it is primarily a matter of global justice and equity' (Misereor 2008: 4).

Particularly in the earlier parliamentary debates until 2005 and then again after 2009, climate change securitisations invoked the danger, but also quite often the risk dimension. In doing so, they combine long-term perspectives and probabilities with short-term concerns of danger. Yet they largely refrain from apocalyptic scenarios and emphasise opportunities to reduce risk through mitigation measures such as the protection of forests (Caesar 2000: 9362) or energy efficiency (Deutscher Bundestag 1999a: 3343; DPG and DMG 1987; DPG 1986). The lack of a strong territorial danger dimension and the emphasis on risk and the individual level has led to a consensus that we have to do something to prevent or limit further climate change. More recently, however, the strengthening of resilience as an adaptive measure to combat individual risk has become a more widespread argument, as we will show in the section on policy consequences. Before we do so, let us first have a look at the dominant actors of the climate security debate.

Discursive entrepreneurs

A multitude of actors is involved in the general climate and climate security debate in Germany. More than 200 organisations are listed in the databases of the Climate Action Network (CAN), the German Climate Consortium (DKK 2013) or the

Climate Alliance (Climate Alliance 2015). Of these, 117 are registered at the UNFCCC as civil society observers (UNFCCC 2013c). As such, we can only address some of the most outspoken actors in this section who stand out as discursive entrepreneurs. However, it is important to bear in mind that the securitisation of climate change in Germany is a consequence of the voices of a multitude of actors and coalitions from different sectors such as science, civil society, bureaucracy, government and the media. The German climate security discourse has a broad basis in society – and thus, individual entrepreneurs such as Goodman, Campbell or Dabelko in the US case do not stand out as much, even if some individuals and organisations can be identified as particularly influential.

Our network analysis of the citations in the sixty-six most important German reports on climate change and security, summarised in Figure 4.1, shows the large number of actors involved. Among the domestic actors, WBGU clearly receives the most references, which further illustrates the importance of its reports – above all the 2007 report *Climate Change as a Security Risk*. We also note the centrality of supra- or international institutions of which Germany is a member, such as the IPCC, UN and EU, reflecting the international orientation of the German climate security debate. On a second tier, the reports often refer to the federal government, the UN Security Council (coded here as separate from references to the UN at large), the World Bank, GIZ and NGOs such as Oxfam, Greenpeace and the WWF. Military actors such as the *Bundeswehr* play only a minor role, substantiating our argument that climate change as an issue of territorial danger is not central to the German debate.

As we have already outlined, scientific actors were crucial in pushing the climate security debate in Germany during the first as well as the second phase of securitisation attempts (Weingart *et al.* 2002; Schmidt 2012: 69). Particularly important in this respect were the 1985 and 1987 DPG and DMG warnings on an impending 'climate catastrophe' (DPG and DMG 1987; DPG 1986). As Weingart et al. (2000: 265) point out, attention for such alarming studies in media, science and politics steadily increased between 1975 and 1995. This trend continued in the climate security debate that followed. For example, the PIK has a media occurrence of three to four articles per month in national media, as becomes evident in its media clipping report (PIK n.d.). Germanwatch, while not a scientific actor per se, mainly produces data on climate security through its Risk Index and regularly appears in core national news outlets (Nicola 2013; Bojanowski 2013). Not only the media, but civil society and governmental actors as well have been keen to take up the arguments from actors such as the DPG, the WBGU, PIK, the Wuppertal Institute or the Max Planck Institute to substantiate their securitising moves and provide them with credibility. Again, the 2007 WBGU study stands out. WBGU was in a good position to influence the debate, not least because its specific function was to provide advice to the government. Other more traditional research institutions such as the German Institute for Economic Research (DIW), the Wuppertal Institute and the Max Planck Institute needed to put more effort into disseminating their findings, yet even they found an open ear in media and politics (Wuppertal Institute 2015a; *Die Welt* 2015; *Frankfurter Rundschau* 2015; Deutscher Bundestag 1995d).

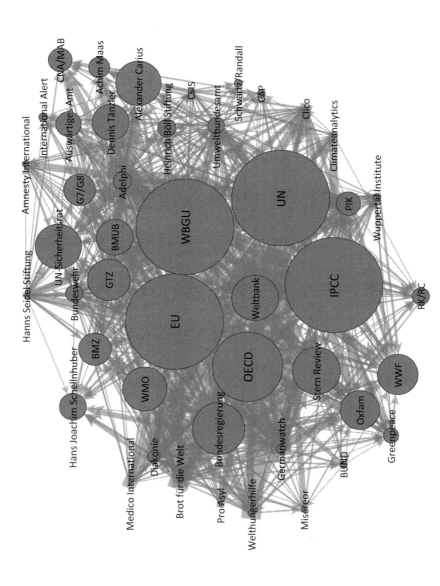

FIGURE 4.1 Network citation analysis (German case)

From early on, the German climate research system had become one of the leaders in the global research community (Krück *et al.* 1999), providing a huge output of data and knowledge, including climate change models and projections (Interview 2014ai). Among other evidence, this is reflected in the think tank ranking of the International Center for Climate Governance (ICCG). German organisations, among them the PIK, MCCI, Wuppertal Institute, IASS and Germanwatch, are recognised as being among the leading climate think tanks worldwide (ICCG 2014). German civil society and politicians tend to not use 'foreign' findings apart from IPCC and UNFCCC publications, preferring the data and models from German research institutions. In parliamentary debates on climate change, PIK, is among other German research organisations, one of the most cited (Deutscher Bundestag 2004b: 8374; 2009e: 599; 2009b: 24252).

Among the think tanks that have influenced the climate security debate, Adelphi, a private consultancy working for German state institutions at federal and state level as well as for European and international institutions and organisations, is by far the most important (Institute for Environmental Security 2015). Adelphi has particularly strong links with the Foreign Office (Interview 2014as), and has been involved in the securitisation of climate change from as early as 2001. The Ministry of Environment, Nature and Nuclear Safety, the GIZ, as well as the Foreign Office and important international actors such as the EU and G7, continued to use Adelphi as a main consultancy (EUISS 2015a; Adelphi 2009b; Maas *et al.* 2011; Fritzsche and Ruettinger 2013). In 2004, Adelphi set up a platform for climate change vulnerability and conflict in the context of the implementation of the Foreign Office's Action Plan on Civilian Crisis Prevention (ECC n.d.). Despite the link between conflict and climate change in the title, the platform focuses on individual risks in the most affected areas and advocates building up increased resilience among local populations. On the EU level, in 2009–10 Adelphi was responsible for drafting the *Roadmap on Climate Change and International Security*, the aim of which was to integrate the security challenges of climate change systematically into EU policies, and conducted several studies for the EU Commission (Adelphi 2011a; 2011b). In 2014, G7 members commissioned an international consortium involving International Alert, the Woodrow Wilson International Center for Scholars, the EU Institute for Security Studies (EUISS) and Adelphi as the lead partner to conduct an independent study on climate change and state fragility. The consortium launched the Environment, Conflict and Cooperation (ECC) online platform that aimed to share and disseminate the collected knowledge and research in May 2015 (EUISS 2015b).

Moreover, a huge number of development and church organisations has participated in the German climate security debate. As we have already seen, actors such as *Diakonie Katastrophenhilfe* and *Brot für die Welt* from the Protestant churches and Misereor from the Catholic Church, as well as development NGOs such as Oxfam Germany, drove individual and planetary securitisations. They often worked together with state-funded development organisations such as the GIZ and the DIE, which in turn had strong links to the WBGU and other climate change organisations. Finally, yet importantly, in contrast to our other case studies, the Green Party, founded in 1979 and represented in the *Bundestag* since 1983, plays an important role in German politics. Given that the party sees climate change as one of the central challenges for foreign and security policy (Bündnis 90/Die Grünen Bundestagsfraktion 2014), climate change has a direct 'spokesparty' in Parliament, and provides an access point for environmentalist groups.

Climate change NGOs and think tanks in Germany have a comparatively high level of institutionalisation and professionalisation. Taken together with the broad societal consensus, this implies a rather weak influence of individual discursive entrepreneurs. Yet their role should not be underestimated. Although not as influential as in the US, individual discursive entrepreneurs have also played a role in Germany. A closer look at articulations of climate security shows that some key actors have participated in the debates over longer periods and in different functions. A first example is the physicist Peter Heinloth, who first had the role of a securitising scientist in two important reports of the 1980s, and shortly after became a member of the Enquete Commission that was founded as a consequence of the successful politicisation and follow-up securitisation of climate change, first in science and then the media and politics (Weingart *et al.* 2000: 269).

Moreover, as our network analysis shows, Hans-Joachim Schellnhuber, director of PIK and the WBGU, is another important individual discursive entrepreneur. Sometimes also called Chancellor Merkel's 'climate whisperer', his impact exceeds national boundaries and he has decisively shaped not only the national but also the international climate security debate (PNN 2015). In 2004, he participated in a visit of international climate scientists to brief the White House and then president George W. Bush on international climate policies. From 2007 onwards, he became chief advisor on climate change to the Federal Government during the German presidencies of the G7 and the Council of the European Union, and was at the same time director of both the WBGU and PIK (PIK 2015a). Later, on 15 February 2013, Schellnhuber spoke as the only participating scientist at an informal meeting of the UN Security Council on climate change (PIK 2013b). Moreover, Schellnhuber gave the inaugural speech at the preparatory conference of the EU Commission for the UN Climate Conference in Paris in 2015 (PIK 2015b). In summer 2015, together with Pope Francis in the Vatican, he presented the papal encyclical *Laudatio Si*, focusing on environmental security threats (Dehmer 2015).

Other key individual discursive entrepreneurs are Alexander Carius, director of Adelphi, and Dennis Tänzler, director of the international climate policy unit at Adelphi. Besides Carius' and Tänzler's work for Adelphi in general, their good personal relations with the German Federal Foreign Office and other ministries such as the BMUB enabled Adelphi to conduct an influential series of studies for different important ministries and state organisations on the domestic and international level (Carius and Maas 2009; Maas and Tänzler 2009; Adelphi 2009b; EUISS 2015a; Maas and Tänzler 2009; Adelphi 2013a). During the time of the German EU and G7 presidencies in 2007 and 2008, Tänzler was an expert member of the planning staff of the Federal Foreign office in the field of energy and climate policies (Adelphi n.d.b; Interview 2014as). He has participated in consultancy projects since the 2000s, has worked as a consultant for, and has led and managed the Environment, Conflict and Cooperation Platform, which the German Federal Foreign Office has been supporting since 2004. Since 2014, Tänzler has also been leading a project on the narratives of climate diplomacy for the European Commission (ibid.).

Compared to our other case studies, insurance companies play a much greater role in the German climate security debate, which further illustrates the risk focus in the German case. This is significant for the global debate on climate change not least because German companies such as Munich Re own a decisive share in the international (re-)insurance market (Statista and Standard & Poor's 2015). While only twenty years ago Munich Re had seen itself as 'a business organisation that cannot act politically' (Kulke 2013), it now cooperates closely with environmental organisations such as Germanwatch and the PIK. It has even started two initiatives of its own that work on climate change and provide funding for research, for instance in the PIK (ibid.). Its Geo Risk Research Unit has been researching and documenting loss events caused by natural hazards around the globe for more than forty years, creating an unrivalled database on natural disasters that is now of crucial relevance for climate security debates (MCII n.d.; Höppe 2008). GIZ, WBGU, PIK and the publications of other actors regularly employ Munich Re data (Endlicher and Gerstengarbe 2007; DiakonischesWerk der EKD e.V. *et al.* 2008: 64; PIK 2007: 118; WBGU 2006: 109; 2012: 37).

Already before the publication of the Stern Report in 2006, Munich Re representatives had argued that climate change was not only an ecological but also an economic risk that insurers and especially re-insurers had to be concerned about (Höppe 2008). It now maintains the Munich Re Foundation, which funds climate research, and the Munich Climate Insurance Initiative (MCII) as a think tank. Other insurance-related organisations include, for instance, the Allianz Environmental Foundation (*Allianz Umweltstiftung*). All of them play a crucial role in research and advocacy of climate change policies, using a risk framework. Munich Re, for example, has been present at the most recent COP meetings (Munich Re 2015; Kulke 2013). The Munich Re Foundation has funded a seven-year study by the United Nations University on 'Addressing Loss and Damage in the Context of Social Vulnerability and Resilience', which it presented at COP-18 in Doha in 2012 (UNU-EHS 2012). Hannoversche Rück, too, has published a series of reports on emerging risks and climate change (Hannover Re 2013).

Interestingly, there are strong connections on the level of funding, as well as between personnel and insurance-related organisations and other civil society actors involved in the climate security debate. For example, the PIK has conducted a study on the financial damage caused by climate change in the German insurance sector (*Auswirkungen des Klimawandels auf die Schadensituation in der Deutschen Versicherungswirtschaft*) for the German Insurance Federation GDV (GDV 2012). Christoph Bals, managing director of Germanwatch, is at the same time vice-chair member of the Munich Climate Insurance Initiative (MCII n.d.).

While the discursive consensus is that climate change presents a threat, a relatively small group of climate sceptics continues to follow the antithetic narrative that the climate catastrophe, global warming or climate change are lies produced by an overly hysterical coalition of national and international climate scientists (cf. Weingart et al. 2000; Bachmann 2007; Vahrenholt and Lüning 2012). These sceptics, however, are much less influential than, for example, their counterparts in the US. The successful securitisation of climate change in Germany has certainly contributed to their marginalisation.

Political impact

> Climate change is one of the greatest challenges of the twenty-first century and a key foreign policy task.
>
> (Federal Foreign Office 2015)

In Germany the task of addressing climate change as a global issue and a security task has mainly been assigned to the Federal Foreign Office (Interview 2014as; 2015b; 2014ae). While experts acknowledge that classical defence policy is important in addressing climate change within a narrow understanding of security (SWP 2011), preventive security and development policy is regarded to have the important tasks of avoiding an escalation of the risks and dangers related to climate change. The general attitude of German foreign policy to climate change is to address it as a challenge that is not necessarily connected to violence, but first and foremost requires cooperative policy approaches that reduce the need for security policy interventions (ibid.).

The political elite, or at least significant parts of it, have been relatively quick in picking up climate security arguments, and they themselves have become securitising actors at a relatively early stage. Climate security discourses appeared in the *Bundestag* as early as the early 1990s, when terms such as the 'climate catastrophe' and 'climate death' (*Klimatod*) began to emerge (Deutscher Bundestag 1995c: 1662; 1997a; 1993d: 2–4; 1993b: 13011). Generally, we can distinguish four stages of climate security in German parliamentary debates. In the first phase from 1990 to 1998, *Klimatod* and *Klimakatastrophe* appear frequently, yet mostly without any further definition. Apart from invoking danger, it remains unclear what the climate catastrophe exactly is (Deutscher Bundestag 1993a: 12646). This can be explained by the fact that both were already established as keywords by the earlier articulations of scientists and the media. In those debates both notions approximate to and are a mixture of individual and planetary danger, as evident in the following statement by Klaus-Dieter Feige of the Green Party:

> Considering the threatening climate catastrophe, it is simply a decision between a somewhat secure and human survival of human society as we know it, or the crash into chaos with unmanageable consequences.
>
> *(Deutscher Bundestag 1993a: 12646D)*

The debates between 1990 and 1998 centre on distinct measures such as CO_2 emission reductions as proposed by the Enquete Commission, and proposals for an ecological and energy tax reform (Deutscher Bundestag 1997b: 18328; 1998a: 19413; 1995d: 2529). Debates are dominated by an opposition–government divide and parliamentarians of the CDU/CSU such as MdBs Ruck and Lippold rather proposed to transfer capital and know-how to developing countries (Deutscher Bundestag 1995b: 809) and to further support nuclear energy (Deutscher Bundestag 1996: 8942).

After the Red–Green coalition took office in 1998, and based on rising scientific evidence, debates on climate change became more nuanced. Securitising moves became less widespread, and the invocation of horror scenarios such as *Klimatod* receded into the background and at times was even heavily disputed. Thus, MdB Peter Paziorek (CDU) criticised the government for portraying environmental problems as a matter of life and death:

> During the past year you have always justified your claims similarly … namely with scenarios of catastrophes and doom … Such scenarios have never served the issue of environmental protection and will also remain useless in the future.
>
> *(Deutscher Bundestag 1999b: 3377B-C)*

Thus, securitisation had achieved its first policy impact of placing the issue on the political agenda, but the debates that followed did not go beyond our security threshold. Yet securitising moves increased again after 2003. References to individual danger (e.g. Deutscher Bundestag 2003: 6439; 2004d: 7668; 2004e: 13417) now became the most frequent ones in this third phase, as this quote from Michaele Hustedt (Green Party) exemplifies:

> According to WHO data, the anthropogenic greenhouse effect has in 2002 already claimed 150,000 deaths. This makes it clear that climate protection is not a Green or Red–Green luxury, but an urgent and necessary precaution. This is not a soft but a hard issue. It concerns everyone.
>
> *(Deutscher Bundestag 2004c: 7675)*

Parliamentary debates continued to invoke planetary danger, but such invocations were less widespread than among civil society organisations. Securitising moves remained on a very general level and often did not justify specific extraordinary measures. References to territorial danger in this phase were rare (e.g. Deutscher Bundestag 2004b), but increased in the last phase from 2007 (Deutscher Bundestag 2007b; 2008c; 2008b; 2007c). Furthermore, calls for adaptation measures such as increasing resilience now became more widespread (Deutscher Bundestag 2008c; 2007c). They linked securitising moves to concrete, although still largely non-military measures (Deutscher Bundestag 2008c).

Because of the successful securitisation of climate change in Germany with an emphasis on individual and planetary security discourses, legitimised policies differ considerably from those in the US. Most importantly, Germany has pursued an energy policy that some analysts have described as 'very idealistic, ambitious and overly optimistic' (Umbach 2008: 1). The German energy turn, consisting of a withdrawal from nuclear energy and a commitment to significantly increase the share of renewable energy, constitutes an extraordinary measure in that it is a radical shift in the national energy culture and infrastructure. Its radical nature becomes clearer if we consider that some of the main German energy companies, often state-owned in the past and still with heavy state investment, were forced to significantly shift their investments towards renewables and have made large financial losses as a consequence (Interview 2014j). Despite the fact that the final decision for the nuclear phase-out, for example, was motivated by the Fukushima nuclear incident, the ground for such a move was prepared by the anti-nuclear and sustainable energy discourse, which is strongly entangled with the climate security discourse (Seils 2012; BMZ 2013a). Thus, in its reports the WBGU had repeatedly called for an 'energy transition' even on a European scale (WBGU 2003; 2007c: 9).

As a consequence of the security representations of climate change as an existential threat, Germany continually sets itself high emission reduction goals. The GHG reduction target of 40 per cent by 2020 and 80–95 per cent by 2050 (compared to 1990) was set in 2007 (BMUB 2014). Such reductions had already been proposed in the DPG and DMG warnings of the 1980s (DPG and DMG 1987: 348–349; DPG 1986: 10–13). Furthermore, government documents routinely refer to NGO reports and scientific studies such as the 2007 WBGU report (WBGU 2007b: 226, 278).

Beyond domestic energy politics, climate security debates have influenced German development and foreign policy, but have had rather limited effects on military planning (Interview 2014ae). This is evident in the fact that the German Federal Armed Forces to date have published only two reports that have considered climate change as a security threat (Bundeswehr 2012; 2014); and security experts as well as military officials have refrained from pointing out tasks for the military apart from technical and logistical assistance, mainly in development policies directed at climate security hotspots (Interview 2014ae; Bundeswehr 2014: 24–26; 2012: 143–149). The reports appeared relatively late in the debate and mainly contained statements that explicitly denied the ability of the armed forces to tackle climate change militarily apart from stabilisation measures: 'Increasing resilience is in the first place not a military task but rather a challenge for the state as a whole' (Bundeswehr 2012: 9).

While according to some analysts, the *Bundeswehr* is well aware of climate change as a security issue, partly through reports such as the CNA or CSIS reports in the US, army officials have been rather cautious in articulating this publicly (Interview 2015e). However, as we have noted before, both the 2012 and 2014 *Bundeswehr* reports did contain references to territorial danger (Bundeswehr 2012: 110–112; 2014: 7–12). Even so, their referent object is not primarily Germany or the territory of another state, but what McDonald (2013) would call international security (Bundeswehr 2014: 1). The report concludes that even the melting Arctic is still a sufficiently stable region that does not represent a direct threat or challenge for defence policy (Bundeswehr 2014: 24).

Even from the viewpoint of German defence institutions and decisionmakers, the Foreign Office is the main actor in climate security (Interview 2014ae; 2014as). The notion of 'climate diplomacy', which has become increasingly popular in Germany in the 2010s, confirms this impression (Adelphi 2013b; Federal Foreign Office 2015). Part of this diplomacy is to motivate actors in other states to act and increasingly comply with and strengthen the international climate change regime. Thus, German diplomats have been particularly concerned about how to convince decisionmakers in Africa that climate change is a security threat (Interview 2015c). Germany's Federal Foreign Office furthermore did not only influence the international climate security debate by initiating a UN Security Council debate in 2011, but together with the UK brought the EU Foreign Affairs Council to focus on climate diplomacy in 2011 and again in June 2013. In 2011, the concept of 'foreign climate policy' (*Klima-Außenpolitik*) was put on paper for the first time. A mandate was agreed on for European Foreign Policy. Since then, the EU has been called to minimise systemic risks that result from climate change before these can transform into crises (Federal Foreign Office 2015). Meanwhile, German and European development policy has shifted its financial and technical assistance to countries, regions and communities regarded as particularly vulnerable to the effects of climate change. The Clean Development Mechanism of the Kyoto Protocol supports investments of OECD countries in developing countries.

The links between the insurance industry and its climate risk discourse and policy are particularly strong in Germany. Government documents such as the German Adaptation Strategy for Climate Change (*Deutsche Anpassungsstrategien den Klimawandel*) explicitly mention the MCII (Bundesregierung 2008: 37) and demonstrate the increasing relevance of adaptation measures. In May 2015, the BMZ organised a stakeholder conference on climate risk insurance in preparation for the G7 summit in June 2015 and invited representatives of developing countries, industrialised countries, the insurance sector and the German Development Bank (KfW). The federal government promised to support the creation of finance mechanisms for the insurance industry with 150 million euros until 2016. The mechanisms aim at covering the increased risks of 500 million individuals through climate change by 2020 (Munich Re 2015).

Facilitating conditions and context for climate securitisation in Germany

In Germany the context of climate security discourses, especially for individual and planetary discourses, has been favourable compared to our other case studies. Our analysis has shown that the structure, the financial and organisational capabilities of securitising actors, and the discursive environment that they have encountered, have shaped their success.

In particular, we have emphasised that climate security discourses in Germany have not been a matter solely of the environmentalist movement or elite. Instead, they fitted into a societal discourse and self-construction that easily accommodated individual and planetary framings. The political landscape of actors in Germany is strongly infused by environmental interests (WBGU 2001), and environmental awareness has a long record in German society, providing a friendly milieu for discursive entrepreneurs of climate security (Kuckartz et al. 2006; Interview 2014af). This culture of environmental awareness itself is both evidence of successful securitisation and leads to further engagement in securitising moves. Indeed, according to a public survey conducted at the peak of the climate security debate in 2007, almost every second German felt personally threatened by climate change (Kuckartz et al. 2006: 20). Thus, and in marked contrast to the US, civil society actors who wanted to advocate policies of mitigating or adapting to climate change did not have to set their climate security framing apart from an environmentalist discourse to generate attention. Thus, they did not resort to a territorial danger discourse that might legitimise military action, and in fact would not even contemplate doing so.

Many individuals from a generation of activists and protesters of the 1970s ecological and peace movement who were influenced by the debates on the limits to growth and sustainability, in time came to occupy influential positions in German politics and society, not only in the Green Party. They have, as one journalist put it, 'their fingers in the pie' (Interview 2014af). The environmental movement and Germany's subsequent leading position in environmental politics demonstrate how the ideas of a generation, set here in the context of confronting a society dominated by a rather conservative middle class and values in the aftermath of the Holocaust, have been able to shape policymaking over a long period of time.

The proximity of NGOs and research institutions to each other as well as to governmental actors further eased the passage of climate security articulations. Research institutions such as the Wuppertal Institute, PIK and WBGU receive large parts of their base funding from the state. One of their explicit tasks is to advise political decisionmakers on questions of climate change from a scientific point of view. Due to their relative autonomy and independence, however, the broader public considers them to offer reliable sources of information, and their securitising moves therefore carry significant weight.

In addition to these domestic factors, Germany's self-conception as a civilian power in world politics makes it open to multilateral engagement and receptive to transnational framings of security threats. In climate security, we therefore witness a strong link between German, EU and international policymaking. Thus, securitisation of climate change differs from the US, but less so from prevailing EU discourses (Hayes and Knox-Hayes 2014; Springer 2008). Actors and institutions in Germany and on the EU level, as well as in other EU member states, cooperate closely with each other, such as in the case of the Adelphi project 'Developing and Implementing the European Roadmap on Climate Change and Security' (Adelphi 2009a) or the 'Climate Change, Hydro Conflicts and Human Security' project of

Ecologic (CLICO 2015). Thus, it is sometimes difficult to draw the line between EU and German attempts to securitise climate change, as organisations such as Adelphi, Ecologic, the European Climate Foundation, Climate Analytics or the Mercator Foundation act on both levels. However, this also shows how the international context influences the domestic discourse in Germany. Parliamentarians in the *Bundestag*, German ministries, NGOs and think tanks all often referred to the Stern Report and UK politicians (Fuhr 2008; Steinmeier and Miliband 2008; GTZ 2008b; BMUB 2006). Then UK foreign secretary Margaret Beckett (2006–2007) as well as her successor David Miliband (2007–2010) had a strong influence on the German climate security discourses (Interview 2014ad; Richert 2012; Scott 2012: 221). Beckett, for instance, gave a keynote address on climate change security in the British embassy in Berlin on 24 October 2006, in which she alerted the foreign policy community to the need for action on climate security (Richert 2009b; Germanwatch 2006):

> What should concern us here in the foreign policy community is that an unstable climate will place huge additional strain on these tensions which we spend our time trying to resolve. They are already at breaking point and climate change has the potential to stretch them far beyond it.
>
> *(Beckett 2006)*

In 2007, together with the German state secretary Georg Boomgaarden of the Federal Foreign Office, Beckett argued that the nature of security threats had fundamentally changed (Brauch 2009b: 101). Foreign ministers Frank Walter Steinmeier and David Miliband together issued a pamphlet for the German Federal Foreign Ministry in 2008, in which they stressed the role and importance of the European Union within the process of international climate negotiations (Steinmeier and Miliband 2008):

> From the melting Arctic glaciers to the growing African deserts, climate change is a reality. It threatens our prosperity and well-being, not just in Europe but beyond. Moreover, it will reshape the geopolitics of the world in which we live, with important consequences for peace and security. Climate change will act as a stress multiplier. It will exacerbate existing pressure on scarce resources, particularly energy, water and food.
>
> *(Steinmeier and Miliband 2008)*

However, despite strong attempts to securitise climate change, in developing countries and on the international level, Europeans do not only perceive themselves affected by global warming as such. The strong dependency on fossil fuel imports renders measures for climate protection also economically attractive, as these reduce the need for imports (BMUB 2014; WBGU 2001: 77) and in the long run open new business opportunities for Germany's 'green economy':

> For us this [the support of the industrialised countries for developing countries with 100 billion dollars from 2020 onwards] signifies: World society is heading towards climate protection. We will do good if we use these economic opportunities. The world needs our efficient technologies and our know-how. Herein lies the economic success of the future. We should enforce and not block it.
>
> *(CDU/CSU Parliamentary Group 2010)*

Such economic considerations, together with the participation of the insurance industry and the presumed positive effect of a strengthening of European policymaking and identity in light of Germany's general support for European integration (Hayes and Knox-Hayes 2014), have added to the favourable context for securitising climate change. None of these factors, however, is tied to conceptions of territorial danger – instead, they all work in favour of individual and planetary climate security articulations.

Conclusion

Germany presents an antipode to the securitisation of climate change in the US. Our analysis has demonstrated the prevalence of individual and planetary security. Individual risk has been particularly prominent in the later stages of the debate, but articulations often blend danger and risk into each other. A broad range of highly organised discursive entrepreneurs appear and act in multiple contexts and positions. While Adelphi as a security think tank did play a role in the securitisation process, scientific organisations and environmental, church and developmental NGOs have been a lot more influential than in the US, while the military's historically tarnished societal standing caused it to keep out of climate security debates for most of the time. This broad coalition of climate security protagonists met a highly favourable societal and political context, shaped by the peace movement and environmentalist campaigns since the 1970s. They promoted a policy of mitigation, tackling climate change at the root cause and reducing carbon emissions, which, in combination with contextual factors such as the Fukushima nuclear accident, led to the implementation of an 'energy turn' that combines a withdrawal from nuclear power with an increasing share of renewable energies in Germany's energy mix.

Furthermore, we saw a focus on developmental policies, both in assisting developing countries in their efforts to grow sustainably, and in helping those at the highest risk to adapt to potential climate catastrophes and increase their resilience, while not ignoring the economic opportunities that a reorientation of world society towards climate change mitigation and adaptation implies for the German insurance industry, technologies and 'green economy' (CDU/CSU Parliamentary Group 2010). Yet we have also noted the related ambivalences in Germany's domestic policies, and that its heavy industries, in particular the automobile sector, have sometimes imposed limits on climate change policies. Towards the end of our study period, in the 2010s, we saw adaptation strategies rising in their importance for Germany itself, combined with a few articulations of territorial danger. Whether these will be characteristic of the German climate change debate in the future remains to be seen. Yet we did note a relatively strong influence of the insurance industry through financing research and personnel connections. Together with an increasingly differentiated climate science, this has reinforced the risk framing of climate security in Germany.

5
MEXICO
A case of politicised securitisation?

Introduction

Compared to many other developing countries and emerging economies, including Turkey, Mexico is a forerunner in climate policies, and is highly integrated into the international climate regime. This is surprising given the rapid social, political and economic development the country has undergone in the last three decades and the severe problems we would expect this to pose for climate policy. On the one hand, Mexico's population grew from 86 million in 1991 to 113 million in 2010 (World Bank 2012a), the country saw a gradual democratisation since the late 1990s (Peters and Maihold 2007: 8), and its economy became the second biggest in Latin America and the thirteenth largest worldwide (Akerberg 2011: 38). On the other hand, Mexico still struggles with severe problems of organised crime and widespread violence, which have even led to a categorisation of some areas of the country as a failed state (Bertelsmann Stiftung 2012: 6). Moreover, social and economic inequality and severe poverty are widespread, with a Gini coefficient of 48.3 in 2010 and a majority of 51 per cent living below the poverty line (World Bank 2012a; Bertelsmann Stiftung 2012: 12). While in other countries, these factors have served as an excuse for not adopting climate policies, Mexico has managed to position itself as one of the most progressive countries in the global climate regime. From 2005 to 2014, it has always ranked among the top fifteen of the Climate Change Performance Index (Germanwatch and CAN 2015), and its efforts to fight climate change are in the 'medium' category of the Climate Action Tracker (Höhne et al. 2012). This is particularly striking in comparison to its economically much better-off US neighbour.

In the light of this surprisingly progressive stance towards climate action, one might suspect that a successful securitisation of climate change was the driving force behind this development. Yet, as we show in this chapter, this is only partly true and the reality is in fact more ambiguous. Climate security articulations, mostly in line with our individual risk discourse, have frequently appeared in parliamentary debates and some actors (mostly foreign to Mexico) have persistently tried to securitise climate change by relying on individual but also territorial risk and danger articulations. In the end, these efforts in Parliament and by NGOs to securitise climate change were moderately successful in terms of transforming the climate debate in Mexico and influencing concrete policies. While the individual risk discourse has been fairly successful, at least since 2005, in influencing the debate and legitimising policy, territorial discourses failed to gain traction in Mexico. What is more, other influences outside of securitisation such as pressure from the US, the legacy of Mexico's progressive environmental agenda of the past and the dedication of discursive entrepreneurs also played an important role in the progressive development of Mexico's climate policy. Eventually, the successful politicisation of climate change, the prevalence of other security problems and severe diplomatic misunderstandings between the external securitising actors and their Mexican counterparts hindered a more successful securitisation of climate change, especially in relation to territorial discourses and national security conceptions. Thus, climate change largely remained an environmental and economic problem. Individual risk articulations have played a supporting role and have been successful in contributing to the legitimisation of new policies and in infusing them with concepts such as risk management, insurance schemes and civil protection measures. Thus, Mexico presents itself as a case where politicisation and securitisation went hand-in-hand in advancing a relatively progressive climate agenda. This is an important finding in relation to our theoretical model because it underscores the idea that certain securitisation discourses, such as individual risk, are more compatible with politicisation and more likely to legitimise genuine climate policy instead of security policy.

This chapter is based on the analysis of twenty-seven core publications that include securitising articulations of relevant climate change actors among think tanks, in civil society and government institutions and 126 parliamentary debates on climate change between 1990 and 2014. To further substantiate the findings, we have conducted over fifteen mainly semi-structured and informal interviews with think tanks, NGOs and state representatives in the country, and additionally conducted a network citation analysis.

Before we go into the climate security debate, to contextualise the analysis, the next section provides a brief introduction to the overall climate debate in the country since its beginnings in the 1980s (for a more thorough discussion of Mexico's general climate politics and policies see Sánchez Gutiérrez *et al.* 2009).

The general climate debate: Mexico as climate vanguard

While the first precursors of a growing importance of environmental issues already appeared in the 1970s, which included the integration of environmental concerns into the Mexican Constitution in 1971 and the adoption of the first environmental law in 1972 (Mumme *et al.* 1988: 12; Mumme and Lybecker 2002: 314), Mexico's active involvement in environmental policy properly began in the 1980s. After years of political and economic isolation under the authoritarian regime of the *Partido Revolucionario Institucional* (PRI), the government then started a gradual policy of economic opening (Peters and Maihold 2007: 8; Sánchez Gutiérrez *et al.* 2009: 4). This entailed an increased focus on environmental problems such as air pollution and the contamination of water resources. Eventually it led to a reform of the environmental law in 1981, to an integration of environmental problems into the National Development Plan 1983–1988 and to the adoption of a new environmental law in 1988 (Mumme *et al.* 1988: 15–19; Assetto *et al.* 2003: 255). Apart from the administration under President Miguel de la Madrid (1982–1988), important actors pushing the environmental agenda were academic and governmental research institutions such as the *Universidad Nacional Autónoma de México* (UNAM) and the Ministry of Health (Mumme *et al.* 1988: 12). A further crucial factor was the strengthening of economic and political ties particularly with the United States. The US was at that time still a forerunner in environmental and climate policy (see Chapter 3). Thus, after the Mexican environmental law of 1972 had already been loosely modelled in accordance with the US National Environmental Protection Act, the political opening towards the US further increased environmental regulation in Mexico (Mumme and Lybecker 2002: 314). Hence, Mexico started several joint projects for environmental protection at its border with the US (Mumme *et al.* 1988: 15). These progressive developments notwithstanding, the effective enforcement of environmental policy, especially on the local level, remained a problem (Mumme and Lybecker 2002: 317), which later would also become an issue for the implementation of climate policy.

Similar to the development of the environmental agenda in general, the first actors to considerably push the topic of climate change came from the scientific sector and from governmental research institutions. UNAM and the *Instituto Nacional de Ecología* (INE) – a state-owned environmental think tank – stood out in this respect. After the establishment of the UNFCCC, ratified by Mexico in 1993, UNAM and INE were mostly responsible for the creation of Mexico's *Programa Nacional Científico sobre Cambio Climático Global*, which helped to coordinate climate research within the country. When in the course of the 1990s the climate debate entered the political sphere on a global scale and research on the issue intensified, it became apparent that Mexico was quite vulnerable to the effects of climate change. Thus, Mexico's government became increasingly eager to address the topic domestically as well as internationally (Salazar and Masera 2010; Wolf 2007).

The establishment of the North American Free Trade Agreement (NAFTA) in 1994 further increased the pressure from the US on Mexico to strengthen environmental policy and led to a growth in joined border projects (Assetto *et al.* 2003: 256; Mumme and Lybecker 2002: 320). An additional facilitating factor in the formulation of Mexico's climate strategy was the US Countries Studies Program, which was supposed to support developing countries in designing a strategy towards climate change (Pulver 2006: 51; Sánchez Gutiérrez *et al.* 2009: 3–5). It eventually led to the publication of Mexico's national greenhouse gas inventory in 1995 and the first national communication to the UNFCCC in 1997 (Pulver 2006: 51). Indeed, Mexico is one of the few developing countries that has managed to submit these communications to the UNFCCC on a regular basis ever since (UNFCCC 2014). With the Kyoto Protocol, which Mexico ratified as a non-Annex I country in 2000, the interest in combatting climate change grew even stronger because of the prospect of accumulating foreign investment through the Clean Development Mechanism (CDM) (Pulver 2006: 55–56). As a market-conform instrument of the Kyoto Protocol, the CDM is designed to facilitate mitigation projects in developing countries financed by industrialised countries, which in turn receive Certified Emission Reduction Units that can be used to set off their own emissions.

The early 2000s saw a brief period of neglect of climate matters under President Vicente Fox of the *Partido Acción Nacional* (PAN). Leaving aside Fox's personal preferences, the rejection of the Kyoto Protocol by the United States meant that the opportunities for investments in Mexico through the CDM were seriously restricted. Yet the debate regained momentum after the ratification of Kyoto by all EU member states and especially under the newly elected president, Felipe Calderón (PAN), in 2006, who even received the GLOBE Award (2009) and the Champions of the Earth Award of the UNEP (2011) for his leading international role in environmental issues. During his presidency (2006–2012), combatting climate change became one of the most important political issues in Mexico, especially in foreign policy. The preparations for the sixteenth Conference of the Parties (COP-16) of the UNFCCC, which took place in Cancún in 2010, further added to this development. Mexico was praised for its constructive leadership during the conference. Its role as a mediator for the 'good cause' was particularly underscored by its position between developing and industrialised countries (Peters and Maihold 2007: 2–3). Mexico has ever since acted as a strong vanguard at the level of international climate negotiations, and while reminding the industrialised countries of their historical responsibility, has also committed itself to ambitious climate goals (Detsch 2011: 34–35). This is underscored by its membership in the Cartagena Dialogue and the Environmental Integrity Group, which both stand for a progressive position concerning climate action.

Besides the dedication of Calderón, additional factors pushing Mexico's climate agenda were the heightened vulnerability of parts of the population, the high potential for mitigation and thus economic opportunities in the country (Rong 2010: 4590) and to a certain extent also the securitisation of climate change as individual risk. Concerning its institutional setup and concrete policies, the establishment of the *Comisión Intersecretarial de Cambio Climático* (CICC) in 2005, designed to increase the coordination of climate issues between all relevant departments of government, was one important milestone. Furthermore, the National Development Plan 2007–2013 for the first time explicitly addressed climate change. At the same time, Mexico adopted a National Strategy on Climate Change (*Estrategia Nacional de Cambio Climático*, ENACC) in 2007, which then contributed to the establishment of the Special Programme on Climate Change (*Programa Especial de Cambio Climático*, PECC) in 2008. This was followed by various further policies such as the Sustainable Electricity Programme, the *Programa Nacional de Estadística y Geografía*, which focused on identifying local needs for adaptation measures, and several state level versions of the PECC, called PEACC (Mexican Government 2012: 22–26). Yet the most notable policy outcome was the General Climate Law (*Ley General de Cambio Climático*), which was adopted in 2012. It committed Mexico to emission reductions of 30 per cent below the levels of 2000 by 2020 and of 50 per cent by 2050, and reorganised the INE to become the *Instituto Nacional de Ecología y Cambio Climático* (INECC). The successful adoption of this law was quite a remarkable development, since at that time Mexico was one of the very few countries worldwide to actually adopt a binding domestic climate regulation. After the election of Enrique Peña Nieto (PRI) as president in 2012, the political importance of climate change decreased somewhat. The new government has kept Mexico's international commitments and is implementing the domestic measures foreseen by the Climate Law, yet climate matters have no longer been a priority (Interview 2014e, 2014f).

Dominant securitisation attempts: climate risks for individuals

Despite Mexico's early involvement in environmental and climate change debates, Mexican actors only slowly picked up climate security argumentations. Our analysis of parliamentary debates between 1990 and 2014 revealed that climate security articulations gradually began to play a role during the 1990s. Mostly we can attribute this increase to Mexican parliamentarians adopting arguments from the international climate security debate; hence, they frequently mention international regimes such as the Montreal Protocol or the Convention on International Trade in Endangered Species of Wild Fauna and Flora in connection with climate security articulations (Senado de la República 1993: 75). For our analysis, we searched for the term 'climate change' (*cambio climático*) on the websites of the Mexican Senate and the Chamber of Deputies and downloaded all debates containing the term. In a second step, we analysed whether these debates actually had climate change as a relevant focus and whether they contained instances of securitisation. Out of 143 debates that contain the word 'climate change', we identified 126 as being relevant, and 43 of these include securitising articulations. In general the debates contain much fewer and less intense securitising articulations than is the case in the US or Germany, though more than in Turkey.

The first occasional instances of climate security articulations appeared in 1992 and 1993. As in the US and Germany at that time, these articulations often linked climate change to other environmental problems and the destruction of the ozone layer (Senado de la República 1993: 74). Mario Molina, one of the scientists who discovered the harmful potential of chlorofluorocarbons and himself a Mexican citizen, underscored the importance of the ozone issue in Mexico. In the course of the 1990s, climate change understood as global warming became more important. The first climate security articulations mostly focused on the planetary and individual level and on the risk dimension and were rather low-key in their intensity. Mostly they portrayed climate change as a global problem that pertained to the whole planet and humanity as such, and focused on global solutions. Thus, for example, Senator Guillermo Ulloa Carreón (PRI) was concerned with 'the prevention of pollution of the atmosphere ... the universal concern for the future of the human species and the survival of the planet that we cohabit with other peoples and nations' (Senado de la República 1994: 14).

While the territorial level and the connection between environmental problems and conflict was largely absent in these early parliamentary debates, Thomas Homer-Dixon, who already had been an important discursive entrepreneur in the international and particularly the US environmental security debate was one of the first to connect this argumentation to the Mexican context. In a 1996 article, Homer-Dixon together with Philip Howard drew a connection between the Chiapas uprising and problems in the surrounding environment (Howard and Homer-Dixon 1996). In contrast to the US however, where Homer-Dixon even briefed Vice-President Gore, political actors in Mexico did not directly pick up his arguments. Nonetheless, towards the end of the 1990s, the frequency and intensity of parliamentary debates on climate security increased, although it still remained at a much lower level than in the US or Germany. While we only identified two clearly securitising debates between 1990 and 1996, the number rose to six between 1997 and 2000. Besides the still dominant individual and planetary risk discourses (Cámara de Diputados 1998: 14; Senado de la República 2000: 4), in 1998 the territorial level appeared for the first time, in a statement of Senator José Guadarrama Márquez (PRI) with reference to the possibility of 'environmental conflicts' (Senado de la República 1998: 10). During the first half of the 2000s the climate security framing was less common. It reappeared more frequently from 2005 onwards (Cámara de Diputados 2005b) and particularly gained momentum between 2006 and 2013 (Cámara de Diputados 2007a; Senado de la República 2008; Cámara de Diputados 2009b; Senado de la República 2012). This timing corresponds to the peak of the climate security debate on the global level, and to our other country cases, but also to the non-governmental securitising attempts in Mexico itself that we will discuss in a moment. Between 2005 and 2013, we identified twenty-three securitising debates, which, compared to the earlier periods, contained a higher number of and more intense security articulations, and portrayed climate change particularly as a problem of individual risk. A typical example is the following joint statement of PRI parliamentarians:

> Given its geographical location, Mexico is a country that is highly vulnerable to climate change related phenomena, which entails significant risks in terms of health, availability of natural resources, the protection of ecosystems, infrastructure and security of the population.
> *(Cámara de Diputados 2007a: 63; see also Cámara de Diputados 2007c; Senado de la República 2011b)*

The territorial and the planetary level instances were less widespread, that is they only appeared about half as much as those of the individual level. Planetary arguments mostly highlighted the shared responsibility of humankind to overcome the climate crisis by adopting mitigation measures, as this statement of Augusta Valentina de Rivera Hernández (PAN) exemplifies:

> The problems and risks of climate change for Mexico and for humanity are good reasons for our country to implement and strengthen measures to mitigate it, for which it is necessary to take solid and effective actions concerning energy policy that contribute to the mitigation of climate change.
> *(Cámara de Diputados 2009c: 97)*

While the individual risk discourse remained dominant, the territorial level slowly caught up and in 2005 Senator Fauzi Hamdan Amad (PAN) for the first time linked climate change to national security conceptions (Cámara de Diputados 2005a: 79), a connection which then reappeared more frequently from 2007 onwards (Cámara de Diputados 2007b: 72; 2009b: 212). Yet, in line with the politicised nature of the broader debate, and in contrast to the US, parliamentarians did not normally link climate security to the military, even if they made use of the territorial level and referred to 'national security'. Rather, 'seguridad nacional' was used much more broadly – Jacinto Gómez Pasillas (Nueva Alianza) even explicitly discussed a widening of the concept (Cámara de Diputados 2009b: 211). Articulations regularly linked the territorial and individual level, and placed the threats to individuals at the core of their argument, as this quote by Senator María Elena Barrera Tapia of the *Partido Verde Ecologista de México* (PVEM) from a debate in the Senate exemplifies:

> This scenario requires immediate action and views climate change as a question of national security, yet this conception of security includes food security, health care, water supply, energy consumption and disaster control as important questions of the national interest.
> *(Senado de la República 2013: 4)*

After his election as president in 2006, Felipe Calderón, who became one of the most important discursive entrepreneurs concerning climate change in general, occasionally used climate security articulations to advance his climate agenda, mostly relying on the individual and planetary level. For instance, in 2010 at the COP-16 in Cancún he urged delegates 'to restart the dialogue and make the necessary arrangements to cope, as humanity, with the threat of climate change' (Calderón 2010). Yet, securitising climate change was not his prevailing theme, which rather focused on the moral responsibility of all countries, including Mexico itself, to protect the climate as well as on climate change as environmental topic and economic opportunity in terms of a green economy and energy efficiency (Calderón 2009b, 2009a). We will come back to the role of Calderón in the section on discursive entrepreneurs.

As the last paragraphs have shown, apart from those of Calderón, until 2007 climate security talk in Mexico was present mainly in parliamentary debates rather than the broader civil society. Based on the international climate debate, Mexican parliamentarians mainly constructed climate change as a risk to individuals and to a lesser extent to the planet as a whole, and only occasionally as a national security issue. After the climate security framing had become more popular on the international stage in 2007, the first foreign actors began to link climate change to security in Mexico. Thus, in 2008 the Globe Americas Legislators Forum, organised by GLOBE International and the World Bank, included a discussion of the possible security-related impacts of climate change in Mexico (Sánchez Gutiérrez et al. 2009: 7; World Bank 2008). Thereafter, two attempts to securitise climate change became particularly prominent – yet both showed only limited success. The first came from an international coalition of NGOs called Partners for Democratic Change International (PDCI), which cooperated with a couple of Mexican NGOs; the second from the British think tank, the Royal United Services Institute (RUSI), together with the British Embassy. Although no discourse clearly dominates these attempts, they show a slight tendency to also emphasise risk and the individual. An exception is the first RUSI report that regularly referred to territorial danger, emphasised the already unstable regional security environment, and worried about resource scarcity that could eventually lead to dissatisfaction with the government and to violent conflict:

> Even without additional stress from climate change, the region has multiple risk factors for instability including areas vulnerable to water stress, high population growth, crop decline, hunger, coastal risk from sea level rise, and a history of recent conflict. As climate change intensifies these dynamics, challenges must be handled so as to avoid aggravating current tensions and contributing to an already deteriorating security environment.
> *(Feakin and Depledge 2010: v; see also Deheza and Mora 2013: 7, 20; Brodziak et al. 2011: 7; CCC 2008: 4; Carius and Maas 2009: 3, 9)*

In general, however, articulations of climate change were more cautious. They focused on potential future risks that could gradually worsen existing domestic problems. For instance, a 2013 RUSI report argued that:

> some already populous regions that are attractive to migrants have developed, or are predicted to develop, vulnerabilities associated with climate change that could be exacerbated by the increased concentration of people upon arrival of additional migrants.
> *(Deheza and Mora 2013: 27; see also CCC 2008: 4; Sánchez Gutiérrez et al. 2009: 8; Deheza 2011: 9; Greenpeace México 2010: 19, 24; WWF México 2010: 2, 4)*

Statements particularly pointed to poor people living under already difficult conditions who now were at risk of being hit by a wide range of natural disasters exacerbated by climate change: 'The physical effects ... of climate change, such as hurricanes, droughts, floods, extreme hydrometeorological phenomena, forest fires and heat waves, directly affect the quality of life and increase people's vulnerability' (Brodziak et al. 2011: 11).

Thus, the most common risks associated with climate change were, first, slow-onset changes in the natural environment, such as decreasing natural resources (particularly food and water) due to changing climatic variables (heat, drought, changed precipitation patterns) and sea level rise, which could gradually affect the living conditions of Mexico's inhabitants (Deheza 2011: 8; CCC 2008: 1, 7–8; Brodziak *et al.* 2011: 11). According to most reports, these problems were especially worrying because of the already existing poverty that increased vulnerability to climatic effects decisively (CCC 2008: 4; Sánchez Gutiérrez *et al.* 2009: 8, 21). The further spread of disease due to a warmer or more humid climate was another slow-onset risk that most reports identified in connection to climate change (Deheza 2011: 20). Second, the reports pointed to rapid-onset natural disasters such as severe storms, floods or heatwaves that could seriously affect the Mexican population and especially certain high risk groups and areas such as poor indigenous people in the southern and more rural parts of the country (Deheza 2011: 7, 10; Brodziak *et al.* 2011: 11, 14). Third, in connection to both slow- and rapid-onset disasters, energy security (mostly understood as a problem for individuals and for the economy) was another point of concern as the production of electricity and oil could be affected by water scarcity or extreme weather events (Deheza and Mora 2013: 60–62). The fact that even today power cuts are not uncommon in Mexico (Deheza and Mora 2013: 60), and that the oil industry and Mexico's state-owned PEMEX company are important cornerstones of the Mexican economy and the Mexican state budget, underscores this point (Friedrich 2010: 56). However, in contrast to the debate in Turkey, discourses on energy security in Mexico were not used on a larger scale to argue against climate protection. Rather, the solutions to the climate problem often included energy efficiency measures and the like that at the same time could contribute to energy security (CCC 2008: 4–6; Brodziak *et al.* 2011: 32–33; Mexican Government and CICC 2009: 33). One important reason for this was the fairly open stance of PEMEX to climate measures, which, despite its own significant influence on Mexico's emissions, in the 1990s helped to overcome objections by the Ministry of Energy (SENER) and later implemented mitigation measures itself (Pulver 2006: 52–56; Chandler 2002: 33–34).

Finally, climate security reports in the Mexican case pointed to increased internal and international migration that could lead to problems in the receiving areas (e.g. rapid urbanisation, conflicts with the people already living there) (Deheza 2011: 18) as well as in the communities left behind (drain of knowledge and workforce) (Deheza and Mora 2013: 3, 9, 27). Yet some reports also pointed to the growing trend in migration studies to understand migration as a viable adaptation strategy that could alleviate the effects of climate change (Deheza and Mora 2013: xiii).

Similar to what we have seen in the parliamentary debates, some articulations linked the individual to the territorial level of climate security. Yet, even in most of these statements, and in contrast to the US where we saw the reverse, the territorial argument played only a supporting role, and the core referent object remained the well-being of individuals:

However, an adversarial reaction could exacerbate existing tensions and social anxiety if things are not resolved, which could, in turn, lead to violent conflict and thus further decrease the quality of life and increase the vulnerability of people.

(Brodziak et al. 2011: 21; see also Brodziak et al. 2011: 8, 15; Feakin and Depledge 2010: 29; Deheza 2011: vi)

Even less frequent were references to the planetary referent object level, which also mostly supported the individual level: 'Agriculture and industry are also dependent on so called "ecosystem services" which are predicted to decline over the next twenty years, making production and manufacturing more expensive' (Deheza 2011: 9; see also Sánchez Gutiérrez *et al.* 2009: 3; Greenpeace México 2010: 2, 57).

In terms of countermeasures, first, all reports strongly recommended increased climate adaptation measures in Mexico, in line with the prevailing individual risk framing. The concrete focus was on the encouragement to compile risk and vulnerability atlases and to enhance risk management schemes to prevent problems from getting out of control (Feakin and Depledge 2010: 12, 21; Deheza 2011: 25, 28; Deheza and Mora 2013: xvii, 8). The reports recommended the introduction of early warning schemes for natural disasters and conflict (Brodziak *et al.* 2011: 7). In addition, they urged an increase in the coping capacity and resilience of risk groups within the population (Deheza and Mora 2013: 78; Deheza 2011: 26–27), for example through climate insurance and education on the adverse effects of climate change (Deheza and Mora 2013: xviii, 76; Deheza 2011: 27). A further focus was on integrating questions of climate migration into relevant planning schemes and understanding migration as a positive adaptation strategy (Deheza and Mora 2013: xvii). Second, the reports also recommended the strengthening of research on and the handling of climate-induced risks by improving environmental governance in general and the cooperation between different government institutions on the issue in particular (CCC 2008: 2, 5; Sánchez Gutiérrez *et al.* 2009: 9; Deheza and Mora 2013: xvii). Third, but less frequently, some reports also called for increased mitigation measures either on the global level, or directly in Mexico, for example by improving energy efficiency or transportation options in bigger cities (CCC 2008: 4–6). Finally, some the PDCI and RUSI reports also called for an integration of climate risks into the national security strategy (Deheza and Mora 2013: 63, 79, 80).

Mexico's media also picked up climate security arguments, particularly in the international peak period between 2007 and 2011 (*La Jornada* 2009; *Reforma* 2010). Most pieces focused on the effects of climate change on Mexico's population. Hence, while the term 'seguridad nacional' frequently appeared, similar to the parliamentary debates, this territorial framing was often linked to an individual argumentation or directly to the concept of food and water security (Saavedra 2010):

> But there is a new factor to be included: amongst the major threats to national security are the environmental effects caused by climate change. Its

greatest impact in Mexico itself will be felt concerning scarce natural resources such as water.

(Hernández Díaz 2009)

Naturally, media attention to climate change in general and climate security discourses in particular increased during the COP-16 negotiations in Cancún in 2010 (Elvira Quesada 2010; LuegeTamargo 2010; Amador 2010). Moreover, in general the attention to climate security in Mexico's media, public and political debate, was always high when major reports on climate security appeared, for example those of the UN, World Bank, Mexican Universities or RUSI (*La Jornada* 2008; 2009; Aranda 2011; Eseverri 2009; Alatorre 2010) or in the aftermath of natural disasters that affected parts of the population (Interview 2014c; 2014h).

Summing up, the first instances of securitisation talk in Mexico appeared in parliamentary debates, which mostly discussed climate change as a risk to individuals. While the 1990s saw only very few securitising arguments, they became more numerous and intense between 2005 and 2013, although still on a much lower level than in the US or Germany. The first clearly securitising articulations from NGOs appeared around 2008 and were initiated primarily by foreign organisations. Although the distribution of discourses was more even amongst these, and territorial discourses played a role, the individual risk discourse dominated here as well. Overall, in terms of our first criterion for measuring the impact of securitisation, the transformation of the debate, we classify the securitisation of climate change as moderately successful in Mexico. Hence, while climate security did not become the dominant framing of climate change, which continued to focus on environmental, economic and development considerations (Interview 2014g; 2014k; see also the next section), it frequently appeared in parliamentary debates, speeches of high-ranking government officials and in the media discourse.

Discursive entrepreneurs: Parliament and imported securitisation

As the previous section has shown, before foreign actors took up the framing, climate security articulations had already appeared in parliamentary debates. However, these speech acts came from a range of different individuals from all parties and we could not single out important individual discursive entrepreneurs in these debates. Apart from the parliamentary debates, the single most influential discursive entrepreneur concerning climate change in general was President Felipe Calderón. References to climate security certainly were part of his argumentation. For instance, he called climate change 'one of the major threats to humanity' (Calderón 2010) in his inauguration speech at the COP-16 in Cancún and highlighted the potential negative impacts for individuals, especially for the poor (CNN México 2010). Thus, he mostly focused on our planetary and individual level. However, Calderón did not exclusively rely on securitisation to advance his climate agenda. He also politicised the issue by portraying climate change as an environmental issue (Mexican Government 2007: 237–238) and by discussing it as a question of sustainable development, moral responsibility, international justice and economic opportunity (Forbes México 2015; Saúl and León 2012). For example, after signing the general law on climate change in 2012 he stated that:

> This law paves the way towards a low carbon growth by setting goals for gradual reconfiguration of subsidies to discourage the use of fossil fuels and to renew renewable energy, energy efficiency and sustainable transport and infrastructure development.
>
> *(Quiroz 2012)*

Thus, one recurring message of Calderón in relation to climate change was the possibility of a 'green economy' and of 'green growth' (*El Economista* 2012; González 2012). One reason for his preoccupation with climate change was certainly Calderón's personal dedication to climate matters. Yet probably even more importantly, Calderón also used the climate topic to boost his domestic popularity by taking advantage of the political credit Mexico was accumulating through its role as vanguard in climate matters on the international level (Akerberg 2011: 37; Sánchez Gutiérrez *et al*. 2009: 5–7; Interview 2014e).

Besides the Parliament and Calderón, only a few actors actively tried to construct climate change as a security issue in Mexico. In contrast to the US or Germany, domestic NGOs or think tanks were not highly involved in securitising climate change. Due to its only recent democratisation, the total number of NGOs in Mexico is still small compared to other countries of the same size, and their political influence is limited (CIVICUS 2011: 28; Bertelsmann Stiftung 2012: 24, 26; Peters and Maihold 2007: 36). Moreover, only a few of them directly specialise in climate change. Among the most important players in this respect are the *Centro Mario Molina*, founded by the Mexican scientist who was involved in the discovery of the destruction of the ozone layer, and the *Centro Mexicano de Derecho Ambiental* (CEMDA). Yet, these organisations focused rather on technical assistance to the Mexican government in designing its climate policy and on monitoring the financial pledges concerning climate measures (Interview 2014f; 2014e; Centro Mario Molina 2014; CEMDA 2010; 2015). Nonetheless, they were involved in a joint project of PDCI that we will discuss in the following paragraphs.

Most of the actors that did perform securitising moves came from abroad or were local sections of international NGOs. Apart from the Globe Americas Legislators Forum hosted by GLOBE International and the World Bank, which discussed climate security arguments only briefly, these included reports by Greenpeace (Greenpeace México 2010), the WWF (WWF México 2010) and the German Heinrich Böll Foundation (Jungehülsing 2010). These reports primarily construct climate change as a risk to individuals (Greenpeace México 2010: 2, 24; Jungehülsing 2010: 3, 18; WWF México 2010: 2, 4; AGRIFOR Consult and Europe Aid 2009: 13, 15, 35) or to planetary ecosystems (Greenpeace México 2010: 30, 42; WWF México 2010: 2, 6). The German environmental consultancy Adelphi, which, as we have seen in Chapter 4, has been a major actor in the German climate security debate, also pointed to the security impacts of climate change in Central America and in Mexico. However, in contrast to the other reports, Adelphi focused on the territorial danger discourse and discussed the impact of climate change on violent conflicts and state security in the region (Carius and Maas 2009: 3, 9; Maas and Tänzler 2009: 9). However, the impact of all of these actors on the climate security debate in Mexico was marginal.

The first major and more influential attempt to connect climate change with security that directly drew on this connection came from an international coalition of NGOs called Partners for Democratic Peace International (PDCI). PDCI cooperated with the Mexican NGOs *Centro de Colaboración Cívica* (CCC), *Centro Mario Molina* (CMM), *Centro Mexicano de Derecho Ambiental* (CEMDA) and *Comisión de Estudios del Sector Privada para el Desarollo Sustentable* (CESPEDES), as well as the UNDP to organise a dialogue process in the Chamber of Deputies between November 2008 and 2009. The goal of this initiative, called *Programa de Diálogo y Construcción de Acuerdos: Cambio Climático y Seguridad Nacional*, was to raise awareness of climate matters in political circles. It wanted to encourage mitigation and adaptation policies and create a dialogue between civil society and political practitioners (CCC 2008; Sánchez Gutiérrez et al. 2009: 9–12; Interview 2014k). Contrary to what the title of the project, 'Climate Change and National Security', suggests, it referred to the individual level and risk conceptions in most of its documents and discussions (CCC 2008: 1, 8; Sánchez Gutiérrez et al. 2009: 8). One reason for the use of the notion of 'national security' in the title could have been tactical because of its attention-generating qualities. Moreover, new security conceptions such as human security are still less known in the country and fail to produce the same level of urgency. Quite similar to the discursive entrepreneurs in the US case, PDCI and the other involved organisations reckoned that approaching climate change from a security perspective would turn this often complicated and technocratic issue into a more accessible political argument (Sánchez Gutiérrez *et al.* 2009: 8–9; Interview 2014k).

PDCI and its partners carried out workshops and conducted interviews with various non-governmental stakeholders in the Mexican climate field as well as members of the *Cámara de Diputados* to discuss the connections between climate change and security. The largest share of funding for this undertaking came from the British Embassy with a contribution of 155,580 GBP, and the US-based Tinker Foundation, which focuses on sustainability grants in Latin America (CCC 2008: 11). In 2011, PDCI and CCC published a further study on the connections between climate change and conflict as part of a broader, EU-funded international project, the 'Initiative for Peacebuilding – Early Warning Analysis to Action' (IfP-EW). This study focused slightly more on the territorial level and on the danger dimension, though often linking this to endangered individuals (Brodziak *et al.* 2011: 7, 11, 15). In 2012, the IfP-EW, with the assistance of Adelphi and International Alert, published a synthesis report on climate change and conflict that summarised the findings from several regions around the world, including Mexico (Tänzler *et al.* 2012). However, the 2012 report did not have a great impact on the Mexican debate but was rather aimed at an international and European audience.

The second foreign attempt to securitise climate change in Mexico came from the British security think tank RUSI, together with the British Embassy. One reason for the overall preoccupation of UK actors in Mexico with the security dimension of climate change (and the specific timing of between 2008 and 2011) was the importance of the climate security debate in the United Kingdom itself and at the global level at the time (Rothe 2016: 182–183). Moreover, in 2008 Mexico had not yet developed an all-encompassing climate strategy of its own and was thus still open to suggestions. Consequently, by using the security framing RUSI and the British Embassy hoped to raise awareness of climate change, to link it with their overall development goals in Mexico and to directly steer Mexican policies towards climate security (Deheza and Mora 2013: x; Feakin and Depledge 2010: v, Interview 2014g; 2014ar).

RUSI and the British Embassy conducted two projects between 2008 and 2013, commissioned by the Foreign and Commonwealth Office (FCO) and partly funded by the British Prosperity Fund. The projects included workshops with several Mexican and international climate NGOs as well as two universities (*Universidad Nacional Autónoma de México*, and *Universidad Iberoamericana*), and the publication of three larger reports. Both projects were part of RUSI's Climate Change and Security Programme, which they had been running since 2006 and was supposed to engage traditional security actors in a dialogue about climate change (Feakin and Depledge 2010: title pages 3). The first project was conducted between 2008 and 2010 under the auspices of RUSI together with regional organisations, including the *Fundación para el Ecodesarrollo y la Conservación* (FUNDAECO), the *Comisión Centroamericana de Ambiente y Desarrollo* (CCAD), and the Caribbean Community Climate Change Centre (CCCCC). As the title of the final report, *Climate-Related Impacts on National Security in Mexico and Central America* (Feakin and Depledge 2010) suggests, the project targeted the larger region and not only Mexico. Its aim was to accumulate information about the connection between climate change and security in Central America and gauge the knowledge and views of local stakeholders, as well as to raise their awareness. Although the report included risk articulations as well, it regularly referred to 'national security' and more often applied the territorial danger discourse (Feakin and Depledge 2010: v, 21). Thus it ended with recommendations to include climate change into Mexican security planning schemes as well as to improve inter-departmental and regional cooperation on the issue (Feakin and Depledge 2010: 65–66; Interview 2014g).

Based on the findings of the first report, a second project immediately ensued that focused exclusively on Mexico and especially on climate migration. RUSI chose to focus on Mexico because of the country's vulnerability to the effects of climate change. Furthermore, its many different climatic zones could exemplify the broad variety of climate change effects. Moreover, Mexico was already highly engaged in the international climate debate, and thus an easily accessible showcase. One of the main characteristics of this second project was its close interconnectedness with Mexican stakeholders, especially with various government departments relevant to combatting climate change and security issues. They included the *Instituto Nacional de Ecología y Cambio Climático* (INECC*)*, *Secretaría de Medio Ambiente y Recursos Naturales*

(SEMARNAT), *Centro de Investigación y Seguridad Nacional* (CISEN), and *Comisión Nacional del Agua* (CONAGUA) (Deheza and Mora 2013: v). Through the involvement of these actors, RUSI wanted to create a sense of local ownership (Interview 2014ar; Deheza and Mora 2013: v). Yet, as we will see when discussing the policy consequences in the next section, in the end this endeavour was to fail.

Apart from raising general awareness, especially of the consequences of climate change for individuals, the main aim of this second project was to integrate climate security into Mexican policies, particularly into the fifth communication to the UNFCCC and the Mexican National Security Programme (Deheza and Mora 2013: 82–85; Interview 2014g). The original focus was on the nexus of climate change, migration, organised crime and security. However, in the midst of the project, RUSI and its partners had to drop organised crime because of objections from the Mexican Foreign Ministry, which feared interference in Mexican security policy and deemed the topic of organised crime too sensitive to leave to outsiders to handle. In the final version of the report, RUSI thus actively tried to establish a new conception of security that focused on seemingly 'softer' notions of security. This included an emphasis on risks to individuals due to the physical effects of climate change (Deheza and Mora 2013: 94; Interview 2014ar), which coincided with severe droughts in the northern parts of Mexico at the time (Interview 2014g). Accordingly, the recommendations of this second project were much more focused on the problems of individuals and how the authorities might adequately handle such climate risks (Deheza and Mora 2013: 82–85).

A network citation analysis based on the twenty-one most relevant reports and policies in the climate security debate (Figure 5.1) illustrates the importance especially of RUSI and to a lesser extent of PDCI for the climate security debate in Mexico. The figure reveals that except for RUSI, the focus of reports on climate change is on civilian and environmental government departments and policies such as SEMARNAT, INE, CICC, SAGARPA, PECC, UNAM and ENACC. Furthermore, it illustrates the importance of international and foreign actors such as the UN, the IPCC and the World Bank as well as the US and the EU.

Legitimised policies

Overall, in Mexico the securitisation of climate change has been moderately successful. It has not been as influential in terms of transforming the general debate on climate change and directly influencing political debates and policies as it has been in the US or German case, but much more influential than in Turkey. Thus, in Parliament, climate security articulations were frequently used to legitimise climate legislation and many policies that have been adopted clearly correspond to the dominant individual risk discourse. Beyond that, the two most visible non-governmental attempts to securitise climate change by PDCI and RUSI did raise some awareness for a limited time, were able to place climate security arguments on the agenda of the political debate and influenced some policies. Yet they also encountered severe resistance that limited their impact. The territorial risk discourse

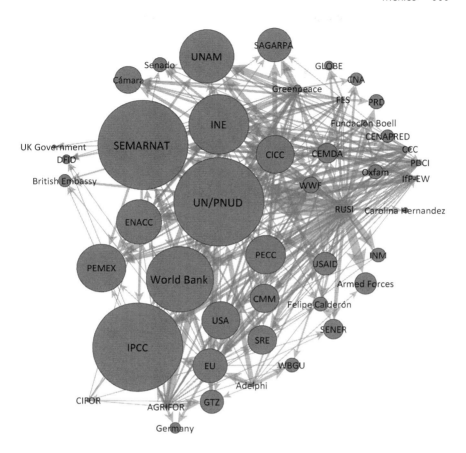

FIGURE 5.1 Network citation analysis (Mexican case)

and direct references to Mexican security policy were especially not well-received in the country, and apart from some exceptions could not gain a foothold on a broader basis. Below, we first look at the attempts by PDCI and RUSI and the problems they encountered, and thereafter analyse how the dominant discourse of individual risk has influenced concrete policies.

The PDCI and its partners had not designed their project as a public campaign, but had aimed it at political actors, especially in the *Cámara de Diputados* (Interview 2014k). While deputies did mention the initiative in their debates on climate change and security (Cámara de Diputados 2008: 48), it nonetheless faced considerable challenges in convincing the political stakeholders of the importance of the climate security framing. First, and in contrast to both Germany and the US at the time, the argument was quite new and unconventional in Mexico (Interview 2014k). Second, the PDCI found it difficult to establish their argument on a long-term basis because the term for parliamentarians in the *Cámara de Diputados* in Mexico is three years, with re-election not being an option. Because the project started in the middle of a legislative period, many deputies left Parliament shortly after having built a connection with it (Interview 2014k). With hindsight, some participants of the project thought that it probably would have been more effective to work with the Senate, as its members are elected for a longer time period and are more influential in general (Interview 2014k). Furthermore, although the project started out to discuss the security aspects of climate change, in the course of it, the focus shifted towards a more general discussion of climate change (Sánchez Gutiérrez *et al.* 2009: 40). In 2009, the project ended prematurely after two workshop sessions in the *Cámara de Diputados*. PDCI and the British Embassy turned out to have very different conceptions of the project's goals so that the embassy cut the funding. While PDCI had wanted to foster an open-ended dialogue, the British were more interested in developing concrete policies (Interview 2014k; Sánchez Gutiérrez *et al.* 2009).

Yet despite these problems, the project succeeded in influencing some minor laws in the environmental and health sector, for instance in reducing the vulnerability of certain sectors (health, fisheries) to climate change effects (see Sánchez Gutiérrez *et al.* 2009: 15, for a detailed list of the outcomes). Furthermore, it led to a non-binding political declaration by all parliamentary committees of the Chamber of Deputies to integrate the security impacts of climate change into Mexican policies, to establish working groups on the topic in the Senate and in the *Comisión Intersecretarial de Cambio Climático* (CICC) and to inform the public about their efforts (Sánchez Gutiérrez *et al.* 2009: 16–17). To date however, the working groups on climate change and security in the CICC and Senate have not been established. Finally, the project strengthened the dialogue between civil society and politicians, and improved the coordination between the various non-governmental actors themselves. Eventually, this led to the founding of the *Grupo de Financiamiento para Cambio Climático* in 2010, a consortium of fifteen climate NGOs that focuses on the effective implementation of Mexican climate polices and has since exerted considerable influence in Mexico (Sánchez Gutiérrez *et al.* 2009: 15; CEMDA 2010). For example, the 'Grupo' has always reserved the single spot available for civil society actors in Mexico's COP delegations for one of its members and has assisted the government in questions of climate financing (Interview 2014e). All of these effects, however, relate to the structure of the political debate and can hardly be seen as extraordinary measures. Instead of linking security and climate change, thus, this first securitisation attempt led to further politicisation.

The second attempt under the leadership of RUSI and the British Embassy was from the beginning supposed to inform the public debate. Its workshops were well attended by various NGOs (e.g. by the Heinrich Böll Foundation and CEMDA) and governmental actors. Due to good connections between the embassy and higher-ranking members of the executive in Mexico, its message found considerable resonance in political circles as well (Interview 2014g). In particular, the close cooperation with the head of GLOBE at that time, Carolina Hernandez, was crucial for getting the ideas of the report to Mexico's senators and deputies (Deheza and Mora 2013: 5; Interview 2014ar). Moreover, major Mexican newspapers such as *La Jornada* and *Reforma* picked up the climate security framing of RUSI on several occasions, and reported on the project's events and reports (*La Jornada* 2008; 2009; Aranda 2011; Eseverri 2009; Alatorre 2010).

Yet despite this temporary resonance in the debate, the project had only a limited impact on concrete policies, at least in the short run until the end of our study period. Its main problem was a misunderstanding between the project leaders and the Mexican Foreign Ministry, which led to considerable diplomatic strains. Despite efforts to avoid traditional security conceptions and to include the Mexican counterparts in the research process, the Foreign Ministry got the impression that the UK and RUSI (as foreigners in Mexico) were interfering with and criticising Mexican security policy. Hence, the Mexican government declined to use the climate security argument in its official policies on climate change but allowed its ministries to use the findings of the 2011 draft project internally (Interview 2014g; 2014ar). They banned publication of the report for six months, and even considered it a threat to Mexico's national security itself. This went as far as communication between the foreign ministries of Mexico and the UK being restricted to letters (Interview 2014ar). Eventually, the publication of an edited version of the report (without the chapter on the nexus of climate change, security and organised crime) became possible after the election of the new Nieto government. However, by then much of the momentum of the debate had evaporated. In particular, the ties to important political practitioners were lost because a large portion of these personnel had been replaced after the election (Interview 2014ar). Subsequently, Mexico increasingly developed its own approach to climate change and was much less receptive to suggestions from the outside. Thus, the window of opportunity for others to influence its policies towards the climate security discourse had closed for the time being.

After having elaborated on the impact of the two concrete foreign attempts for securitisation, we now turn to the question of whether the individual risk discourse, which prevailed in the parliamentary debates and to a lesser extent also in the other attempts at securitisation, actually translated into concrete policies. As discussed earlier, despite the frequent occurrence of this discourse, other non-securitising articulations of climate change kept their importance in Mexico (Interview 2014e), which makes it difficult to link concrete policies exclusively to the security framing. However, based on our analysis of parliamentary debates and the tracking of concepts in policy documents associated with individual risk, we identified certain institutional changes and policies that can be associated with security articulations (Interview 2014h).

As we have seen in the section on the dominant discourses, the first climate security articulations in the Mexican Parliament appeared as early as 1992. However, at that time they only popped up infrequently and were not very intensely securitising. Thus, while considerations about Mexico's vulnerability to climatic effects certainly have contributed to the country's ratification of the UNFCCC and its early climate policies, successful securitisation was not the driving force behind this. Rather, international pressure, especially from the US, the legacy of Mexico's past commitment to environmental issues and the politicisation of climate change contributed to this development. This picture changed somewhat in the late 1990s and early 2000s, when climate security articulations became slightly more numerous and intense. Thus, parliamentarians occasionally legitimised the ratification of the Kyoto Protocol with planetary and individual risk argumentations (Senado de la República 2000: 1). Yet, even at this time, the security framing was not the most important argument and the focus remained on a strategy of politicisation of climate change as an environmental problem, a question of sustainable development and of the moral obligations of humankind (Senado de la República 2000: 2).

When the climate security articulations in parliament grew stronger and became more frequent between 2005 and 2013, and when the climate security framing received more attention due to the efforts of PDCI and RUSI, both the importance of legitimising policies as well as the number of certain concrete concepts in these policies increased. Thus, parliamentarians included individual risk articulations to legitimise the consideration of questions of health in climate policy and the integration of the Ministry of Health in the CICC (Cámara de Diputados 2006: 230–231; 2007c: 204). Furthermore, they also used individual risk arguments in connection with the ENACC strategy (Cámara de Diputados 2006: 229; 2007d: 332; 2009a: 109–110). Consequently, climate security considerations, to a limited extent, ended up in the ENACC strategy's publication in 2007, which refers to climate change as problem of 'strategic security' (Mexican Government and CICC 2007: 13). Despite the traditional ring of this term, it merely means that climate change affects almost all sectors of the country, with a focus on the well-being of the population. Thus, the proposed solutions focus on mitigation and energy efficiency, helping the population to adapt on the basis of monitoring and early warning systems, measures to reduce vulnerability, risk management, insurance schemes and civil protection measures (Mexican Government and CICC 2007: 8–10).

In 2009, parliamentarians underscored the importance of the PECC strategy with reference to individual and planetary risk considerations (Cámara de Diputados 2009a: 108; 2009c: 248). Eventually, the PECC portrayed climate change as 'one of the greatest threats to the process of development and human welfare' (Mexican Government and CICC 2009: 9) with concepts of risk management, human vulnerability and disaster prevention, as well as the security of the population and its food supply, featuring prominently (Mexican Government and CICC 2009: 25, 50–52, 65). Furthermore, the PECC foresees the establishment of a National Risk Atlas concerning climate change and a better integration of climate risk into the civil protection frameworks of the country (Mexican Government and CICC 2009: 25). An overview of Mexico's efforts at climate adaptation published in 2010 reinforces this focus on individual risk by highlighting the vulnerability of the population, and problems of food security, and pushing for a better integration of climate risks into the National Risk Atlas (Mexican Government 2010: 34, 50, 17). The focus on the problems of individuals was further underscored when in 2011, the director of the *Instituto Nacional de Ecología* (INE; now *Instituto Nacional de Ecología y Cambio Climático* or INECC) recognised the impact of climate change on food security (Alatorre 2011).

Moreover, debates in the Mexican parliament used climate security arguments, mostly based on individual and planetary risk discourses, to legitimise the Mexican

Climate Law and its amendments between 2011 and 2013 (Senado de la República 2011a, 2011b, 2012, 2013).Although the law does not explicitly address climate change as a security problem, it contains some references to food security and concerning the adaptation to climate change the law urges to 'Facilitate and promote food security, the productivity of agriculture, livestock, fisheries, aquaculture, and the preservation of ecosystems and natural resources' (Cámara de Diputados 2012: 16). Finally, a focus on climate risks for individuals is also apparent in the new 2013 *Estrategia Nacional de Cambio Climático* (ENCC), which mentions food security (37, 51, 53), the national risk atlas (14–15), the vulnerability of the population towards disasters (33) and risk management as well as civil protection measures (Mexican Government *et al.* 2013: 37).

Due to the focus on individual risk, climate change is also becoming more important in Mexico's disaster management planning, with a clear focus on risk-management-based measures (Interview 2014l). Examples are initiatives by the Ministry of Social Development to create risk and vulnerability atlases, disaster prevention and management plans, and the establishment of disaster funds (FONDEN/*Fondo Nacional para el Desarrollo Nacional*, FOPREDEN/*Fondo para la Prevención de Desastres Naturales*). As the World Bank (2012b: v) argues:

> Mexico stands at the forefront of initiatives to develop comprehensive disaster risk management structures and programs, including disaster risk financing and insurance strategies to manage the fiscal risk posed by disasters.
> *(see also Deheza and Mora 2013: 72–73)*

Likewise, disaster risk management and civil protection measures feature prominently in Mexico's fourth and fifth communication to the UNFCCC (SEMERNAT and CICC 2009, 2012). The fifth communication to the UNFCCC also mentions the 2011 RUSI report on climate change, migration and security (SEMERNAT and CICC 2012: 369), yet only in passing and without a larger section on these dynamics as originally hoped for by RUSI.

Domestically, Mexico's disaster management department, CENAPRED, increasingly integrates the adaptation to climate change and the management of climate risks into its planning with a particular focus on water, agricultural and health issues (CENAPRED and SEGOB 2014). It has also called for the incorporation of climate change into the National Risk Atlas, which the PECC and other strategy documents had already demanded (Interview 2014i). Moreover, there is a widespread distribution of agricultural insurance schemes in Mexico, both by private companies and government agencies (e.g. SAGARPA's Agrosemex) (Deheza and Mora 2013: 76; Agrosemex 2015). Finally, the National Development Plan 2013–2018 explicitly addresses climate change as risk for the population and calls for increased civil protection and disaster prevention measures (Mexican Government 2013: 37, 142).

These policies and developments clearly demonstrate the degree to which the individual risk discourse has not only been prominent in the general debate, but has informed climate change policies and regulations. In a few cases, however, climate change has also found its way into security planning. At first sight, this contradicts the predominant individual risk framing. However, it can be understood with a view to the particular aims of the securitisation attempts by PDCI and RUSI that included the incorporation of climate change into security policy (Sánchez Gutiérrez et al. 2009: 16–17; Deheza and Mora 2013: 82). Although, as we have already shown, these attempts were less successful than the actors had hoped, some of their recommendations were eventually taken up. The change in government and the election as president in 2012 of Nieto, who was less opposed to the recommendations of RUSI, further facilitated this process. Thus, there have been two attempts to reform the Mexican National Security Law. One originated in the Chamber of Deputies, which pushed to make amendments to the law explicitly address climate change as a national security threat under Article 5 of the law (Cámara de Diputados 2007b: 72–76; 2008: 48–49; 2009b: 211–213). A second initiative came directly from the leftist opposition party PRD in 2011, which wanted to include human rights considerations in the law (Deheza and Mora 2013: 79; Taniguchi 2011). As of November 2015, this reform is still pending. In addition, the Mexican National Security Programme 2014–2018 has mentioned climate change as an important topic, which President Nieto addressed in a message at the beginning of the programme (Mexican Government 2014: 17). Interestingly, even in this very traditional document of security policy, climate change is primarily addressed as a problem for individuals and food security (Mexican Government 2014: 86–88), which underscores the predominance of the individual risk discourse in the country.

Apart from these developments, there have been occasional discussions at the Mexican Centre for Intelligence and National Security (CISEN) about doing more research on the security aspects of climate change and including it in the Annual Risk National Agenda (that CISEN develops for the National Security Council and that forms the basis for the National Security Programme). A plan to open a new department focusing entirely on climate change, modelled on the CIA's Center for Climate Change and National Security (see Chapter 3) has not yet materialised (Deheza and Mora 2013: 80; Interview 2014ar). Finally, the cautious reception of territorial discourses by Mexican governments is underscored by the fact that in the UNSC debates on climate change and security in 2007 and 2011, Mexico took a conservative stance. It highlighted the risks for individuals, the need for mitigation and adaptation but expressed its scepticism regarding involvement of the UNSC (UNSC 2007b: 19–20; 2011b: 9–10).

In sum, the securitisation of climate change in terms of transforming the overall debate and legitimising policies has been partly successful. The concrete attempts by PDCI and RUSI had considerable problems in establishing their framing, especially when it came to territorial risk and national security considerations. However, arguments tapping into the individual and planetary risk discourse have frequently appeared in Parliament to legitimise climate policy, and eventually appropriate measures ended up in climate policy documents. Nevertheless, these findings should not overshadow the fact that the impact of securitisation was still less significant in

Mexico than was the case in the US or Germany. Especially in terms of a transformation of the debate, securitising moves were not able to entirely transform the predominant discourse of climate change as environmental or economic issue. Thus, while we have shown that climate security arguments were involved in the legitimisation of Mexican climate policy, politicising arguments pointing to the moral responsibility of humankind, economic opportunities, international pressure, and strategic considerations by the Calderón administration to position Mexico as the climate change vanguard played an equally important role.

Facilitating conditions and the context of climate securitisation

One important precondition for the emphasis on the individual level are the actual climate predictions of the IPCC that project severe environmental changes in Mexico. They include increased temperatures and droughts in the north, more humid weather in the south, sea level rise, and overall an increase in the frequency and intensity of extreme weather events (IPCC 2007b: 79, 92, 153). All these changes particularly affect the Mexican population, and although often classified as an emerging economy, many Mexicans (especially in the southern and rural parts) lack the financial means to adequately cope with adverse climatic effects (Salazar and Masera 2010: 22–25). In addition, the Mexican state is not able to organise climate adaptation measures on a larger scale in many regions of the country, leaving large parts of the population vulnerable to climate change (Wolf 2007: 36).

Thus, a focus on the individual level made sense for discursive entrepreneurs of climate security in Mexico. The tendency to focus on the risk dimension when pointing to the problematic effects of climate change originates from some historic-contextual and some strategic factors. On the one hand, climate projections see Mexico as directly and severely affected by climate change and people attribute considerable importance to its risks (AXA and IPSOS 2012: 4). However, when it comes to the prevailing security problems and top concerns in the country, other issues such as organised crime and widespread violence against civilians still overshadow the climate threat (Interview 2014d; 2014e; Pew Research Center 2011). Thus, it makes sense that climate change is perceived as an important but at the same time rather long-term risk. Moreover, scientific actors, who have dominated the Mexican climate debate in the past, tend to be rather cautious when it comes to articulating threats, the German case notwithstanding. Both of these factors lend themselves to less alarmist articulations of climate risk.

On the other hand, discursive entrepreneurs made a conscious choice to focus on individual risk (Interview 2014g; 2014ar; Deheza and Mora 2013: preface). The restrained use of territorial danger made sense in a country where the concept of security is still associated with organised crime and connected to widespread violent conflict (Bertelsmann Stiftung 2012: 6). Security policy is therefore a very sensitive subject that is directly associated with the core interests of the Mexican state. RUSI and the British Embassy clearly underestimated this sensitivity, and later focused on new security issues as well. Moreover, the linking of seemingly 'soft' political issues, such as climate change, to 'hard' (national) security considerations is not very common in Mexico (Interview 2014k).

Apart from the question of why individual risk frames prevailed in Mexico, several contextual factors impeded an even more successful securitisation of climate change, especially concerning the territorial level and national security conceptions. The political importance of narcotics trafficking and organised crime in Mexico did not leave much space for a 'soft' security problem such as climate change (Interview 2014e; 2014k; Pew Research Center 2011; Bertelsmann Stiftung 2012: 2, 6). Linking environmental issues to security concerns did not have a long tradition in Mexico and thus most political actors did not accept this as a legitimate frame (Interview 2014k). In contrast to industrialised countries such as Germany and the US, Mexico had not seen an influential environmental security debate in the 1990s that could have prepared the actors for such arguments. The sarcastic question of a military officer – whether 'they should chase and arrest hurricanes' – underscores the low priority for climate change and 'new security problems' in the Mexican military (Interview 2014k).

Ironically, one further limiting condition for the climate security framing was the previous and parallel existence of a successful and influential general climate debate in Mexico – the politicisation of climate change. Mexico had integrated climate change quite early into its policies, for reasons that, as we have shown, had only marginally to do with securitisation. Hence, there was only a limited necessity to generate further attention through securitising moves, especially not for a transformation into a military security issue. Indeed, in our interviews many Mexican climate NGOs claimed that they had fairly good relationships with the government, and generally speaking were quite content with what the government had done in terms of climate policies (Interview 2014e; 2014c), although some, including the Heinrich Böll Foundation and Greenpeace, pursued a more confrontational approach. Accordingly, the main problem in Mexico was not a lack of climate policies but their effective implementation, especially on the local level. These enforcement problems originating from a highly centralised institutional structure, the vague formulation of environmental policy and often only voluntary agreements, as well as inadequate funds for implementation, are not new in Mexico but have been present since the early days of its environmental agenda (Mumme and Lybecker 2002: 317). Although there certainly has been progress on these problems, they still play an important role (Höhne et al. 2012: 4–5).

In addition, because of the relatively recent democratisation process, the number of NGOs actively focusing on climate change in Mexico is fairly small, and so is their political influence. Although preparations for the international climate negotiations in Cancún in 2010 led to a rise in NGOs tackling climate change, many of them only took up the topic as an opportunistic strategy. Few organisations have a deeper knowledge of climate matters and a longer tradition in advocating climate policies (for example the Centro Mario Molina or CEMDA) (Interview 2014e). Hence there have been no strong Mexican NGO actors pushing for the climate security framing, which eventually led to the problems described above of foreign actors attempting to work with effective counterparts and understand particular local concerns. In particular, the UK/RUSI attempt eventually failed because these actors were perceived as outsiders and lacked long-term political connections to all relevant parts of government. The problems of such a securitisation from the outside not only hold for Mexico but also apply to other countries of the Global South. Besides touching on sensitive security issues, this 'advice' from outsiders often is perceived as a neo-colonial, imperialistic or 'Western' discourse (see also Chapter 6 on Turkey) that tries to impose certain policies on developing countries (von Lucke *et al.* 2014: 21–26; Boas 2014: 153; Duffield and Waddell 2006).

Finally, despite the occasional articulations of territorial danger in parliamentary debates, the lack of experience of political personnel with climate security matters and the high turnover of politicians and public servants after elections, made it difficult to place the territorial danger framing on the political agenda on a permanent basis (Interview 2014k; 2014ar). This was particularly pertinent in view of the fact that the major securitising actors in this respect came to Mexico from elsewhere and thus had only a limited amount of time to influence the discourse while lacking ties to all relevant political actors.

Conclusion

As we have shown in this chapter, although some initial precursors appeared as early as 1992, climate security discourses began to gain importance in Mexico in the mid-2000s and peaked between 2006 and 2013. Overall, climate security debates have predominantly focused on individual risk and to a lesser extent on planetary risk, while discourses of territorial danger and risk had problems generating attention. Eventually, the individual risk discourse, supported by planetary arguments, was able to facilitate concrete political consequences. It contributed to the legitimisation of major policies and increased the importance of risk management and civil protection measures. However, attempts at an even more widespread distribution of the climate security framing – including territorial danger and risk arguments – by foreign actors (PDCI and RUSI) had considerable problems in convincing political actors. Moreover, the climate security framing was not alone responsible for Mexico's role as a climate change vanguard, but rather other politicising factors played an equally important role. These included the framing of climate change as an environmental issue, as a problem of moral responsibility and as an economic opportunity; as well as international pressure and the populist strategy of Calderón to present Mexico abroad as a progressive country as a way to help him overcome domestic problems. Thus, we classify the securitisation of climate change as moderately successful in Mexico. In comparison to our other cases, it has been less influential than in the US and Germany, but certainly more important than in Turkey.

Our analysis shows that to a certain extent a parallel politicisation and securitisation is possible and can jointly increase attention to an issue and lead to concrete political consequences. The individual risk discourse seems to be particularly suitable in this respect because it operates with less alarmist threat constructions, hence being more compatible with 'normal' politics. In addition, people themselves are less inclined to perceive individual risk discourses as securitisation or as security discourses at all. The findings furthermore underscore our hypothesis postulated in the theoretical chapter that the individual risk discourse lends itself better to legitimising genuine climate policy – including mitigation and adaptation measures – instead of military preparedness. Furthermore, the problems of PDCI and especially RUSI in distributing their framing of climate security shows that securitisation is more likely if strong domestic actors with expertise, long-standing political connections and the trust of the political decisionmakers carry it. In Mexico, such actors have been largely absent with respect to civil society. Moreover, in order to be successful on a broader basis and over a longer period, it does not suffice for only a few actors to pick up the securitising arguments, but instead requires a rather broad coalition, such as in the case of the US. Furthermore, the limited influence of territorial danger and risk discourses in the Mexican case reinforces the argument about the need to include context in our studies of securitisation. Without a longer tradition of security arguments in the respective field, our study suggests, resonance in political circles is likely to be limited, especially if there are other, 'hard' security issues in play.

6
TURKEY
No climate for change?

Introduction

Turkey, during the past two decades, has evolved as a country displaying rapid socio-economic progress and development. This is evidenced in the Human Development Index (HDI), in which Turkey ranked 90 out of 187 countries in 2013. Turkey's HDI value showed an increase of 52 per cent from 0.474 in 1980 to 0.722 in 2012 (UNDP Turkey 2013). Other country indicators showed corresponding increases: While Turkey's GDP had been 68.79 billion dollars in 1980, in 2000 it was 266.6 billion, and it reached 822.1 billion dollars in 2013. Its population grew from 43 million in 1980 to 63 million in 2000 and 74 million in 2013 (World Bank 2015b). The international media since the mid-2000s has thus viewed Turkey as the 'China of Europe' (*The Economist* 2010; CNBC 2013). Indeed, through tight economic and fiscal policies after the international financial crisis of 2001, the country has managed to stabilise macroeconomic indicators, and even since the economic crisis began in 2008, Turkey's growth has remained more stable than that of most other countries (Çetin 2012), although some question marks have appeared about the sustainability of this growth from 2014 onwards.

This development has formed the basis for a broad acceptance and support for the ruling Justice and Development Party (AKP). Especially after progressive policymaking during its first term from 2002 until 2007, it took Turkey on the way to EU accession negotiations agreed in 2004 and opened on 3 October 2005 (ABGS 2015). The AKP, with Tayyip Erdoğan as an at times disputed but charismatic leader, from then on acquired the image of being a party of 'makers', fronted by an effective and pragmatic leader (Pope 2012; Interview 2014af).

Yet when it comes to climate change, the country has generally remained in a position in which it has widely been considered a laggard, even if it displayed some efforts after joining the UNFCCC in 2004 and starting EU accession negotiations in 2005. Accordingly, in the Climate Change Performance Index of 2015, Turkey ranked 51 out of 61 countries (Germanwatch and CAN 2015), and in the climate action tracker, Turkey, along with the UAE, Gabon, Gambia and Saudi Arabia, has not even been rated (Climate Action Tracker 2014). Despite its newly gained economic strength, Turkey has not committed itself to binding emission reductions for fear of placing its further development at risk (DPT 1990; 1996; 2001; *Star Gazete* 2013; *Hürriyet* 2013). Most national as well as international actors, among them the CAN, the EU and the Turkish Climate Network (İklim Ağı) have thus increasingly criticised Turkey for its resistance to take significant steps towards sustainability in the process of economic growth (İzci 2013; İklim Ağı 2012; CAN 2011; *Zaman* 2015; European Commission 2014). But as if this was not enough, Turkey has continued to increase its greenhouse gas emissions (Algedik 2014: 134; European Commission 2014: 70) and consequently received the Fossil of the Day award from the Climate Action Network at COP-17 in Durban for its attitude of 'wanting everything but giving nothing' (CAN 2011).

In this chapter, we argue that Turkey's laggard status is a consequence of little or no politicisation and a lack of climate change securitisation. Because of the absence of successful securitisation, the issue has not made it onto the political agenda, and there has certainly been no legitimisation of extraordinary measures. Instead, Turkish politicians have regularly prioritised economic development, and have justified their stance by referring to questions of climate justice regarding industrialised versus developing countries in the global climate change regime and to the historical responsibilities of those whose emissions have led to the emergence of the problem in the first instance (*Hürriyet* 2014; *Star Gazete* 2013). This does not mean that there are no securitising actors. However, these often lack resources, support and legitimacy and have not been able to influence the broader political debate in any significant sense. Despite one relatively successful securitising move in the military sector, we find at best fragments of the international climate security discourse. Apart from the focus and priority given to economic development in political and societal debates, we argue that another reason for this limited influence is the weakness of civil society, and especially of the environmental movement (Duru 2013). Even in government-supported organisations (i.e. TÜBITAK or the Eastern Mediterranean Climate Centre, EMCC), state funding and policies that encourage climate change research are largely lacking, and funding for the most part is granted to issues that do not put industrial and technological development at risk (Şahin 2014: 74). As in the Mexican case, NGOs, and environmental NGOs in particular, are few in numbers and have little to no strength in Turkey (*Today's Zaman* 2011). However, partly as a consequence of the Gezi Park movement or 'Gezi spirit' (Madra 2015), more environmental activists may organise themselves in the future, and with rising levels of economic standing, their securitising moves may find a more receptive audience, at least in the industrialised urban regions of western Turkey.

This chapter is based on the screening and analysis of forty-five core publications of relevant climate change actors in civil society, scientific and international organisations and ninety parliamentary debates on climate change and global warming that have been analysed according to our framework. To further substantiate our findings, we have conducted more than twenty mainly semi-structured and informal interviews with state representatives, environmental activists, scientists, think tanks and NGOs and conducted a network citation analysis on the basis of the forty-five core publications that we initially identified.

The general climate debate in Turkey

In Turkey, an environmental consciousness started to evolve in the 1980s, when a period of more rapid industrialisation but at the same time also more tangible and visible environmental pollution began to change the attitude of many people towards the environment (Çavlak 2012: 507). This growing environmental concern reached the state level when in 1982 an article on the protection of the environment was included in the Turkish Constitution for the first time, followed by a comprehensive environmental law in 1983 (*Resmi Gazete* 1983). During the period in office of prime minister Turgut Özal (1983–1987), the concept of 'clean energy' was linked to climate and environmental issues and put on the political agenda. In the fifth Five Year Development Plan (1983–1987) of the State Planning Institution (DPT), environmental issues were discussed in relation to social policies and the support of organisations working on these matters was advised (DPT 1985). Yet the focus of state planning continued to be socio-economic development (cf. DPT 1979; 1985; 1990; 1996), and the recognition of environmental matters in state planning can be regarded as a move to a better management of development and energy policies against environmental claims.

Environmental consciousness increased in the second half of the 1980s and early 1990s, as becomes evident in the sixth Five Year Development Plan of 1987–1992. It mentions the environment for the first time in a section on 'Environment and settlement' (DPT 1990: 312–317). Since the second WMO World Climate Conference in Geneva in 1990, Turkey has been present in the international climate policy process, even if not engaging for climate protection but struggling for its status within the UNFCCC (Türkeş 2002; İzci 2013; Şahin 2014: 24). In preparation for the Earth Summit in Rio (1992), a National Climate Change Coordination Group (NCCG) was formed under the general directorate of the State Meteorology Services (MGM) in 1991 and prepared two reports on Protection of the Atmosphere and Climate Change and Energy and Technology (Türkeş 2002; OECD 2008). The reports analysed Turkey's state of development, including its development goals and energy consumption, arguing that emission reductions would have to be adjusted according to Turkey's special circumstances (Türkeş 2002: 3). The government declared that the environment and its protection had the same priority as economic and industrial development, and the Ministry of Environment was founded in 1991 (ÇŞB 1991).

During the preparatory conferences on the way to the Rio Earth Summit, Turkey's position in the UNFCCC regime was hotly debated. At the conference, delegates held that a classification of Turkey as both an Annex I and II country was problematic, but Turkish officials, in line with the views of the Ministry of Foreign Affairs, claimed that Turkey according to its Western principles had to act in line with the European Union and therefore 'as an OECD country had to take the adequate position' (Şahin 2014: 25). By signing the UNFCCC at the Rio Earth Summit in 1992, Turkey confirmed this position. However, later it became obvious that Turkey lacked scientific and technical expertise, and only in the aftermath of the Earth Summit did decisionmakers recognise that it was impossible for Turkey as an Annex II country to provide technical and financial assistance to Annex I countries. Turkey therefore declined to join the UNFCCC (Şahin 2014: 25; ÇOB 2007). As a consequence of this misguided decisionmaking, a ten-year struggle over the acknowledgement of Turkey's 'special circumstances' within the regime began, and blocked any further commitment to climate protection (Erdoğdu 2010; İzci 2013; ÇOB 2007). Nevertheless, the buzzwords of international environmental debates continued to diffuse into Turkish policymaking. For example, during her term in office from 1993 to 1996, prime minister Tansu Çiller was the first to use the term 'sustainable development' (Çavlak 2012: 507). She also emphasised the importance of environmental issues in the process of Turkey's accession to the EU (Çavlak 2012: 507; Baykan 2013). The reality was that priority was continually given to socio-economic growth, and consequently a parliamentary commission on the environment that was set up in 1994 came to the conclusion that commitments with regard to climate change would block investments (Cerit Mazlum 2009; Şahin 2014: 26).

With the customs union in 1995 Turkey proceeded with closer EU integration, and at the EU summit in Helsinki in 1999, Turkey was recognised as a candidate country for accession (Bekmezci 2015). Yet despite an internationally evolving environmental and climate security discourse, in Turkey the PKK and Islamism as domestic threats to the state, as well as the rivalry with neighbouring states including Greece, Russia and Iran, dominated the political and security agenda throughout the 1980s and 1990s. With regard to energy and environmental policies, absolute priority was at the same time given to industrialisation and development (Kuloğlu 2009; Sandıklı n.d.; İzci 2013: 259; *Hürriyet* 2010b).

After the turn of the millennium, at a time when the climate security debates especially in industrialised countries such as Germany, the UK and the US were already advanced, in Turkey discussions as to whether it should ratify the Kyoto Protocol and join the UNFCCC continued. At the same time, the government started to address climate change in its five-year development plans (DPT 2001: 187), and a special expert commission (*İklim Değişikliği Özel İhtisas Komisyonu*) of the State Planning Institution was set up and issued a report on climate change in 2000 within the framework of the eighth Five Year Development Plan (DPT 2000; Algedik 2013: 17–18) . It discussed climate change from a predominantly technical perspective and at the same time suggested the establishment of a Special Commission on Climate Change and a National Climate Change Action Plan (DPT 2000). In 2001, the Coordination Board on Climate Change was established as the coordinating unit and focal point of Turkey's climate change policies (Türkeş 2002).

In spite of this hesitant progress, Turkey continued bargaining over its status in the international climate change regime (Şahin 2014: 7; Türkeş 2002: 4). Turkey vehemently rejected its classification as an Annex I and II state within UNFCCC. Even if that classification had originally been made at Turkey's insistence, Turkish policymakers now viewed the classification as unjust (cf. MFA 2015; Eroğlu 2015: 15; *Star Gazete* 2013; *Hürriyet* 2013). The situation was complex, as even the EU member states rejected Turkey's claims for a long time after it had achieved the status of an EU accession country (İzci 2013). Only after the parties at the COP-7 in Marrakesh (2001) agreed to delete Turkey from Annex II and recognise its 'special circumstances' as a newly emerging economy, did the country take a more proactive stance within the climate change regime (İzci 2013: 249; UNFCCC 2002; Asan 2010: 147). Thus, after a decade of bargaining, in 2004 Turkey was one of the last countries to implement the UNFCCC and ratified the Kyoto Protocol only in 2009 (Türkmenoğlu 2012; Karakaya and Berberoğlu 2007).

The opening of EU accession negotiations in 2005 contributed to the momentum that Turkish climate policymaking had gained after the COP-7. This became obvious in the size and rank of Turkish delegations to the conferences of parties, which increased decisively for the first time in 2005 and afterwards displayed a steady increase (Şahin 2014: 78). Within the EU accession negotiations, the chapter on the environment was opened in 2009, but Turkish politicians had been eager to present themselves as good membership candidates, and had started to align their environmental policies with the EU *acquis communautaire* even before this (Çavlak 2012; Gieler and Çetinyılmaz 2015). Institutions such as the Ministry of Environment and Forestry and the subordinate National Coordination Board on Climate Change were reorganised several times (ÇŞB 2013: 11). In 2004, the EU-financed Regional Environmental Centre (*REC Türkiye*) opened in Ankara. It was set up as an independent non-profit organisation tasked with strengthening the cooperation of government, civil society, the private sector and other relevant actors. Besides environmental policies, climate change is a main concern of REC (REC 2005) and in the period from 2005 to 2008 it conducted several projects to increase awareness of that issue (REC 2008a).

Other events also affected the Turkish agenda after 2000, both intended, such as the activities of distinct actors, and unintended in the form of extreme weather phenomena or natural disasters (King and Gulledge 2013: 33). As in other countries, the 2004 Hollywood movie *The Day After Tomorrow*, depicting the catastrophic consequences of climate change, received a lot of attention (Aksiyon 2004; Interview 2014al). Cinemas screened it for twenty-seven consecutive weeks with a total attendance of 657,350 visitors (Boxoffice Türkiye 2015a) which puts it among the 10–12 most viewed films in a year (Boxoffice Türkiye 2015b). Additionally, hurricane Katrina struck the Gulf Coast of the US, and the Kyoto Protocol went into effect in 2005. This accumulation of events had an impact on public discourse in Turkey (Lütfi-Şen 2013b; Kadıoğlu 2012a: 54). At the same time, the country was hit by severe droughts, and the media increasingly covered climate change and global warming (Lütfi-Şen 2013b; Met Office 2011: 17).

Media representations of climate change shot up especially in 2007. The number of articles in four of the most important national newspapers (*Hürriyet*, *Milliyet*, *Zaman* and *Radikal*) that included 'climate change' as a keyword increased from 245 (2006) to 1,001 (2007), and those that included 'global warming' from 501 to 3,236 (Lütfi-Şen 2013b). A civil movement on climate change evolved in this context after the mid-2000s (Şahin 2014: 10) and discursive entrepreneurs in science, civil society, politics and the security sector started to operate in an environment that was much more friendly and open to their concerns compared to preceding decades.

Moves to securitise climate change in Turkey appeared on the verge of and during the peak of the international climate security debate in 2007, and can be basically divided into two relevant levels: civil society, including some links with science and media; and the military. Moves on the civil society level, despite leading to isolated government reports and strategic action plans (i.e. Kadıoğlu 2012a; 2012b; ÇŞB 2011; ÇOB 2008; 2010) have been rather unsuccessful, largely because they have been mostly reactive to external interferences in the form of international support and compliance with EU legislation. Securitisation attempts on the military level, however, have been at least partly successful, though still on a much lower level than in the US, as a change in Turkish security perceptions of climate change has occurred in their aftermath.

During the peak of the climate security debate in 2007, Turkey, supported by the UNDP, submitted its first National Communication on Climate Change to the UNFCCC secretariat (ÇOB 2007). Due to the extreme droughts the country experienced increasingly after the mid-2000s, public attention to climate change rose until COP-15 in Copenhagen (2009) (Şahin 2014: 6, 25). Previously only a few and mostly individual actors and activists had tried to increase public awareness of a dangerously changing climate. Most importantly, Ömer Madra, an academic, journalist and activist, had been reporting on climate change as a threat regularly since 1998 on the independent radio station *Açık Radio* (Open Radio) (Şahin 2014: 62), of which he was a co-founder (*Açık Radyo* 2015). However, as a non-commercial media channel that has a rather small and limited audience who are anyway more likely to be familiar with the topic, it has been rather difficult to reach or influence actual decisionmakers and a broader public. Still, as an expert on climate change, Madra is a frequent guest and interviewee of the mass media (Özer 2015; Agos 2015; Alpay 2014) where he has called for strong measures to securitise climate change in drastic and alarming words:

> Another study is from the Potsdam Institute. The climate study of the German scientists provides new frightening statistics. The data even exceeds the scenario put forward by Lord Stern … According to the study, extreme heatwaves will double within only seven years and will even quadruple by 2040. If we do not act now, extreme heat and drought will affect 85 per cent of the earth's surface until 2100. Sixty per cent of the land masses will suffer

from draughts. As a consequence there will be forest fires and a loss of harvests. The story goes like this: Drought, crop failure, hunger, fire, war.

(Madra 2013)

In 2007, at the peak of the international climate security discourse, Madra published the book *Global Warming and the Climate Crisis: Why We Should Not Wait Any Longer* (Madra and Şahin 2007) together with Ümit Şahin and wrote the foreword to the Turkish version of Gwynne Dyer's internationally acclaimed *Climate Wars* that included an apocalyptic future scenario for Turkey (Dyer 2013). Even if Madra's framing of climate change as a threat represents a strong attempt to securitise climate change on the individual and planetary security level, there has been no visible outcome or effect on policymaking or other key actors. This illustrates that, as another activist and representative of an environmental foundation confirmed, civil society is still far from being influential in Turkey (Interview 2014aq; 2014ak). Domestic actors have a particularly hard time in generating support, whereas international actors can at least draw on support that is not tied to Turkish policymaking priorities.

Accordingly, the first campaign that addressed climate change explicitly in Turkey was conducted by the Greenpeace Turkey office in 2005. The campaign was directed against the installation of a geothermal power plant (Şahin 2014: 62) and thus typical of the actions of Greenpeace in Turkey, which are usually directed against such specific energy projects. Due to the general lack of knowledge on climate change within the broader population, campaigns against concrete issues such as energy plants are more likely to be successful in Turkey (Interview 2014aq). Successful environmentalist and rural movements against several industrial projects show that the population can be better mobilised by employing more tangible threats. Where a 'not in my backyard' (Interview 2014af) attitude prevails, climate change as a threat with broader implications on the national or global level remains too abstract and vague to be taken seriously.

However, at the peak of the Kyoto debate in Turkey and the international climate security debate in 2007, environmental movements were not only opposed by government and private sector interests, but also divided among themselves: some were against ratifying the protocol while others campaigned for its ratification (Interview 2014aq). During the 'Ratify Kyoto' campaign, civil society actors managed to mobilise a larger amount of organisations and individuals, and similar to the German case, this was the time when new organisations that previously had not included climate change on their agenda entered the discourse (Interview 2014b). However, after Turkey eventually ratified the protocol, a considerable number of actors considered their mission accomplished and left the field, and the climate movement weakened again. To sum up, the attempts to securitise climate change by civil society actors in Turkey, even at times of great awareness and opportunities, faced many obstacles: minimal resources of actors, a lack of credibility, a limited range of communication channels, and a dominance of issues cutting across security sectors and thus not necessarily linked to climate change, such as biodiversity, droughts, water scarcity, that 'have stolen the show' (Interview 2014an).

However, the dynamics of the climate change discourse in Turkey in the second half of the 2000s did not only add momentum to the green movement, but saw the Technical University of Istanbul (ITÜ) and the Water Foundation (*Su Vakfı*) as institutions close to the government organising Turkey's first national Climate Change Congress (TIKDEK 2007). The conference brought together scientific experts from across the country, but by and large excluded social scientists and political think tanks, as did its two successors (TIKDEK 2007; 2010; 2013). This is indicative of the fact that the climate debate in Turkey, to the extent that it has existed at all, has always sought to deal with the issue as a technical and not a political, let alone a security matter. Nevertheless, and notably, the call for papers for TIKDEK III in 2013 finally included contributions on climate change and security – that nobody followed up (TIKDEK 2013). Comparable to TIKDEK, regional governmental organisations such as the Konya-based Agency for Water Supply (KOSKI) organised a conference on 'Global Climate Change and Its Environmental Impact' (*Uluslararası Küresel İklim Değişikliğive Çevresel Etkileri Konferansı*), thereby reflecting a gradual diffusion of the international and scientific climate security debate towards the governmental level. Experts from civil society and the scientific community mainly addressed the local impacts of climate change, such as its effects on Konya's sweet water systems, precipitation patterns and agriculture. Some presentations included references to food security and 'climate refugees' (KOSKI 2007). The thematic priorities of the conference already pointed to a country-specific, Turkish framing of climate security, which mainly focused on water (droughts) and agriculture (food security) (Interview 2014b), as we will elaborate in the next section. Indicative of the albeit limited rise of climate change as a political issue in the second half of the 2000s is the number of publications on the issue that the Library of the Turkish Parliament (*TBMM Kütüphanesi*) holds. While before 2007 only two such publications had been registered, eight were included in 2007 alone, with some clearly employing securitising frames, including titles such as *Climate Change and the Climate Crisis* (Madra and Şahin 2007) or *Apocalypse and Climate Change* (Ayhan 2007). Most of them, however, were international publications, and some continued to question the significance of global warming and referred to the concern over it as 'fetishism' (Şahin 2005).

Finally, not least because of the context of EU accession negotiations and within the framework of UNFCCC assistance, the government pursued a number of projects to improve activities and awareness with regard to global climate change in Turkey (Aladağ 2008). Among these initiatives were programmes such as 'Enabling Activities for the Preparation of Turkey's Initial National Communication to the UNFCCC', 'Enhancing the Capacity of Turkey to Adapt to Climate Change 2008–2011', and 'Evaluating the National Capacity in the Face of Global Environmental Agreements 2008–2010', to name but a few (Gieler and Çetinyılmaz 2015). Meanwhile, concrete projects such as 'Capacity Building for Climate Change Management in Turkey' and 'Developing Turkey's National Climate

Change Action Plan' have been carried out by international organisations such as the UN or FAO (DSI 2013).

Even if in the public and civil society discourses from the mid-2000s onwards, climate change as an urgent and dangerous issue gained attention and the climate movement in Turkey gained momentum, this can nevertheless not count as an indication of successful domestic civil society moves to securitisation. Other, more credible actors emerged in the course of the international climate change debate and addressed the Turkish policy and security establishment directly. Individual discursive entrepreneurs from the armed forces played a significant role in this. Inspired by the 2007 CNA report *National Security and the Threat of Climate Change* (CNA 2007; see Chapter 3), a general of the Turkish Armed Forces and security expert, Nejat Eslen, published a commentary in Turkey's liberal-left newspaper *Radikal* with the title 'Climate Change Is a Security Issue for Turkey' (Eslen 2007), in which he drew attention to the national security implications for Turkey. According to Eslen, Turkey as a country with important water reserves should meet the challenges and effects of climate change and prepare for their consequences (Eslen 2007). Even if Eslen was the first to publicly articulate climate change as a national security threat, there are other indicators that a climate change related security thinking reached the Turkish military establishment in the course and aftermath of the international climate security debate. The Bulletin of the Turkish General Staff for instance published a series of articles on 'The Effects of Climate Change on Turkey's Security Policies' (Aktaş 2009).

Shortly after these publications, on 11 June 2009, the Strategic Research and Exercise Center (*Stratejik Araştırmave Etüt Merkezi*, SAREM) of the Turkish Armed Forces organised a symposium on 'Global Climate Change and its Effects on Turkish Security' (*Küresel İklim Değişikliğininve Türkiye'nin Güvenliğine Etkileri*). SAREM, founded in 2002, has been referred to as the 'think tank of the military' (*Akşam Gazetesi* 2012) and is subordinated to the Head Office of Military History and Strategic Studies (*Askeri Tarihve Stratejik Etüt Başkanlığı*, ATASE) of the Turkish Armed Forces. Among the participants of the Symposium were Eslen, Ayşegül Kibaroğlu, an expert on the conflict potential of trans-boundary water issues (Kibaroğlu n.d.; 1996), retired general Armağan Kuloğlu, Hasan Saygın, an expert on nuclear energy, Volkan Ediğer, an expert on energy systems, and other high ranking bureaucrats, security experts and scientists (Interview 2015a; Kuloğlu 2009; Kibaroğlu n.d.; Ediğer n.d.).

SAREM was closed down by the Turkish Armed Forces in winter 2011. The media commented that the 'brain of the Turkish Armed Forces had stopped working' and 'think is gone and tank is left' (*Hürriyet* 2012; *Akşam Gazetesi* 2012; *Radikal* 2012). The closure was related to the ongoing trials of 'Ergenekon' and 'Sledgehammer' ('*Balyoz*'), in which military officials and an elite of intellectuals were tried for conspiracy (*Aktifhaber* 2012). By closing down SAREM, the dialogue between the military and representatives from research and civil society that had only just begun to address climate change as a security issue, ended. Nevertheless, the security establishment and a few think tanks and scientists continued to discuss climate change as a security issue (ORSAM; Aktaş 2009). Only one day after the workshop, Saygın published an article on the effects of climate change on national security (Saygın 2009). Likewise, in July–August 2009, Kuloğlu published a shorter article on 'Turkey and Threat Perceptions related to Global Climate Change' (Kuloğlu 2009). Both authors were inspired by the presentations at the workshop, most importantly the contribution of Eslen, and drew their arguments from his argumentation.

In his presentation, Eslen had referred to different antecedent studies and scenarios, such as the CNA report (2007), the Schwartz and Randall Study (2003), outcomes of a research project at the Massachusetts Institute of Technology (Chandler 2009) and the Global Water Futures report by CSIS (Peterson and Posner 2008). By linking climate change to the water–security nexus and water security to food security, he pointed to the Middle East as a neighbouring and possible climate security hotspot that could affect the wider region, and therefore also Turkey, first through a destabilisation triggered by climate change and the resultant mass migration movements and conflicts (Eslen 2009). In the follow-up to the Workshop in June 2010, Eslen was asked by SAREM to publish a 40-page study on 'Climate Change and its Effects on Turkey's Security' in the *Journal of Strategic Studies* (Eslen 2010). In the workshop as well as in his publications, Eslen proposed putting climate change on Turkey's national security agenda as well as the creation of an organisational unit within the National Security Council (*Milli Güvenlik Kurulu*) (Eslen 2009; 2010; Interview 2015a). These securitising moves can be regarded as successful as they have verifiably affected other decisionmakers, first of all the workshop participants and later also the bureaucracy. They triggered a series of publications, and in the end climate change had been recognised as a national security threat and been included in Turkey's 'Red Book', its national security policy document, in 2010 (*Hürriyet* 2010a).

As in the Mexican case, outside actors sometimes supported such framings. David Miliband, then British foreign secretary, for instance visited the Environmental Commission of the Turkish Parliament (*TBMM Çevre Komisyonu*) in the run-up to the 2009 climate summit in Copenhagen. In his speech he referred to climate change as a threat that was going to affect Turkey's culture, economy, politics and security (TBMM 2009: 22). As we will discuss further in the impact section of this chapter, Turkish politicians continued to engage with climate change after this peak and into the 2010s, but at a relatively low level, and often if they were able to link climate and energy security. Thus, President Abdullah Gül acted as honorary chairman of the Solar Energy for World Peace conference in 2013, in which plenary speakers included Jürgen Scheffran of the German Climate Campus (see Chapter 4) and two Nobel Prize-winning scientists (Solar4Peace 2015).

In sum, and compared to the German and US country cases, there have been only sporadic events, reports and statements in Turkey that can be regarded as explicit attempts at securitisation, and for the most part they have had no great visible impact, and have been countered by invocations of energy and economic security (İzci 2013: 248). Nonetheless, we have seen an evolution from relative disinterest until the turn of the millennium towards an increased relevance of climate change in Turkish political debates after 2004, with a focus on territorial danger articulations by military staff (Üzelgün and Castro 2014). However, even if securitisation attempts have multiplied, compared to cases such as Germany or the US, they seem rudimentary and sporadic.

A closer look at climate security discourses in Turkey

As our overview has shown, the Turkish debate on climate security involves a relatively small, although growing group of scientists, bureaucrats, civil society actors and security officials. It is thus more appropriate to speak of discourse fragments rather than a fully developed climate security discourse. Furthermore, we have found few explicit securitisations, and often articulations of climate change that refer to threats only 'implicitly'. For example, in the parliamentary debates we have studied, only one speaker explicitly referred to water scarcity and interstate conflict as a potential effect of climate change (TBMM 2014e: 5). The strongest attempts with regard to a securitisation in the territorial danger dimension were made from within the military and security establishment, starting with the securitising moves of General Eslen:

> Climate change in Turkey must be recognised as a serious security issue. On this basis, a comprehensive strategy must be developed. The effects of climate change ... are already tangible. Climate change leads to losses of harvests, health problems, water poverty and migration and can pave the way to tensions and conflict ... Turkey, with its important water reserves, should meet the challenges posed by climate change and prepare for their consequences.
>
> *(Eslen 2007)*

In line with the territorial danger discourse, Eslen predicted future violent conflicts over water and presented climate change as a trigger for potential military conflict along Turkey's borders (Eslen 2007), a discourse that is frequently reiterated by actors, even international ones, who refer to Turkey's 'troubled waters' of the Euphrates and Tigris (NATO Transformation Command 2007: 61). Accordingly, the EU in its reports regarding the country's accession proposed putting the Euphrates–Tigris water basin, together with springs, canals and barrier lakes, under international management (Eslen 2009).

General Eslen's framing and narrative corresponds to the territorial danger dimension and displays similarities to the US climate security discourse, in which the territorial dimension prevails over individual and planetary danger dimensions. As the keeper of some of the most important water resources in the Middle East, Turkey would have to meet the effects caused by climate change and prepare itself for the like (Eslen 2007). Eslen predicted future conflicts over water and presented climate change as a trigger for potential military conflict and existential primary supply problems. In the general's attempt to securitise climate change the focus is on concrete domestic security threats to Turkey and the concrete security implications arising from water issues at its borders (Eslen 2007), a discourse that is frequently iterated by actors when it comes to management of the important transfrontier rivers of the Euphrates and Tigris.

Eslen's articulations are, apart from their strong links to national security, characteristic of the Turkish framing of climate change as a security threat, but they remain a rare exception in the public Turkish climate security framing. Securitisation attempts on the parliamentary level, to the extent that they existed at all, have operated rather on the level of individual danger. Common to both territorial and individual danger framings is the fact that climate change is perceived as a security issue only when concrete effects such as water scarcity and as a consequence profit cuts in agriculture are at stake that could result in a loss of votes or compliance, especially from the rural population (TBMM 2014g: 15; 2014c: 7–18). Some scientists and civil society actors have linked climate change to migration (KOSKI 2007; Yeşil Ekonomi 2015), but we have not found any corresponding references among bureaucrats or the political elite, with the exception of security experts within the military (Kuloğlu 2009). Government officials tend to refer to planetary and individual danger and, more concretely, to threats to agriculture, the economy, the water supply, and health. The following statement is typical of this framing:

> I have already shared with you the dangerous effects of climate change on the world and on Turkey from this podium several times. I have shared with you my view that the threat and destructive potential of climate change is more dangerous than an economic crisis. Agricultural areas may be lost, water shortage will hit us and the health of the population in cities will be damaged; industrial activity will come to a dead end and even water wars may occur.
>
> *(TBMM 2014d: 7–18)*

Most articulations of climate security in Turkey refrain from discussing the territorial level in terms of violent conflict. References to global threats or other countries and regions such as Africa have appeared only towards the end of our study period (TBMM 2014b: 15). Additionally, the elite often still points to the historical responsibility of industrialised countries and emphasises the importance of climate justice and financial aid rather than the possible risks and dangers connected to climate change (*Star Gazete* 2013; *Hürriyet* 2013). In his speech at the 2014 UN Climate Summit in New York, President Erdoğan thus confirmed that the frequency of natural disasters had increased in quantity as well as in severity but then was quick to emphasise that the criteria for a new climate change regime after 2020 would have to be 'transparent, comprehensive, just and fair' (*Hürriyet* 2014).

While emphasising the need for a just and fair regulation and the fact that it is going to be the least developed countries that are most strongly affected by the impacts of climate change, Turkish decisionmakers generally employ individual danger perspectives. A special characteristic of the Turkish case is that even individual danger framings in parliamentary debates and speeches of policymakers remain restricted to the national and even local level, thus mostly ignoring other regions, states and individuals beyond Turkey. A frequent referent object are farmers and the rural population (TBMM 2014g: 15; 2014f: 23–25; 2014c: 7–18; 2013a: 27).

As mentioned already, the fragment of the climate security discourse that occurs often and is closest to the territorial danger dimension is the water–security nexus. Especially since 2005, actors have become increasingly aware of water shortages and related challenges (IPC 2015b), and have increasingly related them to climate change (IPC 2015b; Eslen 2007; IPC 2015a). The water–security nexus has been the only climate issue so far that has been linked to a rhetoric of war in parliamentary debates (TBMM 2014e: 5). In Parliament it has furthermore been framed within the individual danger discourse, though partly combined with territorial danger elements, including concepts of climate justice:

> Climate change is bringing about decisive changes in all areas of human existence. The most problematic aspect of climate change in this regard is that it hits the poorest among us the hardest and increases disparities among already unequal livelihoods. Because of global climate change, severe droughts and water scarcity will affect some areas such that human existence will become impossible there. As a consequence, there will be cross-continental migration and water wars on our future agenda.
> *(TBMM 2014e: 5)*

As a second climate security framing on the individual level, food and agricultural security has become increasingly important. News reporting on the effects of climate change on agricultural production, especially in the central Anatolian region, has increased (*Anadolu Ajansi* 2015). In the Turkish parliamentary debates, speakers make frequent references to the impact of climate change on farming output and the danger to individual economic security that this poses (TBMM 2014i: 10–11; 2014g: 15):

> Heavy rainfalls, droughts and floods, which have become increasingly visible and tangible during the past years as a consequence of climate change, affect agricultural production more and more. This is why our farmers have to sell their goods at a loss and finally they become unable to repay their loans.
> *(TBMM 2014f: 23–25)*

Apart from the emphasis on water and food security, the Turkish debate on climate security focuses on the resilience of large cities, especially Istanbul, to water scarcity, droughts, floods and heatwaves (IBB 2011; Topbaş 2012; Krellenberg 2013). Scientists, policymakers and the media alike have reiterated the vulnerability of such megacities to the impact of climate change (Topbaş 2012; Lütfi-Şen 2013b: 7–21; Krellenberg 2013; Birgün 2015):

Droughts and heat waves are the two most important climate change-related hazards that could negatively affect the urban life of Turkey in the future. Downpours that could be produced because of the excess heating of the surface may also carry serious threats by causing urban floods. In September 2009, a downpour causing torrential rainfall severely hit a highly industrialised area of Istanbul, causing more than thirty deaths and millions of dollars in damage.

(Lütfi-Şen 2013a)

A link to the individual risk discourse of climate security is most visible in the demand for increased 'risk management' in such city hot spots (Kadıoğlu 2012a; Krellenberg 2013). In July 2013, a workshop organised by Kerstin Krellenberg, an environmental scientist from the German Helmholtz Centre, together with the IPC–Sabanci University–Stiftung Mercator Initiative, REC and the UNDP, brought together representatives from academia, civil society, and politics to discuss how response capacities in the Istanbul Metropolitan Municipality to climate change hazards could be strengthened (Krellenberg 2013). Furthermore, the Ministry of Environment and Urbanisation initiated a project on the 'Expansion of Resilient Cities to Climate Change' in 2013. The project's aim was to ensure risk management of climate change in coastal areas and promote sustainable urban development policies. Accordingly, a City Climate Resilience Strategy was part of the expected outcomes (Öztürk 2012).

There are only few discussions of climate refugees and climate-induced migration as a threat (Albayrakoğlu 2011: 63). Ironically, such rare articulations portray Turkey as being vulnerable to migration from Europe due to a 'new ice age' that would stem from an abrupt climate change (Kuloğlu 2009) as was illustrated in earlier US studies (Schwartz and Randall 2003) and in the film *The Day After Tomorrow*. The planetary danger discourse is also rather weak in the Turkish case. At best, it appears in the emphasis on the importance of the protection of forests from threats such as wildfires and droughts (Türkeş 2002; Lütfi-Şen 2013c). According to the minister of environment and urbanisation, Veysel Eroğlu, 'the most important element of the fight against climate change are the forests' (TBMM 2014b: 15–18). While such statements carry an implicit link to individual dangers posed by forest fires, some actors have also pointed to the effects of climate change on the country's particularly rich biodiversity (Interview 2014an; Lütfi-Şen 2013c). However, this framing has not been sufficiently related to climate change in order to speak of a planetary climate danger discourse. One of the rare examples of such a framing is the following:

We are not the owner of nature and we are not the only ones who have the right to use it and profit from it. We are and we should not be free to devastate and demolish it as we like, according to our short-term profit and without thinking of the generations to come. We usurp the right of all living beings that at least have the same rights to live as we have.

(TBMM 2013b: 52)

In sum, climate security discourses are weak in the Turkish political debate and often debated as side topics related to other issues such as farming, water availability or health. The few securitising moves focus on the individual dimension and include both danger and risk articulations. Other securitisations, apart from an isolated military debate on climate security that started in 2007, are mostly absent.

Discursive entrepreneurs: overly motivated but weak activists and strong but discredited internationals

In Turkey, the influence of both civil society and scientific organisations on the climate change debate and its security implications has been far less pronounced than in countries such as Germany or the US. As we will discuss in the section on context below, Turkish civil society is comparatively weak and science is far from producing extensive knowledge on climate change and its possible implications. Decisionmakers often do not see scientific experts or NGOs as competent partners and sometimes even regard them as potential obstacles to country's overall development aims (Interview 2014al). Instead, the military has historically had a much bigger impact on politics, even in times of democratic government. Military personnel have also been linking climate change and security. Former generals Nejat Eslen and Armağan Kuloğlu belonged to this group of securitising actors that have received some attention but have later been discredited due to political tensions.

While the broader Turkish elite worried more about economic and energy security (İzci 2013: 249; Şahin 2014), some environmental activists and NGOs, but also other international organisations and scientists, have tried to push forward the Turkish debate on climate change. Indeed, among the activists those with international links have been particularly engaged and influential. Apart from the usual suspects of international NGOs, organisations from individual countries and most importantly foundations from Germany have been particularly active in their attempts to securitise climate change in Turkey. The Heinrich Böll Foundation (affiliated with the Green Party and also active in Mexico), the Istanbul Policy Center (IPC) funded by the Mercator Foundation, and even the German Embassy have financed and supported projects on climate change. The Böll Foundation has contributed to Turkey receiving the Fossil of the Day award (Interview 2014aq). It has financed and initiated the inclusion of civil society actors as participants in the COPs and as observers in the UNFCCC process (Interview 2014aq; Algedik 2013). While the Böll Foundation itself did not explicitly pursue securitising moves, it nevertheless supported actors and events that at least indirectly contributed to securitisation. Together with the Turkish Green Party, the Böll Foundation organised a symposium on drought, and it invited an expert from the German Wuppertal Institute to a conference on Climate Change and Global Justice. As the conference took place only shortly after hurricane Katrina hit the US, it had a relatively broad media echo in Turkey (Şahin 2014: 157–158).

The IPC is an Istanbul-based think tank at Sabanci University. It has put climate change on its agenda after it formed a partnership with the German Mercator

Foundation in 2010. As we have outlined in chapter four, Mercator belongs to those German organisations that have come to the climate change debate quite late. Yet, ever since the foundation put climate change on its agenda, it has been relatively effective due to its huge financial, institutional and human capacities. IPC has organised several climate change-related events that have also pointed to security, such as the German–Turkish Climate Security Roundtable in spring 2015 (IPC 2015a). For the roundtable, the IPC teamed up with the French Development Agency (AFD) and the International Organisation for Migration (IOM) to increase impact. However, the roundtable demonstrated the distance between such initiatives and Turkish decisionmakers, since most of the seats for Turkish politicians remained empty (IPC 2015a).

It has become obvious that due to the general absence of climate scientists as possible actors in securitisation, interdisciplinary and technical knowledge, especially in the beginnings of the UNFCCC process, problematic decisions have been made, such as Turkey's positioning as both an Annex I and Annex II country. However, in recent years, attention to the topic has been increasing (Şahin 2014: 8). One outstanding scientific contributor is Murat Türkeş, who at the time of the second World Climate Conference in Geneva in 1990 was the only scientific delegate from Turkey. He had then just finished his Ph.D. thesis at Istanbul University on droughts, and was the only individual who was therefore relatively close to the issue of climate change (Şahin 2014: 24). Other national experts on climate change include Levent Kurnaz of Boğaziçi University in Istanbul and Mikdat Kadıoğlu at Istanbul Technical University. All three have long lists of publications on climate change and appear often in the media (see, for instance, A Haber 2013; CNN Türk 2012; Türkeş 2002), but due to their rather technical background as physicists and meteorologists, they have not been able to effectively link climate change to its socio-economic or security implications. Nevertheless, some scientists have become more aware of the security implications of climate change and have also articulated these on several occasions, such as the CPRS Turkey Conference that has been conducted since 2011 within the framework of an 'International Human Security Conference' series through the cooperation of Coventry University's Centre for Peace and Reconciliation and Turkish universities in Istanbul (CPRS 2012).

However, lacking amplification by other actors, the securitising speech acts of scientific individuals in Turkey have until now remained without a strong impact on the political debate, even if in the framework of distinct national projects and reports, when expertise is needed, these scientists serve as the sole human resources that the state and other organisations, including UNDP and EU, can resort to (UNDP 2007; Kadıoğlu 2012a).

In contrast to international or internationally backed organisations such as the Heinrich Böll foundation or the IPC, most national NGOs lack the financial or professional capacity to act as influential discursive entrepreneurs, not to speak of their recognition in the political debate. This has increased the relevance of individuals with international networks to draw on, such as Ömer Madra. Together with Ümit Şahin, Madra is the producer of the radio programme *Open Green*, which supports the climate movement *İklim İçin* that the two initiated in spring 2015. Şahin, a co-founder of the Turkish Green Party who is affiliated with the IPC, made an important contribution to mapping the policy field of climate change in Turkey with his publication of the 'Turkish Climate Change Policy Actors Map' (*Türkiye'de İklim Değişikliği Aktörlerin Haritası* (Şahin 2014), which, however, does not include any links or information on the security implications of climate change. Nevertheless, Şahin, Madra and other discursive entrepreneurs such as Semra Cerit-Mazlum (MURCIR), Gökçen Şahin (French Development Agency) and Mahir Ilgaz (350.org) belong to a group of activists who have undertaken attempts to organise themselves in the Climate Network (*İklim Ağı*) in 2007 and organise several civil society initiatives to make their voices heard (NTV 2007, Interview 2014a; 2014aj). The network launched the 'Ratify Kyoto' (*Kyoto'yu Imzala*) campaign in the same year. It includes a rather diverse set of actors ranging from conservationists such as the Nature Association (*Doğa Derneği*) and the Nature Conservation Centre (*Doğa Koruma Merkezi*), to organisations focused on desertification and soil erosion such as the TEMA Foundation and KADOS (Kadiköy Science, Culture and Friends of the Arts Association), to transnational NGOs such as Greenpeace and the WWF. This diversity on the one hand makes civil society more dynamic and flexible, while on the other hand keeping the debate rather too diffuse for it to have a greater media and societal impact.

In line with the political, judicial, and technical adaptation measures in the process of the implementation of the *acquis communautaire* and UNDP development aid mainly within the framework of the Green Environmental Fund (GEF) that supports projects on energy efficiency, biodiversity and climate change, the Regional Environmental Center (REC) Turkey, founded in 2004, especially during its first years of action effectively operated as an actor supporting dialogue on climate change between the government, private sector and civil society. From 2005 until 2008, REC produced a multiplicity of initiatives, which however remained rather technical and did not explicitly address the security implications of climate change. However, REC cooperated with actors that have more explicitly framed climate change as a threat, such as Greenpeace Turkey, WWF Turkey and the TEMA Foundation (REC 2008b).

The Turkish media has largely refrained from framing climate change as a security issue. News about the impact of global warming in Turkey gradually appeared during the 1990s, albeit on a limited scale (cf. Doğan n.d.: 50). Özgür Gürbüz, co-founder of the Turkish Green party and one of the first journalists to address climate change, has been writing about climate change only since the second half of the 1990s (Interview 2014aq). The online newspaper *Yeşilgazete* (Green News) and *Açık Radyo* are among the few media outlets that persistently report on climate change. Nevertheless, news reporting on climate change has increased since 2005 with a peak in 2007, as we discussed in the overview of the Turkish debate. Still, the media generally prioritises other issues over climate change. Its agenda is usually dominated by the domestically entrenched problems such as poverty and terror, which are not directly related to climate change or global warming (Lütfi-Şen 2013b). As one expert noted, the media does not even report on climate change at the times of international climate conferences or disasters that are related to climate change. There are reports on droughts, temperature rises and heavy rainfall, but they are not interpreted as effects of climate change (*Radikal* 2014).

Figure 6.1 shows the result of our network analysis of relevant reports and sixty-one key actors, including key individuals, reports, international organisations and domestic actors. It displays the relative importance of international organisations and key actors of the international climate change regime such as IPCC, Kyoto Protocol and UNFCCC. Other external actors, such as the US, EU, OECD, FMO, WWF and UNDP/UNEP, also dominate the debate. In contrast, Turkish civil society organisations such as the TEMA Foundation, *Iklim BU* and *Ekolojik Toplum* remain marginalised. Dominant Turkish actors tend to be 'classic' scientific organisations that address climate change technically, such as the General Directorate of Meteorological Management, Istanbul Technical University, and climate scientists such as Murat Türkeş and Mikdat Kadıoğlu. Actors that have pursued strong securitising moves, such as Ömer Madra, remain marginalised.

Political impact

Because the level of securitisation of the Turkish climate security debate has been relatively low, it is difficult to see any impact in the strict sense. However, some examples demonstrate that at least fragments of the climate security discourse have been acknowledged and adopted by Turkish policymakers. Already in 2007, then prime minister Erdoğan acknowledged at the UN General Assembly's High Level Event on Climate Change (UN 2007) that 'climate change is the biggest environmental threat of our time' (AKP 2007). Furthermore, then president Gül participated in COP-15 in Copenhagen, reflecting the importance given to the event (Şahin 2014). Likewise, in October 2010 Prime Minister Erdoğan attended the Mediterranean Climate Change Initiative in Greece (Tanlay and Yardımcısı 2010). Even if the discourse on climate change in Turkey, as in other countries, had slowed down after the failed Copenhagen summit, government publications and institutional changes still reflect a relatively and steadily growing importance of the issue. For example, in 2013, Istanbul hosted an event of Al Gore's 'Climate Reality Project' with over 600 participants from 97 countries (World Bulletin 2013). Then Turkish deputy prime minister Ali Babacan attended the conference, stating that 'climate change as a global problem must be solved with global solutions'. Gül and Erdoğan both adopted securitising speech acts, such as in Erdoğan's 2014 speech at the UN climate summit in New York (*Hürriyet* 2014). Furthermore, in 2015, the chief of the Turkish General Staff, General Özel, stated in an interview that 'climate change belongs together with migration movements, terrorism, cyber-attacks and other new threats to a new security environment surrounding us', thus indicating that even if there have been no drastic measures taken yet, climate change is being considered in Turkish national security thinking (*Hürriyet* 2015).

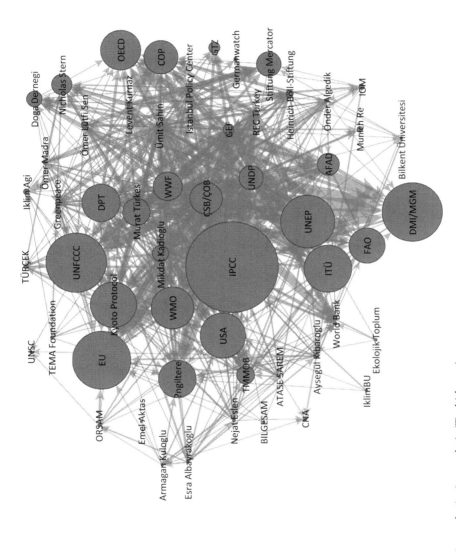

FIGURE 6.1 Network citation analysis (Turkish case)

Following the peak of securitisation in 2007–2009, the number of government reports on climate change increased (ÇŞB 2010; 2011; 2012a; 2012b). Representations of climate change as a threat have become most apparent in the National Climate Change Strategy 2010–2020 (ÇŞB 2010), Turkey's National Climate Change Adaptation Strategy and Action Plan (DSI/Devlet Su İşleri) and the National Security Document (*Hürriyet* 2010a). Although the latter is not publicly available, other sources indicate that it includes climate change as a security issue for Turkey (*Hürriyet* 2010a). This integration and recognition of climate change as a security issue happened only shortly after the appearance of various publications and presentations by General Eslen, who in his speech at the SAREM workshop and later also in his 45-page report proposed to arrange a security strategy and unit for climate change within the Secretariat-General of the National Security Council (*Milli Güvenlik Kurulu Genel Sekteterliği*).

The Authority of Disaster Management and Emergency of the Prime Ministry (AFAD) produced a roadmap for climate change and disaster management for the period 2014–2023 (AFAD 2014), reflecting the importance given to adaptation measures rather than mitigation (Kadıoğlu 2012a; 2012b). Likewise, the Ninth Development Plan for the period 2007–2013 (DPT 2007) highlights the importance of addressing climate change impacts and managing water and ecological resources in a sustainable way, but does not address emission reductions (European Commission 2011).

At the same time, the documents consider Turkey's energy supply as an important issue for national security, offsetting climate security. This demonstrates the importance of counter-securitising discourses in energy or development policy that negatively affect environmental and climate policymaking. Furthermore, Turkish politicians commonly justify their reluctant stance in the climate regime by pointing to the debate on 'climate justice' and to the 'polluter pays' principle (*Hürriyet* 2014; 2013; *Star Gazete* 2013). They argue that those least responsible for climate change will experience most of its consequences, and that those historically responsible for climate change should have to pay and act. Interestingly, discourses of climate justice also appeared in our Mexican case, but supported by a partly successful securitisation and politicisation of climate change, they have rather been articulated to reinforce progressive climate policies.

All in all, representations of climate change as a security threat have usually only translated into policies when linked to financial, technical or political benefits provided by outside actors such as the EU, UN or in the context of the International Climate Change Regime (İzci 2013: 259). According to Turkey's national climate experts, the country has no national strategic planning policy to explicitly address climate change, despite the bulk of strategy documents published in the aftermath of COP-15 in Copenhagen. The fossil fuel industry is growing rapidly and, at least in the energy sector, most policies that are in place lack implementation (Germanwatch and CAN 2015).

The detrimental context for climate securitisation in Turkey

One of the obstacles to the successful securitisation of climate change in Turkey is to be found in its political structure. Frequently changing governments, and thus also bureaucracies, have made long-term policymaking difficult in Turkey since the end of the one-party rule in the 1950s. This changed only with the election of the AKP government in 2002 with Erdoğan as a prime minister who, despite his at times contested ideas, 'is finally the one who gets the things done that others may have started' (Interview 2014af). While the AKP's continuity has raised difficulties from the point of view of democracy, it has allowed more decisive steps in environmental and climate policies. EU negotiations have reinforced this, especially the opening of the environmental chapter (İzci 2013: 258). Thus, EU pressure and the financial support of international organisations such as UNDP have been the main driver of climate change projects and policy implementation in Turkey (Gieler and Çetinyılmaz 2015; Interview 2014am; 2014aq; 2014ao). After EU accession became more unlikely in the late 2000s, the interest in climate change declined somewhat but never stopped entirely.

On this level, however, securitisation has not been in the forefront. Instead, most of the policy adjustments in the context of EU accession negotiations and UN development aid have been technical and financial in nature, as for example the project 'Enhancing the Capacity of Turkey to Adapt to Climate Change', that ran from 2008 until 2012. The project had a 7 million USD budget and was, together with support from UNDP, UNEP, FAO and UNIDO, conducted under the leadership of the Turkish Ministry of Environment and Urbanisation (MDG Achievement Fund 2010). The EU's 'Twinning Project on Improved Emissions Control' ran for the period 2011–2013 and was aimed at bringing Turkey's emission management closer to EU regulations (Öztürk 2012).

Securitising moves, as we have seen, figured more prominently among civil society actors and a few military officials and scientists (Eslen 2007; Kuloğlu 2009). In the case of some of the environmental civil society actors, their own environmentalist convictions have been only part of the picture – funding from international organisations such as the German foundations or the EU (partly through the REC) allowed them to pursue their activities but also shaped their projects in format and content (Interview 2014aq; UNFCCC 2013; Mühlenhoff 2015). This has even led to conspiracy theories about the work of different, especially German, foundations (Erandac 2011).

As we have pointed out, Turkish civil society in general is not as developed as in most other EU countries or the US, and resources are lacking (Interview 2014aq). According to the CIVICUS Civil Society Index, Turkish civil society organisations lack financial, human, technical and infrastructural resources. NGOs often lack knowledge of fundraising and financial management skills. Money is difficult to come by, and the government as well as the private sector have adopted roles as 'grantmakers' only from the 2000s onwards (Bikmen and Meydanoğlu 2006: 54–55). The environment in which civil society operates in Turkey is furthermore difficult due to a lack of adherence to the rule of law, corruption, and a highly centralised state administration (Bikmen and Meydanoğlu 2006: 13). However, the EU accession process had a direct impact considering the support and facilitating conditions for civil society (Dereci 2013). Due to democratic reforms and amendments that facilitated the procedures to establish civil society organisations, the number of such organisations in Turkey increased by 44 per cent (from 60,931 in 2000 to 88,210 in 2011) in the first decade of the 2000s (*Todays Zaman* 2011) and in 2013 reached 97,686. This is still a very small number compared to countries such as Germany, where the number of registered civil society organisations was about 580,000 in 2009, and the United States, where more than 1.5 million welfare organisations are registered (T.C. İçişleri Bakanlığı 2013: 12). However, even within this small number of civil society actors, environmental organisations are a minority (1,594) compared to 15,289 sports organisations, 14,789 aid, 10,291 development and 3,707 cultural organisations (*Todays Zaman* 2011). One explanation for Turkey's generally weak climate science, environmental movements and civil society sector, and consequently its reluctant climate policies, lies in its lingering characteristics as a developing country. A delay in industrialisation and urbanisation led to a delay in environmental movements as a reaction to developmental challenges (Duru 2013).

Adding to the lack of governmental support and low priority of climate change in Turkish civil society, actors in the environmental sector are also badly networked, despite their small numbers. Some organisations refrain from cooperating with others because they perceive each other as illegitimate or rivals (Interview 2014al) or put forward conflicting priorities (Interview 2014an). Furthermore, civil society actors that do attempt to securitise climate change are not taken seriously enough by policymakers and decisionmakers (Interview 2015a). They often have to draw on international research findings because of the weak development of domestic scientific research on climate change (Şahin 2014: 8, 180–184). Experts capable of linking rather technical climate science with political or economic aspects are especially lacking, as has become evident not only at the TIKDEK conferences (TIKDEK 2010; 2013). For example, for the period 1995–2014, the Social Sciences Citation Index (SSCI) lists 525 articles with the keyword 'climate change' and only 82 with 'climate change policy' or 'politics' that have been authored or co-authored by Turkish academics, while for other Mediterranean countries such as Italy or Spain, these numbers are significantly higher – Italy boasts 3,298 and Spain 3,751 references (Şahin 2014: 182). There is little financial support for, nor institutionalisation of, such research in Turkey. Few research institutes at universities such as Boğaziçi, Marmara and Istanbul Technical University engage in research on climate change (cf. Şahin 2014: 63, 180–185; TBMM 1992). Within these institutions, a technical rather than a societal perspective prevails, and in contrast to Germany, scientists have not yet build strong links between climate change and security.

Yet because of general scepticism towards 'foreign' data and policies, NGOs are often regarded as foreign agents with double standards who ignore questions of climate justice. In earlier parliamentary debates this scepticism has been articulated more drastically, such as in a parliamentary report of 1992, which argued that 'by refraining from becoming a party to the UNFCCC, we will be released a bit from Western double standards' (TBMM 1992: 270). In line with such scepticism, some Turkish individuals, organisations and groups (e.g. TMMOB) lobbied against ratification of the Kyoto Protocol even as late as 2007 (Şahin 2014: 63; TBMM 1992: 270). The Water Foundation (*Su Vakfı*) that was founded during Erdoğan's term as mayor of Istanbul and is rather close to the government, has even developed its own climate modelling programme because it regarded international modelling tools as inadequate for Turkey's geography (Şahin 2014: 167).

Invocations of climate justice in turn reflect the continuing importance of economic development and energy security in the Turkish debate, which has made the securitisation of climate change difficult. Thus, 'commitments arising from environmental agreements are sometimes regarded as a serious burden for the competitiveness and development of the country' (TBMM 1992: 270; İzci 2013: 250). Instead, even the minister of environment and urbanisation, Veysel Eroğlu, downplayed Turkey's climate responsibilities by pointing out that 'from a long-term perspective, the greenhouse gas emissions of Turkey among all countries only amount to 0.4 per cent' (TBMM 2014a). Similarly, minister of energy Taner Yıldız emphasised at the 2013 World Energy Congress in South Korea:

> We say this all the time: whoever has polluted the earth should clean it. We have not polluted it and we will not pollute it in the future. This is also why we are not thinking about a separate fund for cleaning. Of course we will act in line with the world, but it goes without saying that the ones who are responsible will have to pay the big amount.
>
> (Star Gazete *2013*)

The highlighting of Turkey's low long-term emission rates serves as an excuse for the country not to commit to and pursue emission reductions (*Star Gazete* 2013; TBMM 2014a). Thus, in documents on climate change in Turkey, mitigation is not a strong part of the debate and rather than talking of 'emission reductions' the policy on emissions is labelled as 'emissions management' (UNDP 2007).

Conclusion

For the most part of our study period, climate change has played a marginal role in Turkish politics, and security frames have been the exception. This does not mean a complete absence of securitising moves, but they have been limited in number and impact. Some military actors have made territorial danger claims, but largely, the climate–security linkages that did exist mostly focused on the individual level, emphasising food and water security, and health and economic (mainly agricultural) security, as well as threats posed to megacities. Yet, such articulations have remained fragments rather than a fully-fledged climate security discourse. Instead, external pressure and funding seems to have been more effective in achieving change in climate policy. We have explained this absence of climate security as caused by the lack of a functioning and resourceful civil society and research infrastructure. In addition, while there is no direct link between developmental standing and climate policy, Turkish politicians have used the development argument and linked it to historical justice claims to reject calls for climate security.

However, such a context is not unchangeable, and the articulations of discursive entrepreneurs on climate change, combined with a changing economic and educational social structure, may lead to increased climate securitisation in the future. For the international climate security discourse to be successful in Turkey, building trust in foreign institutions will be necessary, given the weak domestic scientific infrastructure. As long as the suspicion towards foreign actors remains, measures such as financial or technical help can only be partly successful and serve to reinforce a policy that wants everything but commits to nothing (CAN 2011).

Our research has furthermore shown that after a first peak of climate security talk in the late 2000s, the discourse has picked up again towards the end of our study period (see also Üzelgun and Castro 2015). Indeed, public opinion polls indicate that climate change is becoming a prime concern among the wider public, which increasingly recognises it as an important global threat (AXA and IPSOS 2012: 4; Pew Research Center 2015). As İzci notes, 'it is just recently that climate change appeared as a great concern on the state level in Turkey' (İzci 2013: 258). Among environmentalists, the 2013 Gezi events have generated much hope for activists that the time is ripe for such increased climate securitisation; yet the 2015 elections and the military campaigns against ISIS and the PKK have quickly brought military security issues to the foreground again. Thus, while the historical, institutional and societal context allows us to understand the development of the Turkish climate security debate in the past, predictions about the future remain difficult. If EU accession negotiations move forward again, we may see a further alignment of Turkey with EU climate policies on technical grounds and with securitisation focused on individual risk. If this does not happen, and military concerns dominate the agenda, discursive entrepreneurs in climate policy may have to turn to arguments of territorial danger and link up with the military if they want to bring climate change back on to the agenda – yet the US case has shown the downsides of such a strategy.

7
CONCLUSION
The politics of securitising climate change

Securitisations, not securitisation

Our starting point in writing this book was the academic dispute about whether climate change had been securitised or not, and what securitisation might mean for the political debate and measures to tackle climate change. In line with much of the literature, and against the narrow conceptualisation of securitisation at the core of the Copenhagen School, we developed a six-fold matrix to capture different types of securitisation. We proposed a differentiation along two dimensions: the first distinguishing between threatification and riskification; and the second taking into account the different referent objects of securitisation.

The analysis of securitisation processes in our four country cases has demonstrated the utility of such an approach. It allowed us to show how specific securitising discourses prevailed in each country. In the United States, we saw the predominance of territorial danger, whereas the debate in Germany focused on the individual level, with the invocation of danger still prevalent, but also frequent risk framings as 'counter-alarmist' moves and attempts of a perceived objectification. In Mexico, we found an emphasis on individual and planetary risk, while the overall debate was less securitised than in Germany and the US. An outside attempt to insert territorial threatification into the Mexican debate was only partially successful, and initially at least was met with a significant degree of resistance. In Turkey, the securitisation of climate change has been largely unsuccessful. While we observed attempts to invoke territorial danger, other security concerns from terrorism to energy, and a strong emphasis on further economic development, dominated the debate.

With the exception of Turkey, where we have found only fragments of climate security discourse, we observe an increasing securitisation of climate change across countries over time. Nonetheless, the assessment that there has been no securitisation on the global level may still hold – not because there simply is no securitisation, but because there are competing securitisations. In other words, we see a hegemonic struggle over how to frame climate change. Our analysis has illustrated how dominant discourses are tied to particular contexts, which we discuss below. These contexts not only serve as felicity conditions for the success of securitising moves, but they also insert broader understandings of politics and society into the wider debate. Territorial danger reifies the state as the main reference point of security; individual framings inscribe a human security conception that ultimately sees states as less important than the well-being or survival of a global community of human beings, or what in English School terms may be called world society (Buzan 2004). Threatifications stress the urgency of threats and often strengthen a conception of sovereign politics dominated by centralised state structures, whereas riskifications tend to operate with a decentralised notion of political agency that is much more in tune with what Foucauldians may recognise as governmentality (e.g. Dean 2010; von Lucke 2015). Thus, different securitisations not only legitimise different climate policies; they also differ in their construction of political and societal life as a whole, and empower different strategies and actors – indeed, they constitute different political subjects.

Distinguishing securitisations thus allows us to see the contestations within and across countries over the configurations of legitimate governance. We have emphasised that we understand extraordinary measures as new ways of doing things; as policies that would not have been legitimate without a form of securitisation. In our cases, such policies have ranged from preparing the military to deal with climate change-induced conflicts to devising modes of governance that lead actors to regulate themselves. Neither of these is more or less 'extraordinary'. Instead, they move politics and the organisation of societies in different directions. They are articulations of how we want to live in the future.

Our framework has also rejected the idea that there is a binary opposition of politics and security. We have argued that politics, danger and risk form a space in which articulations of climate change move along continua. Politics thus presupposes an initial securitisation that places an issue on the agenda; and even the classic Copenhagen-style form of securitisation is a form of politics. The question is not one of taking an issue out of politics. The question is, when is an issue pushed so far towards the extreme security poles that the legitimacy of policy measures can no longer be questioned? It is fair to say that climate change has not reached this extreme in any of our cases. Yet, as we have argued in the Introduction, this cannot even be said about the security debates at the height of the Cold War. There is always contestation. At issue is the degree to which hegemonies of a new mode of governing can be established. In Germany and the US, we have observed the emergence of such hegemonies. They are still contested, and ambiguities remain. In Germany, the resistance of the car industry to the demands of the individual danger discourse was obvious even before the Volkswagen scandal of 2015 about the floating of environmental rules concerning diesel engines became apparent. In the US, individual states entered the hegemonic struggle by agreeing to environmental standards beyond the dominant federal emphasis on territorial danger and military preparedness. In Turkey, meanwhile, the old hegemony of economic and energy security has prevailed, whereas in Mexico, riskifications were embedded in a debate much closer to the ideal politics corner.

Overall, riskification appeared much less frequently in our analysis than threatification, and much less often than we had expected. This may be an indication that at least in our cases and in the institutional contexts that we looked at, classic understandings of sovereign politics still prevail. Further research may thus focus on the climate security debate among private actors, and especially the insurance industry, which has not been a major reference point in the debates that we have analysed, although it has played an important role in Germany. Likewise, riskification may be more prevalent in countries in which governance has been more governmentalised than in our cases, such as in the United Kingdom (UK). Carvalho and Burgess (2005) thus find that the insurance industry in the UK has been a major advocate of a precautionary approach to climate change within a risk framing. It remains to be seen whether such a framing will become more important even in our cases in the future – perhaps the shift towards risk in security strategies has been too recent to show its full effects in the period that we have studied.

Our analysis should thus not be understood to argue that the differences between cases and the prevalence of threatification are unchangeable. To the contrary, while we can draw conclusions about the importance of context as a felicity condition, and will do so below, this context is in itself not stable, and our emphasis, *pace* Wiener (2007; 2008), on the 'dual quality of discourse' and the struggles over climate security is also an emphasis on the possibility of change. Analysts should never fall into the trap of taking the future for granted. Politics, after all, is also about changing that future. The different national hegemonies and the dominant framings of climate security that we have shown, however, are an indication of some of the tensions to be overcome on the road to an effective global climate regime, and alert us to the broader political and societal implications of different climate securitisations.

The importance of discursive entrepreneurs

In this struggle over the framing of climate security, we have emphasised the role of discursive entrepreneurs. Articulations do not simply happen; they are performed by concrete actors in concrete contexts. We have outlined in Chapter 2 that we do not see these actors as the 'origin' of discourses, and have argued that they need to be decentred and understood as socialised agents within their own specific contexts. Yet nonetheless, our analysis has time and again demonstrated the importance of such actors and how they have pushed the development of the climate security debate in their respective countries in specific directions.

In the United States, we identified Sherri Goodman as an example of such a discursive entrepreneur. A former deputy under-secretary of defense for environmental security, she managed to draw links between military and environmental security in her position as executive director of the Military Advisory Board of the semi-governmental think tank CNA, and together with her personal network, managed to effectively promote a territorial danger rendering of climate security. In Germany, we have noted the importance of scientific actors working at the intersection of science and politics. Scientists such as Hans Joachim Schellnhuber and Dirk Messner played an important role in this context and helped to establish individual danger as the dominant discourse, while generally speaking, the German debate has been less driven by individuals than by collective actors in the form of NGOs and think tanks. The relative absence of environmental NGOs and scientific actors in the US climate security debate in turn also meant that at least on the federal level, the discourse of territorial danger did not confront a serious challenger.

Likewise, the historical weakness of civil society in Turkey, especially in the field of environmentalism, meant that the energy-cum-military security consensus remained largely untouched, with a few isolated attempts by military actors themselves to promote a territorial danger discourse that would not challenge the status of the military in Turkish society. While domestic NGOs have also been largely absent from the Mexican climate security debate, the early uptake of climate change as a political issue by President Calderón meant that securitisation was not necessary in order to place climate change on the political agenda, and allowed the debate to unfold with less securitisation than in the US or Germany.

Mexico and Turkey are also examples of the largely failed intervention of discursive entrepreneurs in the form of external think tanks, such as RUSI, in alliance with foreign governments, such as the UK in the Mexican case. This failure shows the importance of translatability of climate security articulations into the discursive contexts that they try to influence. Similarly, in the US we have shown how Al Gore, who articulated a planetary and individual danger discourse to much acclaim internationally and in countries such as Germany, was relatively unsuccessful at home, at least as soon as territorial danger became more pronounced by 2007. Ironically, through the appointment of Goodman as deputy undersecretary of defense for environmental security, the Clinton–Gore government may have unintentionally helped the dominance of the territorial danger discourse to come about in the long run. To understand these failures, we need to turn to the importance of context.

The importance of context

Context matters in our case studies both in terms of who can successfully articulate climate security, and which securitisations are more likely to prevail. Our analysis has shown the significance of both institutional and broader discursive legacies. These enable and constrain discursive entrepreneurs and their specific articulations, both in relation to what they will say, and whether what they say is successful in the sense of being accepted by a large proportion of the domestic public.

Thus, we have noted the influence of different actors in the climate security debate in our four cases. While in the US and Turkey we saw the importance of actors with a military background or links to the defence sector, and at the same time the relative insignificance of environmental NGOs and science actors, we found the reverse situation to characterise the German debate. In all of these cases, the institutional environment that actors are embedded in can account for these differences. We have shown how the military has a much higher standing in public discourse in the US and Turkey as compared to Germany, and how in turn scientific and civil society actors, especially in the environmental sector, have historically enjoyed a core position in the German public debate. That climate change had been part of Mexican politics from early on had a decisive impact on the pursuit of climate mitigation policies, even in the absence of a strong environmentalist civil society. In all of our cases, thus, climate security discourses unfold within specific national contexts that have grown historically. It is again important to emphasise that such contexts are not unchangeable. Yet at the same time, they provide some actors with the social capital to articulate climate security effectively, and make it harder for other actors to leave their mark on the debate.

The international context was an important background in all of our cases. The emergence of a climate regime on the level of the United Nations and the scientific framing of climate change within the IPCCC cannot be completely ignored by any actor in any country. We have also noted a parallel development of the importance accorded to climate security in our cases, in line with the development of the global debate. Yet the consequences drawn from this in terms of substance differed significantly between countries. In all of our cases, the national climate security discourses ultimately determined how the global debate was understood, and how actors positioned themselves within this debate. Only in the Turkish case did the international context have a determining influence on climate policies in the form of EU conditions in the specific context of the membership accession process. Yet the limited policy change that this induced did not have any important effect on the climate security discourse. Policies remained largely responsive, and while some NGOs may have been enabled by the EU context, financially or ideologically, to raise their voice, they have not become a dominant force, at least not during the time frame of our analysis, and were instead portrayed as foreign agents. In the Mexican case, while accepting some international advice on climate measures in general, we observed resistance to outside climate security influence both because of an anti-colonialist impulse and because of a mismatch between the security framing that RUSI and its partners promoted and the prevailing conceptualisation of climate change as individual risk that had long been established in the Mexican political debate.

Such a mismatch also accounts for the failure of alternative climate security articulations in our other cases. Adelphi's linking of climate security to territorial danger never captured the domestic German discourse as a whole, even if it caught on in some circles, because the post-World War II rules of the German political debate do not confer broad legitimacy on national security articulations, in contrast to the US or Turkey. In the US, in turn, the planetary and individual danger articulations of Al Gore were associated with state interference in individual liberties – not something cherished by the majority view. The territorial danger discourse instead managed to circumscribe the relevance of the securitisation of climate change for individuals, and could be linked to a self-understanding of the US as a global leader in military security. And in Turkey, articulations of climate change generally did not have a strong impact unless they could be linked to the prevailing security frames of energy and economic security.

The political effects of securitisation

This importance of context cautions us against attributing policy impact solely to successful securitisation. Ultimately, the causes of policy change are not reducible to climate security discourses, but in parts reflect long-standing traditions and political cultures. At the same time, however, we have seen how specific dominant climate security frames have brought climate change onto the political agenda in particular ways, and have legitimised particular policy measures – and how their absence has prevented a broader political debate about climate change in the Turkish case – and thus a neglect of climate policies. Thus, in most cases, with EU and UN incentives to Turkey as an exception, we have seen how climate security discourses are one of the crucial factors in moving climate policies into particular directions.

The most obvious example is the US. Widely seen as a laggard in the regime of climate change, our analysis has demonstrated that the point is not that there is no climate policy on the federal level (as opposed to more progressive individual states), but that the policy is focused on adaptation measures within the military, while trying to limit binding targets that could mitigate climate change but at the same time would constrain individual liberties. This is a clear consequence of the way in which the climate security discourse unfolded in its emphasis on territorial danger and its links between military and climate security. We do not argue that there have not, time and again, been attempts to take mitigation more seriously, as during the Clinton and the second Obama administrations, but the fact that they met with severe resistance and, up to now, have remained relatively unsuccessful is an indication of the strength of the territorial danger discourse. Needless to say other factors, such as the strict blockade by most Republicans and influential economic actors, also contributed to hindering a more successful federal climate agenda. Nonetheless, the territorial danger discourse provided a opportunity to act on climate change while still circumventing too-far-reaching mitigation strategies.

The opposite applies to Germany, where the dominance of the individual danger discourse has led to a strong emphasis on policies to mitigate climate change, and has made Germany an important factor in persuading the EU to advocate such policies on the global level. To repeat, we are not attempting to whitewash Germany's policy record, which is characterised by many inconsistencies, especially when it comes to the regulations of the car industry. Nonetheless, as far as the engagement in the global climate regime and the advocacy of binding targets is concerned, there is a clear link between Germany's positions and its 'energy turn' on the one hand, and the prevalence of individual danger in its climate security discourse on the other.

Likewise, we have linked Mexico's relative forerunner position in the climate regime to articulations of individual risk, although we have also emphasised that the overall level of securitising climate change in Mexico is weaker than in the German or US case. Thus, the Mexican political agenda has been less focused on emergency measures, and the Mexican government has pursued a broad policy mix of mitigation and adaptation measures. Securitising moves, domestic or foreign, have so far mostly been channelled into a pragmatic political debate about appropriate measures. The fact that there is no strong civil society involvement has, however, also meant that climate change as such has been a relatively low key issue in the broader public debates, and that voices that substantially question governmental policies have remained limited in numbers and impact.

Judging securitisation

How are we then to assess the normative implications of securitising climate change? One of the core arguments within the Copenhagen School was that securitisation is a problem because of its marginalising and limiting impact on the political debate, and that desecuritisation thus would have to be preferred. In Chapter 2 we have argued against this narrow assessment of securitisation. Building on the debate in the literature on this issue, we proposed that first, securitisation may be politicising rather than depoliticising in that it effectively places an issue on the political agenda, and that second, the normative assessment of successful securitisation depends on the specific ethical standpoint from which one judges it.

The first point has been made by many others in the debate, and is immediately obvious if one reviews our cases. Thus, the Turkish debate on climate change is not more but less politicised in the absence of securitisation. Issues need some degree of securitisation to be heard and recognised. As we have argued in Chapter 2 and throughout the empirical analyses, it is in that sense that security and politics can never be entirely separated. Of course there is always some closure in any opening, and so any prevalent form of securitisation comes with the marginalisation of exclusion of others. Yet this is a trivial point that simply states that there can be no meaning without difference, and thus no meaningful political debate without some sort of framing. As we have argued before, the decisive point rather is whether the political debate moves so far towards the security point that alternative voices are systematically marginalised. The ridiculing of an individual (not to speak of planetary) danger or risk position and the submergence of individual danger under a territorial danger discourse in the US, at least at some moments during our analytical time frame, is an indication of a debate beyond the threshold in our politics/danger/risk space. Yet likewise, one would also have to say that the marginalisation of voices that question the significance or existence of climate change in parts of the German debate, rather than argumentatively engaging with them, is also a sign of depoliticisation. If we believe in the normative desirability of an open democratic debate, marginalising and ridiculing a political position without substantively engaging with it is always problematic.

Yet the 'if we believe' is an important condition. Ultimately, normative desirability is always a reflection of particular standpoints and basic ethical considerations, and often needs to weigh different normative concerns against each other. Thus, few democratic countries allow a completely open public debate without constraints, for instance when it comes to racism or the celebration of fascism. Their exclusion is justifiable because they themselves are exclusionary. Whether to combat such positions through constraining the space of public discourse or opposing them within public discourse, however, is a thorny issue that we do not have to get into in our present context, not least because, arguably, questioning climate change is not quite on the same level as racism, and thus a position of openness can more easily be defended. We simply bring up this example to demonstrate that a rejection of securitisation in principle is too simplistic – which, in fairness, even Buzan et al. (1998: 29) admit.

More pertinent to our analysis is the question of whether some forms of climate security may be preferable to others. Here, the issue of normative beliefs becomes central. We have written this book from our own position that a policy of mitigating climate change is preferable to a focus on adaptive measures, that climate change should not be reduced to an issue of military concern, and that the state should not be the main referent object of security. As a consequence, we find the dominance of the territorial danger discourse in the US to be problematic, and would prefer a strengthening of the individual rather than the territorial security dimension in Turkey. We sympathise with the prevailing climate security discourses in Germany and Mexico, while being critical of their ambiguities. Yet all of this is a matter of normative judgement, which ultimately is also a political judgement. From our point of view, civil society actors are ill-advised to forge links with the military in the securitisation of climate change and focus on the territorial danger discourse, but given the US context, it may well be that another strategy would have never brought climate change on the agenda as an issue to be taken seriously, as the fate of earlier securitising moves by Gore and others suggests. The core question (and political decision) then becomes whether to prefer a situation with no climate change on the federal agenda and put one's faith in the policies of individual states, or whether to live with the territorial danger discourse and speculate that it may prepare the ground for wider securitisations in the future. Likewise, perhaps any kind of securitisation of climate change in Turkey would be preferable to the present marginalisation of climate change in the Turkish political debate.

We do not pretend we have an easy answer to these questions. Perhaps the only guidance that our analysis suggests is that civil society actors ought to be aware of the links between particular climate security frames and specific policies. If they have to run with climate security articulations that they find problematic in order to promote climate change as an issue because of the context they are embedded in, they would be well advised to think about a strategy of moving out of this framing.

Our empirical analysis has not been able to shed more light on the possible preferability of danger or risk than our theoretical discussion in Chapter 2 has already done. This is largely because risk has not been articulated as strongly in our cases as we had expected, and to the extent that we have observed risk articulations, they have mostly been linked to the simultaneous articulation of danger, most obviously in the German case. Our analysis of the Mexican debate suggests that risk may sit more easily within a debate that veers towards the politics end of the spectrum. Yet future research will have to investigate this more closely, not least because in the US case, to the extent that risk popped up as a security frame in the debate, it was articulated mostly by military actors in relation to changing defence strategies and operability.

The politics of securitising climate change thus is part of a struggle not only over the right means to combat climate change, but involves a broader set of questions from democratic openness to the organisation of governmental structures. Securitising climate change is to move climate change across the politics/danger/risk spectrum: it is necessary in order to open the political agenda to include climate change, but may ultimately also close down the political debate. It is a political practice in which discursive entrepreneurs play an important role, while at the same time being dependent on their own institutional and discursive context. Thus, as we have shown in this book, national debates on climate security differ widely, with important consequences for climate policies. Any discussion about the future configuration of national and global climate regimes will have to take these differences into account, as much as anyone engaged in this debate will have to consider seriously the implications of particular climate security discourses.

REFERENCES

A Haber (2013) *A Haber / Prof. Mikdat Kadioğlu: 'Dikkat! Tropikal İklime Doğru Gidiyoruz.'* News Video.
ABGS (2015) Republic of Turkey, Ministry of EU Affairs. Accession Negotiations, available at www.abgs.gov.tr/index.php?p=37&l=2, accessed 28 October 2015.
Açık Radyo (2015) Ömer Madra, available at http://acikradyo.com.tr/default.aspx?_mv=yzr&yid=5, accessed 10 August 2015.
Adelphi (n.d.a) Mitarbeiter: Alexander Carius. Lebenslauf, available at https://www.adelphi.de/de/mitarbeiter/alexander-carius, accessed 21 October 2015.
Adelphi (n.d.b) Mitarbeiter: Senior Projektmanager Dennis Tänzler, available at https://www.adelphi.de/de/mitarbeiter/dennis-t%C3%A4nzler, accessed 26 September 2015.
Adelphi (2009a) Developing and Implementing the European Roadmap on Climate Change and Security. European Commission, DG External Relations; Project Info Sheet, available at www.adelphi.de/en/projects/project_database/dok/43525.php?pid=297&pidpdf=297, accessed 5 November 2015.
Adelphi (2009b) *Klimawandel und internationale Sicherheit. Entwicklung und Umsetzung der europäischen Roadmap*, available at https://www.adelphi.de/de/projekt/klimawandel-und-internationale-sicherheit-entwicklung-und-umsetzung-der-europ%C3%A4ischen-roadmap, accessed 26 September 2015.
Adelphi (2011a) Water, Crisis and Climate Change in Uganda: A Policy Brief. This Initiative is Funded by the European Union IfP-EW Cluster: Climate Change and Conflict. Brussels.
Adelphi (2011b) Workshop Documentation. Security Implications of Climate Change. New York.
Adelphi (2013a) *Adaptation to Climate Change for Peace and Stability. Strengthening of Approaches and Instruments as well as Promotion of Processes to Reduce the Security Risks Posed by Climate Change in the Context of Climate Change Adaptation*. Berlin.
Adelphi (2013b) *Climate Diplomacy. New Approaches for Foreign Policy*. Berlin.
Adger, N.W. (2006) 'Vulnerability', *Global Environmental Change* 16(3): 268–281.

References

Adriazola, P., Carius, A. and Rettberg, A. (2012) *Climate Change and Security in the Andean Region*. Climate Security Dialogue Brief. Berlin.
Adriazola, P., Maas, A. and Scheffran, J. (2011) *Climate Change in Latin America*. Climate Security Dialogue Brief. Berlin.
AFAD (2014) İklim Değişikliği ve buna bağlı Afetlere Yönelik Yol Haritası (2014–2023), available at https://www.afad.gov.tr/Dokuman/TR/121-2014101011130-iklim-son.pdf, accessed 5 February 2015.
Agos (2015) 'İklim krizine karşı yeni hareket başladı', *Agos*, 1 March.
AGRIFOR Consult and Europe Aid (2009) *Climate Change in Latin America*. Brussels.
Agroasemex (2015) Refuerza agroasemex relaciones con reaseguradoras internacionales para proteger el campo ante cambios climáticos, available at www.agroasemex.gob.mx/LoMásReciente/Comunicados/tabid/118/ArticleID/107/REFUERZA-AGROASEMEX-RELACIONES-CON-REASEGURADORAS-INTERNACIONALES-PARA-PROTEGER-EL-CAMPO-ANTE-CAMBIOS-CLIMÁTICOS.aspx, accessed 17 July 2015.
Akerberg, A.Á. (2011) 'Länderperspektive: Mexiko', in N. Netzer and J. Gouverneur (eds) *Zwischen Anspruch und Wirklichkeit : Internationale Perspektiven vor der Weltklimakonferenz in Durban*, Berlin: Friedrich-Ebert-Stiftung, pp. 37–40.
AKP (2007) AK Parti Genel Merkez Kadın Kolları Dış İlişkiler Birim Bülteni. 25.09.-02.10.2007, available at https://www.akparti.org.tr/upload/.../disiliskiler.doc.
Akşam Gazetesi (2012) 'Askerin Think'i gitti, Thank'i kaldı', 19 January.
Aksiyon (2004) 'Yarından sonra kıyamet', 14 June.
Aktaş, E. (2009) 'Küresel İklim Değ, işikliğinin Türkiye'nin Güvenlik Politikalarına Etkisi', *Genelkurmay Bülteni* (Sayı: 83): 44.
Aktifhaber (2012) 'Genelkurmay SAREM'i Kapattı', 20 January.
Aladağ, E. (2008) *Global Climate Change Education in Turkey*. n.a.
Alatorre, A. (2010) 'Advierten que desastres facilitan la inseguridad', *Reforma*, 16 October.
Alatorre, A. (2011) 'Urgen a modificar modelo agrícola', *Reforma*, 20 November.
Albayrakoğlu, E.P. (2011) 'Climate Change and Security – the Case for Turkey', *Akademik Bakis* 5(9): 59–75.
Albright, M.K., Berger, S.R., Browner, C. and Danvers, W. (2006) *Energy Security Energy and Security in the 21st Century. A New National Strategy. Report of the National Security Task Force on Energy*, available at www.americanprogress.org/kf/energy_security_report.pdf, accessed 12 March 2014.
Algedik, Ö. (2013) *Iklim Degisikligi Eylem Plani Degerlendirme Raporu*, Ankara.
Algedik, Ö. (2014) 'Climate Negotiations without Turkey?', *Turkish Policy Quarterly* 13(2): 129–137.
Allenby, B.R. (2000) 'Environmental Security: Concept and Implementation', *International Political Science Review* 21(1): 5–21.
Allenby, B.R. (2001) 'New Priorities in US Foreign Policy: Defining and Implementing Environmental Security', in P.G. Harris (ed.) *The Environment, International Relations, and U.S. Foreign Policy*, Washington, D.C.: Georgetown University Press.
Allianz Umweltstiftung (2007) Informationen zum Thema 'Klima. Grundlagen, Geschichten und Projektionen', available at https://umweltstiftung.allianz.de/v_1434294358000/media-data2/publikationen/wissen/download/klimamappe_lesezeichen.pdf, accessed 2 September 2015.
Alpay, Ş. (2014) 'Gündem: Et yemenin insanlığa bedeli', *Zaman*, 29 November.

References

Altenhof, R. (2002) *Die Enquete-Kommissionen des Deutschen Bundestages,* Wiesbaden: Westdeutsche Verlag.

Amador, R.G. (2010) 'Amenaza el cambio climático la producción alimentaria en el país. Reporte del Banco Mundial anticipa que México enfrentará eventos extremos con frecuencia', *La Jornada,* 3 November.

American Security Project (ASP) (2012) *Climate Security Report.* Washington, D.C.

Anadolu Ajansi (2015) 'İklim değişikliği en çok iç Anadolu'yu vuracak. Uzmanlar, 2100'de Türkiye'de iklim değişikliklerinden en fazla İç Anadolu Bölgesinin olumsuz yönde etkileneceğini belirtiyor', 19 February.

Angenendt, S. (2011) 'Klimaflüchtlinge – ein neues Sicherheitsrisiko?', in S. Angenendt, S. Dröge and J. Richert (eds) *Klimawandel und Sicherheit. Herausforderungen, Reaktionen und Handlungsmöglichkeiten,* Baden-Baden: Nomos, pp. 177–194.

Aradau, C. (2004) 'The Perverse Politics of Four-Letter Words: Risk and Pity in the Securitisation of Human Trafficking', *Millenium Journal of International Studies* 33(2): 251–277.

Aradau, C. and van Munster, R. (2007) 'Governing Terrorism Through Risk: Taking Precautions, (Un)Knowing the Future', *European Journal of International Relations* 13(1): 89–115.

Aranda, J. (2011) 'Sugieren a México contemplar amenazas a la seguridad nacional distintas al crimen: Aseguran los organismos que existe una compleja interacción entre ésta y el cambio climático', *La Jornada,* 21 November.

Arnold, M., Dressel, G. and Viehöver, W. (2012) *Erzählungen im Öffentlichen. Über die Wirkung narrativer Diskurse.* Wiesbaden: VS Verlag für Sozialwissenschaften.

Asan, Ü. (2010) 'National Researches, Data and Projects on Climate Change in Turkey'. Conference Paper, FAO Conference 'Climate Impacts on Forest Management in Southeastern Europe and Central Asia', 14–16 April 2010, Sopron, Hungary.

Assetto, V.J., Hajba, E. and Mumme, S.P. (2003) 'Democratization, Decentralization, and Local Environmental Policy Capacity. Hungary and Mexico', *The Social Science Journal* 40(2): 249–268.

Atkin, E. (2014) 'I'm not a Scientist': A Complete Guide to Politicians who Plead Ignorance on Climate Change, available at http://thinkprogress.org/climate/2014/10/03/3575849/not-a-scientist/, accessed 11 June 2015.

Austin, J.L. (1975) *How to Do Things with Words,* Cambridge, MA: Harvard University Press.

Auswärtiges Amt (2007) *Sicherheitsrisiko Klimawandel. 17. Forum Globale Fragen,* Berlin: Auswärtiges Amt.

AXA and IPSOS (2012) Individual Perceptions of Climate Risks, available at www.axa.com/lib/axa/uploads/cahiersaxa/Survey-AXA-Ipsos_climate-risks.pdf, accessed 10 August 2015.

Ayhan, B. (2007) *Kıyamet ve Küresel Isınma.* Ankara.

Bachmann, H. (2007) *Die Lüge der Klimakatastrophe. Das gigantischste Betrugswerk der Neuzeit; manipulierte Angst als Mittel zur Macht,* Berlin: Frieling.

Balzacq, T. (2005) 'The Three Faces of Securitization: Political Agency, Audience and Context', *European Journal of International Relations* 11(2): 171–201.

Balzacq, T. (2011) 'A Theory of Securitization: Origins, Core Assumptions, and Variants', in T. Balzacq (ed.) *Securitization Theory. How Security Problems Emerge and Dissolve,* London: Routledge, pp. 1–30.

References

Balzacq, T., Guzzini, S., Williams, M.C., Wæver, O. and Patomaki, H. (2015) 'What Kind of Theory – if any – is Securitization?', *International Relations* 29(1): 96.

BAMF (n.d.) Bundesamt für Migration und Flüchtlinge – Themendossiers – Migration und Klimawandel – Tagung zu Migration und Klimawandel, available at www.bamf.de/SharedDocs/Dossiers/DE/migration-und-klimawandel.html?docId=2050892&notFirst=true, accessed 4 September 2015.

Barnett, A. (2004) Bush Attacks Environment 'Scare Stories'. Secret Email Gives Advice on Denying Climate Change, available at www.guardian.co.uk/environment/2004/apr/04/usnews.theobserver, accessed 8 March 2013.

Barnett, J. (2001) *The Meaning of Environmental Security*, London: Zed Books.

Bayerisches Landesamt für Umwelt (2011) Klimaschutzpolitik in Deutschland und Bayern, available at www.lfu.bayern.de/umweltwissen/doc/uw_99_klimaschutzpolitik_deutschland_bayern.pdf, accessed 15 October 2013.

Baykan, B.G. (2013) Türkiye'nin AB Çevre Mevzuatı'na Uyumu:15 Yılda Neredeyiz?, available at http://ekoiq.com/turkiyenin-ab-cevre-mevzuatina-uyumu15-yilda-neredeyiz/, accessed 29 September 2015.

Beck, S. (2004) 'Localizing Global Climate Change in Germany', in S. Jasanoff and M. Long Martello (eds) *Earthly Politics: Local and Global in Environmental Governance*, Cambridge, MA: MIT Press, pp. 173–194.

Beck, S., Kuhlicke, C. and Görg, C. (2009) Climate Policy Integration, Coherence, and Governance in Germany, available at www.ufz.de/export/data/1/26701_PEERdownload.pdf, accessed 15 October 2013.

Beck, U. (2000) *World Risk Society*, Cambridge: Cambridge University Press.

Beck, U. (2002) 'The Cosmopolitan Society and Its Enemies', *Theory, Culture and Society* 19(2): 17–44.

Becker, M. (2007) 'Happy Ending on Bali Climate Change Deal Reached after US U-Turn', *Spiegel Online*, 15 December.

Beckett, M. (2006) Speech on Climate Change and Security at British Embassy, Berlin.

Bekmezci, I. (2015) *Analyse und Beurteilung des EU-Beitritts der Türkei. Die Dimensionen der Debatte unter Berücksichtigung der europäischen Perspektiven*, Norderstedt, Germany: Books on Demand.

Below, A. (2007) 'The Missing Link: Regionalism as a First Step Toward Globalizing U.S. Environmental Security Policy', *Politics and Policy* 35(4): 702–715.

Bender, B. (2013) 'Chief of US Pacific Forces Calls Climate Biggest Worry', 9 March.

Bendery, J. (2014) 'Chuck Hagel: We Should Worry About Climate Change Like We Worry About ISIS', *Huffington Post*, 29 October.

Benford, R.D. and Snow, D.A. (2000) 'Framing Processes and Social Movements: An Overview and Assessment', *Annual Review of Sociology* 26: 611–639.

Berger, T.U. (2012) *War, Guilt, and World Politics After World War II*, Cambridge: Cambridge University Press.

Bertell, R. (2001) *Planet Earth: The Latest Weapon of War*, Montreal: Black Rose.

Bertelsmann Stiftung (2012) *BTI 2012 — Mexico Country Report*. Gütersloh.

Biazoto, J. (2010) *AFK-Jahreskolloquium. Klimawandel und Konflikt: Versicherheitlichung versus präventive Friedenspolitik?* Hamburg.

Bigo, D. (2002) 'Security and Immigration: Toward a Critique of the Governmentality of Unease.', *Alternatives: Global, Local, Political* 27(supplement): 63–92.

Bigo, D. (2008) 'Globalized (In)Security. The Field and the Ban-Opticon', in D. Bigo and A. Tsoukala (eds) *Terror, Insecurity and Liberty. Illiberal Practices of Liberal Regimes after 9/11,* London: Routledge, pp. 10–48.

Bikmen, F. and Meydanoğlu, Z. (2006) *Civil Society in Turkey: In an Era of Transition.* Civicus Civil Society Index. Country Report for Turkey. http://www.tusev.org.tr/en/research-publications/online-publications/civil-society-in-turkey-an-era-of-transition-civicus-civil-society-index-country-report-for-turkey.

Birgün (2015) Olümcül sicaklar bizi de vuracak, available at www.birgun.net/haber-detay/olumcul-sicaklar-bizi-de-vuracak-82322.html, accessed 21 July 2015.

Blair, D.C. (2009) *Annual Threat Assessment of the Intelligence Community for the Senate Select Committee on Intelligence.* Washington, D.C.

BMUB (2006) Gabriel: 'Deutschland setzt auf eine ökologische Innovations- und Industriepolitik. Britischer Umweltminister Miliband sichert Unterstützung zu. Pressemitteilung', available at www.bmub.bund.de/presse/pressemitteilungen/pm/artikel/gabriel-deutschland-setzt-auf-eine-oekologische-innovations-und-industriepolitik/, accessed 21 October 2015.

BMUB (2014) Selbstverpflichtungen Aktuell, available at www.bmub.bund.de/themen/wirtschaft-produkte-ressourcen/wirtschaft-und-%20umwelt/selbstverpflichtungen/selbstverpflichtungen-aktuell/, accessed 7 January 2014.

BMZ (2013a) Klimapolitik in Deutschland und in der Europäischen Union, available at www.bmz.de/de/was_wir_machen/themen/klimaschutz/klimapolitik/deutscher_beitrag/index.html, accessed 18 November 2013.

Boas, I. (2014) 'Where is the South in Security Discourse on Climate Change? An Analysis of India', *Critical Studies on Security* 2(2): 148–161.

Bodansky, D. (2001) 'The History of the Global Climate Change Regime', in U. Luterbacher and D.F. Sprinz (eds) *International Relations and Global Climate Change,* Cambridge, MA: MIT Press.

Bode, I. (2012) *The People of the United Nations: Individual Agency and Policy Change at the United Nations,* Tübingen.

Bode, I. (2014) 'Francis Deng and the Concern for Internally Displaced Persons: Intellectual Leadership in the United Nations', *Global Governance: A Review of Multilateralism and International Organization* 20(2): 277–295.

Bojanowski, A. (2013) 'Rangliste: Umweltschützer strafen Deutschlands Klimapolitik ab', *Spiegel Online,* 18 November.

Bourdieu, P. (1986) 'The Forms of Capital', in J.G. Richardson (ed.) *Handbook of Theory and Research for the Sociology of Education,* New York: Greenwood Press, pp. 241–258.

Boxoffice Türkiye (2015a) Yarından Sonra [The Day After Tomorrow], available at http://boxofficeturkiye.com/film/yarindan-sonra-2004081, accessed 18 July 2015.

Boxoffice Türkiye (2015b) Yıllık (Annual data), available at http://boxofficeturkiye.com/film/yarindan-sonra-2004081, accessed 18 July 2015.

Brauch, H.G. (2002) *Klimawandel, Umweltstress und Konflikt.* AFES-PRESS Studie für das Bundesministerium für Umwelt, Naturschutz und Reaktorsicherheit.

Brauch, H.G. (2009a) *Facing Global Environmental Change. Environmental, Human, Energy, Food, Health and Water Security Concepts,* Berlin: Springer.

Brauch, H.G. (2009b) 'Securitizing Global Environmental Change', in H.G. Brauch, Ú. Oswald Spring, J. Grin, C. Mesjasz, P. Kameri-Mbote, N. Chadha Behera, B. Chouru and H. Krummenacher (eds) *Facing Global Environmental Change: Environmental, Human, Energy, Food, Health and Water Security Concepts,* Berlin: Springer, pp. 65–104.

Briggs, C.M. (2012) 'Climate Security, Risk Assessment and Military Planning', *International Affairs* 88(5): 1049–1064.

Broder, J.M. (2012) 'C.I.A. Closes Its Climate Change Office', *New York Times*, 20 November.

Brodziak, F., García, A.L. and Chow, L.G. (2011) *Climate Change Impacts on Socio-Environmental Conflicts: Vulnerability in Facing Climate Change and Social Conflicts in Mexico*, Brussels.

Brot für die Welt (2010) *'Klimaflüchtlinge nach Kopenhagen'. Rechtliches Konzept, politische Folgen, normative Überlegungen*, Stuttgart.

Brown, L.R. (1977) *Redefining National Security*. Washington, DC: Worldwatch Institute.

Browning, C.S. and McDonald, M. (2013) 'The Future of Critical Security Studies: Ethics and the Politics of Security', *European Journal of International Relations* 19(2): 235–255.

Brulle, R.J., Carmichael, J. and Jenkins, J.C. (2012) 'Shifting Public Opinion on Climate Change: An Empirical Assessment of Factors Influencing Concern over Climate Change in the U.S., 2002–2010', *Climatic Change* 114(2): 169–188.

Brunner, R.D. and Klein, R. (1999) 'Harvesting Experience: A Reappraisal of the U.S. Climate Change Action Plan', *Policy Sciences* 32: 133–161.

Bruyn, S.M. de (2000) *Economic Growth and the Environment. An Empirical Analysis*, Dordrecht: Springer.

Bryner, G. (2000) 'Congress and the Politics of Climate Change', in P.G. Harris (ed.) *Climate Change and American Foreign Policy*, New York: St. Martin's Press, pp. 111–130.

Brzoska, M. (2009) 'The Securitzation of Climate Change and the Power of Conceptions of Security', *Sicherheit und Frieden* 27(3): 137–145.

Brzoska, M. (2012) 'Climate Change as a Driver of Security Policy', in J. Scheffran, M. Brzoska, H.-G. Brauch, M.P. Link and J.P. Schilling (eds) *Climate Change, Human Security and Violent Conflict. Challenges for Societal Stability*, Berlin: Springer, pp. 165–179.

Brzoska, M. and Oels, A. (2011) '"Versicherheitlichung" des Klimawandels? Die Konstruktion des Klimawandels als Sicherheitsbedrohung und ihre politischen Folgen', in M. Brzoska, M. Kalinowski, V. Matthies and B. Meyer (eds) *Klimawandel und Konflikte. Versicherheitlichung versus präventive Friedenspolitik?* Baden-Baden: Nomos, pp. 51–67.

Buhaug, H. (2010) 'Climate Not to Blame for African Civil Wars', *Proceedings of the National Academy of Sciences* 107(38): 16477–16482.

Buhaug, H., Nordkvelle, J., Bernauer, T., Böhmelt, T., Brzoska, M., Busby, J.W., Ciccone, A., Fjelde, H., Gartzke, E., Gleditsch, N.P., Goldstone, J.A., Hegre, H., Holtermann, H., Koubi, V., Link, J.S.A., Link, P.M., Lujala, P., O'Loughlin, J., Raleigh, C., Scheffran, J., Schilling, J., Smith, T.G., Theisen, O.M., Tol, R.S.J., Urdal, H. and Uexkull, N. von (2014) 'One Effect to Rule them All? A Comment on Climate and Conflict', *Climatic Change* 127(3-4): 391–397.

Bundesministerium der Verteidigung (2006) Weißbuch 2006 zur Sicherheitspolitik Deutschlands und zur Zukunft der Bundeswehr, available at www.bmvg.de/portal/a/bmvg/!ut/p/c4/DcLBDYAgDADAWVyg_ftzC_VXsIEGaIlUXF9zhyf-lKYkcjGlijseUdbwQmgzwZCY-c4sPrpVcSlAmjiYM1xWnsbqjL1sywdHoTKR/, accessed 25 August 2015.

Bundesregierung (2008) *DAS. Deutsche Anpassungsstrategie an den Klimawandel*. Vom Bundeskabinett am 17. Dezember 2008 beschlossen.

Bundesregierung (2009) G8 Gipfel 2007 Heiligendamm – Klimawandel bedroht Weltsicherheit, available at www.g-8.de/Content/DE/Artikel/2007/06/2007-06-06-klimawandel-wird-zum-sicherheitsrisiko.html, accessed 28 August 2015.

Bundeswehr (2012) *Klimafolgen im Kontext: Implikationen für Sicherheit und Stabilität im Nahen Osten und Nordafrika. Streitkräfte, Fähigkeiten und Technologien im 21. Jahrhundert: Teilstudie 2.* Berlin.

Bundeswehr (2014) *Future Topic: Klimawandel und Sicherheit in der Arktis nach 2014. Hat die friedliche und kooperative internationale Arktis-politik eine langfristige Zukunft?* Berlin.

Bündnis 90/Die Grünen Bundestagsfraktion (2013) CO2-Grenzwerte für Pkw: Merkel attackiert erfolgreich Klimaschutz, available at www.gruene-bundestag.de/themen/klimaschutz/merkel-attackiert-erfolgreich-klimaschutz_ID_4390270.html, accessed 7 January 2014.

Bündnis 90/Die Grünen Bundestagsfraktion (2014) Unsere Position: Außen- und Sicherheitspolitik, available at www.gruene-bundestag.de/themen/sicherheitspolitik_ID_207027.html, accessed 1 September 2014.

Burck, J., Hermwille, L. and Krings, L. (2012) *The Climate Change Performance Index. Results 2013,* Bonn, Berlin.

Busby, J.W. (2007) *Climate Change and National Security. An Agenda for Action,* Washington, D.C.

Bush, G.W. (2008) President Bush Discusses Climate Change, available at http://georgewbush-whitehouse.archives.gov/news/releases/2008/04/20080416-6.html, accessed 26 May 2015.

Butts, K.H. (1993) *Environmental Security: What is DOD's Role?* Carlisle, PA: Strategic Studies Institute, U.S. Army War College.

Buzan, B. (1983) *People, States and Fear. The National Security Problem in International Relations,* Brighton: Harvester Wheatsheaf.

Buzan, B. (2004) *From International to World Society? English School Theory and the Social Structure of Globalisation,* Cambridge: Cambridge University Press.

Buzan, B. (2007) *People, States and Fear. An Agenda for International Security Studies in the Post-Cold War Era,* Colchester: ECPR Press.

Buzan, B. and Hansen, L. (2009) *The Evolution of International Security Studies,* Cambridge and New York: Cambridge University Press.

Buzan, B. and Wæver, O. (2003) *Regions and Powers. The Structure of International Security,* Cambridge: Cambridge University Press.

Buzan, B., Wæver, O. and Wilde, J. de (1998) *Security. A New Framework for Analysis,* Boulder, CO: Lynne Rienner.

C.A.S.E. Collective (2006) 'Critical Approaches to Security in Europe: A Networked Manifesto', *Security Dialogue* 37(4): 443–487.

C2ES (2007/2008a) Legislation in the 110th Congress Related to Global Climate Change, available at www.c2es.org/federal/congress/110, accessed 6 September 2012.

C2ES (2007/2008b) National Security and Climate Change Proposals from the 110th Congress, available at www.c2es.org/federal/congress/110/natl_security, accessed 6 September 2012.

C2ES (2008) Legislation in the 110th Congress Related to Global Climate Change, available at www.c2es.org/federal/congress/110, accessed 8 March 2013.

C2ES (2009) Policy Brief: National Security Implications of Global Climate Change, available at www.c2es.org/docUploads/national-security-brief.pdf, accessed 26 March 2013.

C2ES (2012) State Legislation from Around the Country, available at www.c2es.org/us-states-regions/key-legislation, accessed 8 March 2013.

Caesar, C. (2000) *Rede im Deutschen Bundestag. Drs. 14/99.* 9362. Deutscher Bundestag.

References

Calderón, F. (2009a) Joint Press Conference with President Barack Obama and President Felipe Calderón of Mexico, 16 April 2009, Mexico City.

Calderón, F. (2009b) *Palabras del Presidente Felipe Calderón Hinojosa durante su intervención en la sesión plenaria de la 15° conferencia de las Naciones Unidas sobre cambio climático.* Copenhagen.

Calderón, F. (2010) *Mensaje a medios de comunicación del Presidente Calderón con motivo de los logros y resultados de la COP16/CMP6.* Mexico City.

Cámara de Diputados (1998) *Diario de los Debates: Organo Oficial de la Cámara de Diputados del Congreso de los Estados Unidos Mexicanos. Correspondiente al Primer Periodo de Sesiones Ordinarias Segundo Año de Ejercicio; no. 13.* Mexico City.

Cámara de Diputados (2005a) *Diario de los Debates órgano oficial de la cámara de diputados del congreso de los estados unidos mexicanos Poder Legislativo Federal, LIX Legislatura. Correspondiente al Primer Periodo de Sesiones Ordinarias del Tercer Año de Ejercicio; no. 18.* Mexico City.

Cámara de Diputados (2005b) *Diario de los Debates órgano oficial de la cámara de diputados del congreso de los estados unidos mexicanos Poder Legislativo Federal, LIX Legislatura. Correspondiente al Segundo Periodo de Sesiones Ordinarias del Tercer Año de Ejercicio; no. 22.* Mexico City.

Cámara de Diputados (2006) *Diario de los Debates órgano oficial de la cámara de diputados del congreso de los estados unidos mexicanos Poder Legislativo Federal, LX Legislatura. Correspondiente al Primer Periodo de Sesiones Ordinarias del Primer Año de Ejercicio; no. 32.* Mexico City.

Cámara de Diputados (2007a) *Diario de los Debates órgano oficial de la cámara de diputados del congreso de los estados unidos mexicanos Poder Legislativo Federal, LX Legislatura. Correspondiente al Primer Periodo de Sesiones del Primer Año de Ejercicio; no. 6.* Mexico City.

Cámara de Diputados (2007b) *Diario de los Debates órgano oficial de la cámara de diputados del congreso de los estados unidos mexicanos Poder Legislativo Federal, LX Legislatura. Correspondiente al Segundo Periodo de Sesiones Ordinarias del Primer Año de Ejercicio; no. 9.* Mexico City.

Cámara de Diputados (2007c) *Diario de los Debates órgano oficial de la cámara de diputados del congreso de los estados unidos mexicanos Poder Legislativo Federal, LX Legislatura. Correspondiente al Primer Periodo de Sesiones Ordinarias del Segundo Año de Ejercicio; no. 5.* Mexico City.

Cámara de Diputados (2007d) *Diario de los Debates órgano oficial de la cámara de diputados del congreso de los estados unidos mexicanos Poder Legislativo Federal, LX Legislatura. Correspondiente al Primer Periodo de Sesiones Ordinarias del Segundo Año de Ejercicio; no. 31.* Mexico City.

Cámara de Diputados (2008) *Diario de los Debates órgano oficial de la cámara de diputados del congreso de los estados unidos mexicanos Poder Legislativo Federal, LX Legislatura. Correspondiente al Primer Periodo de Sesiones Ordinarias del Tercer Año de Ejercicio; no. 28.* Mexico City.

Cámara de Diputados (2009a) *Diario de los Debates órgano oficial de la cámara de diputados del congreso de los estados unidos mexicanos Poder Legislativo Federal, LX Legislatura. Correspondiente al Segundo Periodo de Sesiones Ordinarias del Tercer Año de Ejercicio; no. 13.* Mexico City.

Cámara de Diputados (2009b) *Diario de los Debates órgano oficial de la cámara de diputados del congreso de los estados unidos mexicanos Poder Legislativo Federal, LX Legislatura. Correspondiente al Segundo Periodo de Sesiones Ordinarias del Tercer Año de Ejercicio; no. 27.* Mexico City.

Cámara de Diputados (2009c) *Diario de los Debates: Organo oficial de la camara de diputados del congreso de los Estados Unidos Mexicanos, Poder Legislativo Federal, LXI Legislatura. Correspondiente al Primer Periodo de Sesiones Ordinarias del Primer Año de Ejercicio; no. 29.* Mexico City.

Cámara de Diputados (2012) *Ley General de Cambio Climático.* Mexico City.

Campbell, D. (1992) *Writing Security. United States Foreign Policy and the Politics of Identity,* Manchester: Manchester University Press.

Campbell, K.M., Gulledge, J., McNeill, J., Podesta, J., Odgen, P., Fueth, L., Woolsey, R.J., Lennon, A.T.J., Smith, J., Weitz, R. and Mix, D. (2007) *The Age of Consequences. The Foreign Policy and National Security Implications of Global Climate Change,* Washington, D.C.

CAN (2011) Turkey Earns its First Fossil of the Day for Wanting Everything but Giving Nothing, available at www.climatenetwork.org/fossil-of-the-day/turkey-earns-its-first-fossil-wanting-everything-giving-nothing, accessed 10 April 2013.

Carius, A. and Lietzmann, K.M. (1998) *Umwelt und Sicherheit. Herausforderungen für die internationale Politik,* Berlin: Springer.

Carius, A. and Maas, A. (2009) *Climate Change and Security. Three Scenarios for Middle America,* Berlin.

Carius, A., Tänzler, D. and Winterstein, J. (2007) *Weltkarte von Umweltkonflikten – Ansätze zur Typologisierung. Externe Expertise für das WBGU-Hauptgutachten 'Welt im Wandel: Sicherheitsrisiko Klimawandel',* Berlin.

Carmen, H.E., Parthermore, C. and Rogers, W. (2010) Broadening Horizons: Climate Change and the U.S. Armed Forces, available at www.cnas.org/files/documents/publications/CNAS%20Publication_Climate%20Change%20and%20the%20US%20Armed%20Forces_April%2020.pdf, accessed 14 March 2014.

Carson, M. (2011) 'Treadmills, Modernization, and the Crooked Path of US Climate Policy'. Paper for European Council for Political Research Conference, Reykjavik, Iceland, 10 August.

Carvalho, A. and Burgess, J. (2005) 'Cultural Circuits of Climate Change in U.K. Broadsheet Newspapers, 1985–2003', *Risk Analysis* 25(6): 1457–1469.

Çavlak, H. (2012) *The Impact of the European Union on the Environmental Discourse of Turkish Governments since the 1980s*, II. Uluslararası Turgut Özal Ekonomive Politika Kongresi, 19–20 April 2012, Malatya.

CCC (2008) *Cambio climático y seguridad nacional. Programa de colaboración entre la H. Cámara de Disputados, el Centro de Colaboración Cívica (CCC), El Programa de las Naciones Unidas para el Desarollo (PNUD), Centro Mario Molina (CMM), Centro Mexicano de Derecho Ambiental, Comisión de Estudios del Sector Privado para el Desarollo Sustentable (CESPEDES).* Mexico City.

CCS (2015) The Center for Climate and Security: Research Hub, available at http://climateandsecurity.org/resources/, accessed 11 June 2015.

CDU/CSU Parliamentary Group (2010) 'Ruck: Cancun hat Gabriel entlarvt – Wir haben jetzt große wirtschaftliche Chancen beim Klimaschutz', 15 December.

CEMDA (2010) El Grupo de financiamiento para cambio climático, available at www.cemda.org.mx/financiamiento-cambio-climatico/, accessed 14 October 2014.

CEMDA (2015) Financiamiento cambio climático, available at www.cemda.org.mx/financiamiento-cambio-climatico/, accessed 3 September 2015.

CENAPRED and SEGOB (2014) *Cambio Climático. Information on the Work of CENAPRED.* Mexico City.

Centro Mario Molina (2014) *Analysis of Barriers in Implementing Low Carbon Technologies and Proposals for their Elimination,* Mexico City.

Cerit Mazlum, S. (2009) 'Turkey's Foreign Policy on Global Atmospheric Commons – Climate Change and Ozone Depletion', in P.G. Harris (ed.) *Climate Change and Foreign Policy. Case Studies from East to West,* London and New York: Routledge.

Çetin, S. (2012) 'The Turkish Economy and the Global Crisis', *International Business: Teaching, Research and Practice – The Journal of the AIB-SE* 6(2): 45–58.

References

Chandler, D. (2009) 'Climate Change Odds much Worse than Thought. New Analysis Shows Warming Could Be Double Previous Estimates', *MIT News*, 19 May.

Chandler, W. (2002) Climate Change Mitigation in Developing Countries: Brazil, China, India, Mexico, South Africa, and Turkey, available at www.c2es.org/docUploads/dev_mitigation.pdf, accessed 2 August 2013.

CIA (2009) CIA Opens Center on Climate Change and National Security, available at https://www.cia.gov/news-information/press-releases-statements/center-on-climate-change-and-national-security.html, accessed 22 June 2015.

CIVICUS (2011) A Snapshot of Civil Society in Mexico. Analytical Report on the CIVICUS Civil Society Index, available at http://civicus.org/images/stories/csi/csi_phase2/mexico%20acr.pdf, accessed 22 February 2013.

Clarke, S. (2005) 'Bush Acknowledges "Problem" of Global Warming', *Guardian*, 6 July.

Clean Energy Wire (2015) Germany's Greenhouse Gas Emissions and Climate Targets, available at https://www.cleanenergywire.org/factsheets/germanys-greenhouse-gas-emissions-and-climate-targets, accessed 2 September 2015.

CLICO (2015) Climate Change Hydro-Conflicts and Human Security, available at www.ecologic.eu/3295, accessed 5 September 2015.

Climate Action Tracker (2014) Climate Action Tracker. Rating Countries, available at http://climateactiontracker.org/, accessed 19 September 2015.

Climate Alliance (2015) Members of Climate Alliance: 1715 (as of July 2015), available at www.climatealliance.org/fileadmin/inhalte/dokumente/2015/Members_List_international_July_2015.pdf, accessed 5 September 2015.

Clisap (n.d.) Beteiligte Institutionen, available at https://www.clisap.de/de/clisap/ueber-uns/exzellenzcluster/clisap-mitglieder/.

CNA (2007) *National Security and the Threat of Climate Change*, Alexandria, VA: Center for Naval Analysis.

CNA and Oxfam (2011) *An Ounce of Prevention: Preparing for the Impact of a Changing Climate on US Humanitarian and Disaster Response*, Alexandria, VA and Boston.

CNA Military Advisory Board (2014) *National Security and the Accelerating Risks of Climate Change*, Alexandria, VA.

CNBC (2013) 'Can Turkey Become the "China of Europe?"' 18 January.

CNN México (2010) Calderón: Inundaciones o huracanes, ejemplos del cambio climático, available at http://mexico.cnn.com/nacional/2010/09/29/calderon-inundaciones-o-huracanes-ejemplos-del-cambio-climatico, accessed 3 September 2015.

CNN Türk (2012) *mikdat kadıoğlu küresel ısınma*.

Coaffee, J. and Wood, D.M. (2006) 'Security Is Coming Home. Rethinking Scale and Constructing Resilience in the Global Urban Response to Terrorist Risk', *International Relations* 20(4): 503–517.

ÇOB (2007) First National Communication on Climate Change. Republic of Turkey, available at http://unfccc.int/resource/docs/natc/turnc1.pdf, accessed 7 August 2015.

ÇOB (2008) İklim Değişikliği ve yapılan çalışmalar [Climate Change and Actions Taken], available at http://laboratuvar.cevre.gov.tr/download/iklim.pdf.

ÇOB (2010) *Türkiye Cumhuriyeti Ulusal İklim Değişikliği Strateji Belgesi (2010 – 2020)*. Ankara.

Corry, O. (2012) 'Securitisation and 'Riskification': Second-order Security and the Politics of Climate Change', *Millennium – Journal of International Studies* 40(2): 235–258.

CPRS (2012) The Center for Peace and Reconciliation Studies Turkey. *Human Security – Risks, Threats and Crisis*. Ankara.

References

ÇŞB (1991) *Çevre ve Şehircilik Bakanlığı Kuruluş ve Görevleri hakkında kanun hükmünde kararname*. Ankara.

ÇŞB (2010) *Climate Change Strategy 2010–2020*. Ankara.

ÇŞB (2011) *Turkey's National Climate Change Adaptation Strategy and Action Plan*. Ankara.

ÇŞB (2012a) Climate Change in Turkey, available at www.csb.gov.tr/db/iklim/editordosya/BROSUR_ENG.pdf, accessed 7 August 2015.

ÇŞB (2012b) Türkiye'de İklim Değişikliği Risk Yönetimi [Climate Change Risk Management in Turkey] Türkiye Çevre ve Şehircilik Bakanlığı, UNDP, GEF, available at www.undp.org/content/dam/turkey/docs/projectdocuments/EnvSust/UNDP-TR-Iklim_Degisikligi_Risk_Yonetimi.pdf, accessed 23 July 2015.

ÇŞB (2013) *Turkey's Fifth National Communication Under the UNFCCC*. Ankara.

Cudworth, E. and Hobden, S. (2010) 'Securing What from Whom? Multiple Complex Inequalities and the Politics of Environmental Security in Europe'. Paper presented to the European Consortium for Political Research, 5th pan-European Conference on the EU, University of Oporto, Porto, Portugal, 24–26 June.

Dabelko, G.D., Dabelko, D.D., Matthew, R., Sherbinin, A.d., Claussen, E. and Levy, M.A. (1995) *Environmental Change and Security Program (ECSP) Report 1*, Washington, D.C.

Dahl, R.A. (1957) 'The Concept of Power', *Behavioral Science* 2(3): 201–215.

Dalby, S. (1992a) 'Ecopolitical Discourse: Environmental Security and Political Geography', *Progress in Human Geography* 16(4): 503–522.

Dalby, S. (1992b) 'Security, Modernity, Ecology. The Dilemmas of Post-Cold War Security Discourse', *Alternatives* 17(1): 95–134.

Dalby, S. (2002) *Environmental Security*, Minneapolis: University of Minnesota Press.

Dalby, S. (2009) *Security and Environmental Change*, Cambridge: Polity.

Dalby, S. (2013) 'Biopolitics and Climate Security in the Anthropocene', *Geoforum* 49(0): 184–192.

Damm, W. (1996) 'Energiekonzepte in Westdeutschland. Umsetzungsergebnisse und -bedingungen auf Bundes- Länder- und Kommunalebene' Dissertation, Freie Universität Berlin.

Davenport, C. (2014a) 'Kerry Quietly Makes Priority of Climate Pact', *New York Times*, 2 January.

Davenport, C. (2014b) 'Climate Change Deemed Growing Security Threat by Military Researchers', *New York Times*, 13 May.

Davenport, C. (2014c) 'Pentagon Signals Security Risks of Climate Change', *New York Times*, 13 October.

Dean, M. (2010) *Governmentality. Power and Rule in Modern Society*, London: Sage.

Debiel, T. (ed.) (2007) *Globale Trends 2007. Frieden, Entwicklung, Umwelt*, Frankfurt am Main: Fischer-Taschenbuch-Verl.

Deheza, E. (2011) *Climate Change, Migration and Security. Best Practice Policy and Operational Options for Mexico*. Interim Report. London.

Deheza, E. and Mora, J. (2013) *Climate Change, Migration and Security. Best Practice Policy and Operational Options for Mexico*. London.

Dehmer, D. (2015) 'Der Grüne Papstflüsterer. Klimaforscher Hans Joachim Schellnhuber', *Der Tagesspiegel*, 18 June 2015, available at www.tagesspiegel.de/politik/klimaforscher-hans-joachim-schellnhuber-der-gruene-papstfluesterer/11931986.html.

Der Spiegel (1986) 'Das Weltklima gerät aus den Fugen', 11 August.

Der Spiegel (2004) 'The Day After Tomorrow': Klimaforscher streiten über Emmerichs Eismaschine, available at www.spiegel.de/wissenschaft/natur/the-day-after-

References

tomorrow-klimaforscher-streiten-ueber-emmerichs-eismaschine-a-299652.html, accessed 2 September 2015.

Der Spiegel (2012) 'Interview mit Dennis Meadows: "Für eine globale Mobilmachung ist es zu spät"', 4 December.

Dereci, S. (2013) 'Reassessing the Impact of the Europeanisation on Civil Society of Turkey', *Centre for Policy and Research on Turkey (ResearchTurkey)* 2(9): 36–41.

Detraz, N. and Betsill, M.M. (2009) 'Climate Change and Environmental Security. For Whom the Discourse Shifts', *International Studies Perspectives* 10(3): 303–320.

Detsch, C. (2011) 'Regionale Perspektive: Lateinamerika', in N. Netzer and J. Gouverneur (eds) *Zwischen Anspruch und Wirklichkeit: Internationale Perspektiven vor der Weltklimakonferenz in Durban,* Berlin: Friedrich-Ebert-Stiftung, pp. 33–38.

Deudney, D.H. (1990) 'The Case Against Linking Environmental Degradation and National Security', *Millennium* 19(3): 461–476.

Deutsche Welle (2015) Renewables Help Cut German CO2 Emissions, available at www.dw.com/en/renewables-help-cut-german-co2-emissions/a-18176835, accessed 2 September 2015.

Deutscher Bundestag (1949) Deutscher Bundestag – Grundgesetz, available at https://www.bundestag.de/grundgesetz, accessed 28 August 2015.

Deutscher Bundestag (1989) *Erste Beschlussempfehlung und Bericht des Ausschusses für Umwelt, Naturschutz und Reaktorsicherheit (21. Ausschuss) zu dem Ersten Zwischenbericht der Enquete-Kommission 'Vorsorge zum Schutz der Erdathmosphäre'. Gemäß Beschluss des Deutschen Bundestages vom 16 Oktober und 27 November 1987, Drs. 11/533, 11/787, 11/971, 11/1351, 11/3246.* Berlin.

Deutscher Bundestag (1991) Parliamentary Speech, MdB Klaus-Dieter Feige (Bündnis 90/Die Grünen), 27.09.1991, *Plenarprotokoll 12/45*, 3786. Bonn.

Deutscher Bundestag (1992) *Erster Bericht der Enquete-Kommission „Schutz der Erdathmosphäre' zum Thema „Klimaänderung gefährdet globale Entwicklung – Zukunft sichern – Jetzt handeln'. Gemäß Beschluss des Deutschen Bundestages vom 25. April 1991, Drs. 12/419.* Berlin.

Deutscher Bundestag (1993a) Parliamentary Speech, MdB Klaus-Dieter Feige (Bündnis 90/Die Grünen), 12.03.1993, *Plenarprotokoll 12/147*, 12646. Bonn.

Deutscher Bundestag (1993b) Parliamentary Speech, MdB Dagmar Enkelmann (PDS), 22.04.1993, *Plenarprotokoll 12/152*, 13004. Bonn.

Deutscher Bundestag (1993c) Parliamentary Speech, MdB Monika Ganseforth (SPD), 23.06.1993, *Plenarprotokoll 12/165*, 14256. Bonn.

Deutscher Bundestag (1993d) *Große Anfrage. Klimaschutz in Europa.* Drucksache 12/5854. Berlin.

Deutscher Bundestag (1994) *Erster Bericht der Enquete-Kommission 'Schutz der Erdathmosphäre' zum Thema Mobilität und Klima – Wege zu einer klimaverträglichen Verkehrspolitik. Eingesetzt durch den Beschluss des Deutschen Bundestages vom 25. April 1991; Drs. 12/419.* Berlin.

Deutscher Bundestag (1995a) *XX Bericht der Enquete-Kommission 'Schutz der Erdathmosphäre' zum Thema Mehr Zukunft für die Erde – Nachhaltige Energiepolitik für dauerhaften Klimaschutz.* Berlin.

Deutscher Bundestag (1995b) Parliamentary Speech, MdB Christian Ruck (CDU/CSU), 20.01.1995, *Plenarprotokoll 13/13*, 809. Bonn.

Deutscher Bundestag (1995c) Parliamentary Speech, MdB Gerold Häfner (Bündnis 90/Die Grünen), 09.03.1995, *Plenarprotokoll 13/24*, 1761. Bonn.

Deutscher Bundestag (1995d) Parliamentary Speech, MdB Dagmar Enkelmann (PDS), 26.04.1995, *Plenarprotokoll 13/33*, 2529. Bonn.

166 References

Deutscher Bundestag (1995e) Parliamentary Speech, MdB Michaele Hustedt (Bündnis 90/ Die Grünen), 26.04.1995, *Plenarprotokoll 13/33*, 2525. Bonn.

Deutscher Bundestag (1996) Parliamentary Speech, MdB Klaus W. Lippold (CDU/CSU), 25.04.1996, *Plenarprotokoll 13/101*, 8926. Bonn.

Deutscher Bundestag (1997a) *Kleine Anfrage. Fünf Jahre nach Rio: Kritische Bilanz beim Klimaschutz.* Berlin.

Deutscher Bundestag (1997b) Parliamentary Speech, MdB Michael Müller (SPD), 13.11.1997, *Plenarprotokoll 13/203*, 18328. Bonn.

Deutscher Bundestag (1998a) Parliamentary Speech, MdB Liesel Hartenstein, 15.01.1998, *Plenarprotokoll 13/213*, 19413. Bonn.

Deutscher Bundestag (1998b) *Unterrichtung durch die Bundesregierung Forschung zur CO2-Minderung in den wichtigsten Industriestaaten einschließlich China.* Drucksache 13/10703. Berlin.

Deutscher Bundestag (1999a) Parliamentary Speech, MdB Jürgen Trittin (Bündnis 90/Die Grünen), 06.05.1999, *Plenarprotokoll 14/39*, 3343. Bonn.

Deutscher Bundestag (1999b) Parliamentary Speech, MdB Peter Paziorek (CDU/CSU), 21.01.1999, *Plenarprotokoll 14/16*, 1086. Bonn.

Deutscher Bundestag (1999c) Parliamentary Speech, Walter Hirche (FDP), 16.12.1999, *Plenarprotokoll 14/79*, 7258. Berlin.

Deutscher Bundestag (2000) *Unterrichtung durch die Bundesregierung Nationales Klimaschutzprogramm. Fünfter Bericht der Interministeriellen Arbeitsgruppe 'CO2-Reduktion'.* Drs. 14/4729. Berlin.

Deutscher Bundestag (2003), Parliamentary Speech, MdB Michaele Hustedt (Bündnis 90/ Die Grünen), 13.11.2003, *Plenarprotokoll 15/75*, 6439. Berlin.

Deutscher Bundestag (2004a), Parliamentary Speech, MdB Reinhard Loske (Bündnis 90/ Die Grünen), 28.05.2004, *Plenarprotokoll 15/112*, 10244. Berlin.

Deutscher Bundestag (2004b) Parliamentary Speech, MdB Reinhard Loske (Bündnis 90/ Die Grünen), 04.03.2004, *Plenarprotokoll 15/94*, 8374. Berlin.

Deutscher Bundestag (2004c) Parliamentary Speech, MdB Michaele Hustedt (Bündnis 90/ Die Grünen), 16.01.2004, *Plenarprotokoll 15/87*, 7675. Berlin.

Deutscher Bundestag (2004d) Parliamentary Speech, MdB Ulrich Kelber (SPD), 16.01.2004, *Plenarprotokoll 15/87*, 7668. Berlin.

Deutscher Bundestag (2004e) Parliamentary Speech, MdB Jürgen Trittin, 02.12.2004, *Plenarprotokoll 15/145*, 13417. Berlin.

Deutscher Bundestag (2004f) Parliamentary Speech, MdB Reinhard Loske, 28.05.2004. *Plenarprotokoll 15/112*, 10244. Berlin.

Deutscher Bundestag (2007a) Parliamentary Speech, MdB Michael Kauch (FDP), 26.04.2007, *Plenarprotokoll 16/94*, 9484. Berlin.

Deutscher Bundestag (2007b) Parliamentary Speech, MdB Georg Nüßlein CDU/CSU), 22.06.2007, *Plenarprotokoll 16/106*, 10953.

Deutscher Bundestag (2007c) Parliamentary Speech, MdB Gabriele Groneberg (SPD), 16.11.2007, *Plenarprotokoll 16/127*, 13377 Berlin.

Deutscher Bundestag (2008a) Parliamentary Speech, MdB Katherina Reiche (CDU/CSU), 17.01.2008, *Plenarprotokoll 16/136*, 14268. Berlin.

Deutscher Bundestag (2008b) Parliamentary Speech, Mdb Frank Schwabe (SPD), 29.05.2008, *Plenarprotokoll 16/163*, 17247. Berlin.

Deutscher Bundestag (2008c) Parliamentary Speech, MdB Sigmar Gabriel (SPD), 17.12.2008, *Plenarprotokoll 16/195*, 21071. Berlin.

Deutscher Bundestag (2008d) Unterrichtung durch die Bundesregierung. Hauptgutachten 2007 des Wissenschaftlichen Beirats der Bundesregierung Globale Umweltveränderungen 'Welt im Wandel – Sicherheitsrisiko Klimawandel' und Stellungnahme der Bundesregierung, 22.12.2008, *Plenarprotokoll 16/11600*. Berlin.

Deutscher Bundestag (2009a) Parliamentary Speech, MdB Hans Eichel (SPD), 02.07.2008, *Plenarprotokoll 16/230*, 25623. Berlin.

Deutscher Bundestag (2009b) Parliamentary Speech, MdB Frank Schwabe (SPD,) 13.05.2009, *Plenarprotokoll 16/221*, 24253. Berlin.

Deutscher Bundestag (2009c) Parliamentary Speech, MdB Bärbel Höhn (Bündnis 90/Die Grünen), 13.05.2009, *Plenarprotokoll 16/221*, 24255. Berlin.

Deutscher Bundestag (2009d) *Antrag der Fraktion der SPD. Die Klimakonferenz in Kopenhagen zum Erfolg führen – Deutschlands und Europas Vorreiterrolle nutzen und stärken*. Berlin.

Deutscher Bundestag (2009e) Parliamentary Speech, MdB Christisan Ruck (CDU/CSU), 03.12.2009, *Plenarprotokoll 17/9*, 599. Berlin.

Deutscher Bundestag (2010) *Antrag. Internationaler Klimaschutz vor Cancún – Mit unterschiedlichen Geschwindigkeiten zum Ziel*. Drucksache 17/4016. Berlin.

Deutscher Bundestag (2011a) *Antrag. Klimakonferenz Durban: 10 Punkte für ein besseres Klima*. Drucksache 17/7828. Berlin.

Deutscher Bundestag (2011b) *Antrag der Abgeordneten Frank Schwabe, Dirk Becker, Gerd Bollmann, Marco Bülow, Petra Ernstberger, Iris Gleicke, Christel Humme, Ulrich Kelber, Dr. Bärbel Kofler, Ute Kumpf, Dr. Matthias Miersch, Thomas Oppermann, Ute Vogt, Waltraud Wolff (Wolmirstedt), Dr. Frank-Walter Steinmeier und der Fraktion der SPD. Die Klimakonferenz in Durban zum Erfolg führen – Kyoto-Protokoll verlängern, Klimaschutz finanzieren und Cancún-Beschlüsse umsetzen*. 1-8. Berlin.

Deutscher Bundestag (2012) *Der Einstieg zum Ausstieg aus der Atomenergie*. Berlin.

Deutscher Bundestag (2013) Datenhandbuch Bundestag: Tabellarische Übersicht der Enquete-Kommission, available at www.bundestag.de/dokumente/datenhandbuch/08/08_10/08_10_01.html.

Deutscher Bundestag (2014a) *Bericht des Ausschusses für Bildung, Forschung und Technikfolgenabschätzung (18. Ausschuss) gemäß § 56a der Geschäftsordnung*. Drucksache 18/2121. Berlin.

Deutscher Bundestag (2014b) Parliamentary Speech, MdB Kathrin Göring-Eckhardt (Bündnis 90/Die Grünen), 10.09.2014, *Plenarprotokoll 18/50*, 4650. Berlin.

Deutscher Bundestag (2014c) *Antrag der Abgeordneten Annalena Baerbock, Bärbel Höhn, Oliver Krischer, Dr. Julia Verlinden, Peter Meiwald, Claudia Roth (Augsburg), Sylvia Kotting-Uhl, Christian Kühn (Tübingen), Steffi Lemke, Harald Ebner, Matthias Gastel, Kai Gehring, Stephan Kühn (Dresden), Nicole Maisch, Friedrich Ostendorff, Markus Tressel, Dr. Valerie Wilms und der Fraktion Bündnis 90/Die Grünen. Ein Scheitern der nationalen Klimapolitik abwenden und international an Glaubwürdigkeit zurückgewinnen*. Drucksache 18/2744. Berlin.

Deutscher Bundestag (2015) *Kleine Anfrage der Abgeordneten Bärbel Höhn, Oliver Krischer, Annalena Baerbock, Matthias Gastel, Sylvia Kotting-Uhl, Stephan Kühn (Dresden), Steffi Lemke, Nicole Maisch, Peter Meiwald, Markus Tressel, Dr. Julia Verlinden, Dr. Valerie Wilms und der Fraktion Bündnis 90/Die Grünen*. Drucksache 18/3692. Berlin.

Deutschlandfunk (2008) Der Klimawandel als kultureller Wandel, available at www.deutschlandfunk.de/der-klimawandel-als-kultureller-wandel.1184.de.html?dram:article_id=185273, accessed 4 September 2015.

References

DHS (2013) *NIPP 2013 Partnering for Critical Infrastructure Security and Resilience.* Washington, D.C.

Diakonisches Werk der EKD e.V., Germanwatch and Brot für die Welt (2008) Climate Change, Food Security and the Right to Adequate Food, available at https://germanwatch.org/de/download/2798.pdf, accessed 28 August 2015.

Die Welt (2007a) 'Wer ein mutiges Wort riskiert muss mit Widerspruch leben. Bundeskanzlerin Angela Merkel beantwortet die Fragen der Welt Leser', 15 October.

Die Welt (2007b) 'Klimakatastrophe' ist das Wort des Jahres, available at www.welt.de/kultur/article1438096/Klimakatastrophe-ist-das-Wort-des-Jahres.html, accessed 4 September 2015.

Die Welt (2015) 'So klimafreundlich ist ihr Mittagessen', 31 August.

Diez, T. (1999) 'Speaking Europe: The Politics of Integration Discourse', *Journal of European Public Policy* 6(4): 598–613.

Diez, T. (2001) 'Europe as a Discursive Battleground. Discourse Analysis and European Integration Studies', *Cooperation and Conflict* 36(1): 5–38.

Diez, T., Bode, I. and da Costa, A.F. (2011) *Key Concepts in International Relations,* Los Angeles: Sage.

Dionne, E.J. (1989) 'Washington Talk. Greening of Democrats: An 80's Mix of Idealism and Shrewd Politics', *New York Times,* 14 July.

DIW (2010) *Wochenbericht des DIW Berlin Nr. 13-14/2010 2 Ökosteuer hat zu geringerer Umweltbelastung des Verkehrs beigetragen. Wochenbericht des DIW Berlin Nr. 13-14/2010.* Berlin.

DIW/SPRU (2001) Treibhausgasminderung in Deutschland und UK: Folge 'glücklicher' Umstände oder gezielter Politikmaßnahmen? Ein Beitrag zur internationalen Klimapolitik, available at www.isi.fraunhofer.de/isi-wAssets/docs/e/de/publikationen/treibgasminderung.pdf, accessed 2 September 2015.

DKK (2013) Mitglieder des Deutschen Klima-Konsortiums, available at www.deutsches-klima-konsortium.de/de/mitglieder.html, accessed 18 November 2013.

DOD (2008) *National Defense Strategy.* Washington, D.C.

DOD (2010) *Quadrennial Defense Review Report 2010.* Washington, D.C.

DOD (2011) *Trends and Implications of Climate Change for National and International Security. Report of the Defense Science Board Task Force.* Washington, D.C.

DOD (2012) *Climate Change Adaptation Roadmap (CCAR).* Washington, D.C.

DOD (2014a) *2014 Climate Change Adaptation Roadmap.* Washington, D.C.

DOD (2014b) *Quadrennial Defense Report 2014.* Washington, D.C.

DOD (2014c) *Strategic Sustainability Performance Plan FY 2014.* Washington, D.C.

DOD (2014d) *USCENTCOM Climate Change Assessment.* Washington, D.C.

DOD (2015) About SERDP, available at https://www.serdp-estcp.org/About-SERDP-and-ESTCP/About-SERDP, accessed 10 June 2015.

Doğan, D. (n.d.) *Global Climate Change and Its Effects in Turkey.* n.a.

Donner, S. and Faltin, F. (2007) *Klimapolitische Entwicklungen in den USA. Initiativen auf bundesstaatlicher und regionaler Ebene – Info Brief – Deutscher Bundestag Wissenschaftliche Dienste.* Berlin.

Doran, P. (2000) 'Upholding the "Island of High Modernity"', in P.G. Harris (ed.) *Climate Change and American Foreign Policy,* New York: St. Martin's Press, pp. 51–70.

DPG (1986) *Warnung vor einer drohenden Klimakatastrophe. Pressekonferenz in Bonn.*

DPG and DMG (1987) 'Deutsch Physikalische Gesellschaft, Arbeitskreis Energie. Gemeinsamer Aufruf der DPG und der DMG Warnung vor drohenden weltweiten Klimaänderungen durch den Menschen', *Physikalische Blätter* 43(8).
DPT (1979) *Kalkınma Planı (Dördüncü Beş Yıl) 1979–1983.*
DPT (1985) *Kalkınma Planı (Beşinci Beş Yıl) 1985–1989.*
DPT (1990) *Kalkınma Planı (Altıncı Beş Yıllık) 1990–1994.*
DPT (1996) *Kalkınma Planı (Yedinci Beş Yıllık) 1996–2000.*
DPT (2000) İklim Değişikliği Özel İhtisas Komisyonu Raporu [Report of the Expert Commission on Climate Change]. Sekizinci Beş Yıllık Kalkınma Planı [8th Five Year Development Plan], available at http://igemportal.org/Resim/İklim%20Raporu.pdf, accessed 15 July 2014.
DPT (2001) *Uzun vadeli Strateji ve Sekizinci Beş Yıllık Kalkınma Planı 2001–2005.*
DPT (2007) *Dokuzuncu Kalkınma Planı 2007–2013.*
DSI (2013) *İklim değişikliği.*
DSI/Devlet Su İşleri (2010) *Turkey's National Climate Change Adaptation Strategy and Action Plan (2010–2020).*
Duffield, M. and Waddell, N. (2006) 'Securing Humans in a Dangerous World', *International Politics* 43(1): 1–23.
Duru, B. (2013) '"Sustainability" of the Green Movement in Turkey', *Perspectives* (4).
Dyer, G. (2013) *İklim Savaşları. Ömer Madra'nın önsözü ile.* Türkiye 2035 senaryosu. İstanbul: Paloma Yayinevi.
Eakin, H. and Luers, A.L. (2006) 'Assessing the Vulnerability of Social-Environmental Systems', *Annual Review of Environment and Resources* 31(1): 365–394.
Eastin, J., Grundmann, R. and Prakash, A. (2011) 'The Two Limits Debates. "Limits to Growth" and Climate Change', *Futures* 43(1): 16–26.
Eberwein, W.-D. and Chojnacki, S. (2001) Stürmische Zeiten? Umwelt, Sicherheit und Konflikt, available at http://edoc.vifapol.de/opus/volltexte/2009/1927/pdf/p01_303.pdf, accessed 21 October 2015.
ECC (n.d.) Environment, Conflict and Cooperation, available at https://www.ecc-platform.org/, accessed 5 September 2015.
Eckersley, R. (2007) 'Ambushed: The Kyoto Protocol, the Bush Administration's Climate Policy and the Erosion of Legitimacy', *International Politics* 44(2/3): 306–324.
Ederer, M. (2007) *Energie- und Klimasicherheit während der deutschen EU-Ratspräsidentschaft.* Akademie für Politik und Zeitgeschehen der Hanns-Seidel Stiftung.
Ediğer, V.S. (n.d.) *Özgeçmiş ve Eserler Listesi*, Istanbul.
EED and Brot für die Welt (2009) *Klimawandel – Eine Arbeitshilfe für die Gemeindearbeit zur Studie 'Zukunftsfähiges Deutschland in einer globalisierten Welt'.*
Egle, C., Ostheim, T. and Zohlnhöfer, R. (eds) (2003) *Das Rot-Grüne Projekt. Eine Bilanz der Regierung Schröder 1998-2002*, Wiesbaden: Westdeutscher Verlag.
Ehrlich, P. (1968) *The Population Bomb*, New York: Ballantine.
El Economista (2012) 'G20 servirá para alianza por crecimiento verde: Calderón', *El Economista*, 15 June.
Elbe, S. (2006) 'Should HIV/AIDS Be Securitized? The Ethical Dilemmas of Linking HIV/AIDS and Security', *International Studies Quarterly* 50(1): 119–144.
Elbe, S. (2009) *Virus Alert. Security, Governmentality, and the AIDS Pandemic*, New York: Columbia University Press.
Elvira Quesada, J.R. (2010) 'Colaborador invitado: México frente al cambio climático', *Reforma*, 21 November.

170 References

Endlicher, W. and Gerstengarbe, F.-W. (2007) Der Klimawandel – Einblicke, Rückblicke und Ausblicke, available at https://www.pik-potsdam.de/services/infothek/buecher_broschueren/.images/broschuere_cms_100.pdf.

EPA (1994) Memorandum of Understanding between the U.S. Environmental Protection Agency and the U.S. Department of Defense, available at http://www2.epa.gov/fedfac/memorandum-understanding-between-us-environmental-protection-agency-and-us-department-defense, accessed 10 June 2015.

Erandac, B. (2011) 'Alman Vakıflar Dosyası acılınca neler çıkacak, neler ...', *Takvim Gazetesi*, 3 October.

Erdoğdu, E. (2010) 'Turkish Support to Kyoto Protocol: A Reality or Just an Illusion', *Science Direct* 14(3): 1114–1117, www.sciencedirect.com/science/article/pii/S1364032109002512. doi:10.1016/j.rser.2009.10.020

Eroğlu, V. (2015) *Susuzluk yaşatmayacağımızın sözünü veriyorum*. Haberler, 9 January 2015, available at www.haberler.com/bakan-eroglu-susuzluk-yasatmayacagimizin-sozunu-6851843-haberi/.

Eseverri, J. (2009) 'Arriesga clima la seguridad en alimentos', *Reforma*, 12 November.

Eslen, N. (2007) 'İklim değişikliği bir güvenlik sorunu', *Radikal*, 30 April.

Eslen, N. (2009) 'Küresel ısınma ciddi bir güvenlik sorunudur'. Presentation at the 'Global Climate Change and Turkey's Security' Symposium. Genelkurmay Stratejik Araştırmalar ve Etüt Merkezi, Ankara.

Eslen, N. (2010) 'İklim değişikliği ve Türkiye'nin güvenliğine etkileri', *SAREM Stratejik Araştırmalar Dergisi* 8(15): 237–275.

EUISS (2015a) *A New Climate for Peace. Taking Action on Climate and Fragility Risks – Executive Summary*. Independent Report Commissioned by the G7 members. Paris: EUISS.

EUISS (2015b) *EUISS Yearbook of European Security. YES 2015*. Paris: EUISS.

European Commission (2011) *EU IPA Enlargement Monitoring GHG Emissions Turkey. Part 2: Climate Change Component*. Brussels: European Commission.

European Commission (2014) Turkey Progress Report, available at http://ec.europa.eu/enlargement/pdf/key_documents/2014/20141008-turkey-progress-report_en.pdf, accessed 10 August 2015.

European Council (2003) A Secure Europe in a Better World. European Security Strategy, available at www.consilium.europa.eu/uedocs/cmsupload/78367.pdf, accessed 21 September 2015.

Falkner, R. (2005) 'American Hegemony and the Global Environment', *International Studies Review* 7: 585–599.

Faust, J. and Messner, D. (2004) *Europe's New Security Strategy – Challenges for Development Policy*. Bonn: Deutsche Institut für Entwicklungspolitik.

Feakin, T. and Depledge, D. (2010) Climate-Related Impacts on National Security in Mexico and Central America. Reasearch project, London: Royal United Services Institute.

Federal Foreign Office g-8.de. Homepage of G8 Summit in Heiligendamm, Germany, available at http://g-8.de/Webs/G8/DE/Homepage/home.html, accessed 22 September 2015.

Federal Foreign Office (2008) 17. Forum Globale Fragen am 13. und 14. Juni 2007 im Auswärtigen Amt. Sicherheitsrisiko Klimawandel, available at www.auswaertiges-amt.de/DE/Aussenpolitik/GlobaleFragen/ForumGF/17-GF/17GF_node.html, accessed 5 September 2015.

References

Federal Foreign Office (2015) Climate and Security, available at www.auswaertiges-amt.de/EN/Aussenpolitik/GlobaleFragen/Klima/KlimaUndSicherheit_node.html, accessed 5 September 2015.

Feindt, P. (2002) 'Gemeinsam gegen Niemanden. Nachhaltigkeitsdiskurs in Deutschland', *Forschungsjournal Neue Soziale Bewegungen* 15(4): 20–29.

FEMA (2012) *Crisis Response and Disaster Resilience 2030: Forging Strategic Action in an Age of Uncertainty.* Washington, D.C.

Fincham, M.W. (2014) The Day before Yesterday: When Abrupt Climate Change Came to the Chesapeake Bay, available at https://www.climate.gov/news-features/features/day-yesterday-when-abrupt-climate-change-came-chesapeake-bay, accessed 18 August 2015.

Fingar, T. (2008) *National Intelligence Assessment on the National Security Implications of Global Climate Change to 2030.* Washington, D.C.

Finnemore, M. and Sikkink, K. (1998) 'International Norm Dynamics and Political Change', *International Organization* 52(4): 887–917.

Fischer, F. (2014) 'Climate Crisis and Ecological Democracy'. Workshop on 'Environment, Energy, Climate'. Free University, Berlin.

Fletcher, A.L. (2009) 'Clearing the Air: The Contribution of Frame Analysis to Understanding Climate Policy in the United States', *Environmental Politics* 18(5): 800–816.

Floyd, R. (2007a) 'Human Security and the Copenhagen School's Securitization Approach:. Conceptualizing Human Security as a Securitizing Move', *Human Security Journal* 5: 38–49.

Floyd, R. (2007b) 'Towards a Consequentialist Evaluation of Security: Bringing Together the Copenhagen and the Welsh Schools of Security Studies', *Review of International Studies* 33(2): 327–350.

Floyd, R. (2010) *Security and the Environment. Securitisation Theory and US Environmental Security Policy,* Cambridge: Cambridge University Press.

Floyd, R. (2011) 'Can Securitization Theory be Used in Normative Analysis? Towards a Just Securitization Theory', *Security Dialogue* 42(4–5): 427–439.

Floyd, R. (2013) 'Whither Environmental Security Studies? An Afterword', in R. Floyd and R.A. Matthew (eds) *Environmental Security. Approaches and Issues.* Abingdon and New York: Routledge, pp. 279–297.

Focus Online (n.d.) 'Es kostet nicht die Welt, den Planeten zu retten'. UN-Weltklimarats-Bericht, available at www.focus.de/wissen/un-weltklimarat-stellt-wege-der-treibhausgasminderung-vor_id_3768067.html, accessed 22 September 2015.

Focus Online (2013) Berlin verhindert CO2-Kompromiss: Die Auto-Kanzlerin tritt auf die Klimaschutz-Bremse, available at www.focus.de/politik/deutschland/berlin-verhindert-co2-kompromiss-die-auto-kanzlerin-tritt-auf-die-klimaschutz-bremse_aid_1028513.html, accessed 7 January 2014.

Foley, C. (2012) *Military Basing and Climate Change.* Washington, D.C.

Foley, C. and Holland, A. (2012a) *Climate Security Report: Part One, Climate Change and Security.* Washington, D.C.

Foley, C. and Holland, A. (2012b) *Climate Security Report: Part Three, Climate Change and the Homeland.* Washington, D.C.

Foley, C. and Holland, A. (2012c) *Climate Security Report: Part Two, Climate Change and Global Security.* Washington, D.C.

Forbes México (2015) 'Combatir cambio climático beneficia economía: Felipe Calderón', *Forbes México*, 3 September.
Frankfurter Rundschau (2015) 'Das Radeln mit dem Hilfsmotor boomt. E-Bikes', 13 August.
Friedrich, S. (2010) 'Chancen zur Umsetzung einer effektiven Klimapolitik in Mexiko', in H.M. Calderón and U. Tietz (eds) *Klimapolitik in Lateinamerika*. Berlin: Berliner Debatte Initial, pp. 55–59.
Fritzsche, K. and Ruettinger, L. (2013) *Environment, Climate Change and Security in the Southern Mediterranean. Literature Review*, Berlin.
Fuhr, L. (2008) Steinmeier zu Klimawandel und Sicherheit. Klima der Gerechtigkeit Blog, available at http://klima-der-gerechtigkeit.boellblog.org, accessed 1 September 2014.
Gallup (2014) Confidence in Institutions, available at www.gallup.com/poll/1597/confidence-institutions.aspx, accessed 25 August 2014.
Ganseforth, M. (1996) 'Politische Umsetzung der Empfehlungen der beiden Klima-Enquête-Kommissionen (1987–1994): eine Bewertung', in H.G. Brauch (ed.) *Klimapolitik. Naturwissenschaftliche Grundlagen, internationale Regimebildung und Konflikte, ökonomische Analysen sowie nationale Problemerkennung und Politikumsetzung*, Berlin and Heidelberg: Springer, pp. 215–224.
Gaufman, E. (2015) 'Enemies at the Gates: Threat Narratives in Putin's Russia'. Doctoral thesis, Eberhard Karls University, Tübingen.
GDV (2012) *Auswirkungen des Klimawandels auf die Schadensituation in der deutschen Versicherungswirtschaft. Kurzfassung Hochwasser*. Studie im Auftrag des Gesamtverbandes der Deutschen Versicherungswirtschaft e. V.
Germanwatch (2006) *Beckett: Berliner Grundsatzrede zu Klimasicherheit*. Bonn.
Germanwatch (2013) *Auf der Flucht vor dem Klima*. Bonn.
Germanwatch (2014) *Global Climate Risk Index 2015. Who Suffers Most From Extreme Weather Events? Weather-related Loss Events in 2013 an 1994 to 2013*. Bonn: Germanwatch Nord-Süd Initiative e.V.
Germanwatch, Amnesty International, Brot für die Welt, Deutsche Gesellschaft für die Vereinten Nationen, Oxfam, Pro Asyl, and Welthungerhilfe (2013) Auf der Flucht vor dem Klima, available at https://germanwatch.org/de/download/7343.pdf, accessed 2 September 2015.
Germanwatch and CAN (2015) The Climate Change Performance Index. Results 2015, available at https://germanwatch.org/en/download/10407.pdf.
Gieler, W. and Çetinyılmaz, H. (2015) *Die Klimapolitik der Türkei zwischen Anspruch und Wirklichkeit*, Berlin: LIT.
Giroux, H.A. (2006) 'Reading Hurricane Katrina: Race, Class, and the Biopolitics of Disposability', *College Literature* 33(3): 171–196.
Gleditsch, N.P. (ed.) *1997: Conflict and Environment*, Dordrecht: Kluwer Academic Publishers.
Gleditsch, N.P. (2012) 'Whither the Weather? Climate Change and Conflict', *Journal of Peace Research* 49(1): 3–9.
Goede, M. de (2008) 'Beyond Risk: Premediation and the Post-9/11 Security Imagination', *Security Dialogue* 39(2–3): 155–176.
González, I. (2012) 'Calderón dice que modelo económico es insostenible', *Excelsior*, 24 March.

Goodman, S.W. (2014) Testimony Before the U.S. Senate Budget Committee: The Cost of Inaction: The Economic and Budgetary Consequences of Climate Change. Washington, D.C.

Gore, A.A. (2007) Nobel Peace Prize Lecture. Oslo.

Greenpeace (2007) *Klimaflüchtlinge. Die verleugnete Katastrophe.* Hamburg.

Greenpeace México (2010) *México ante el cambio climático. Evidencias, impactos, vulnerabilidad y adaptación.* Mexico City.

Greenpeace USA (2011) *Koch Industries: Still Fueling Climate Denial. 2011 Update.* Washington, D.C.

Grundmann, R. (2007) 'Climate Change and Knowledge Politics', *Environmental Politics* 16(3): 414–432.

Grundmann, R. and Scott, M. (2014) 'Disputed Climate Science in the Media: Do Countries Matter?', *Public Understanding of Science* 23(2): 220–235.

GTZ (2008a) *Klimawandel und Sicherheit. Herausforderungen für die deutsche Entwicklungszusammenarbeit.* Eschborn.

GTZ (2008b) *Klimawandel und Sicherheit. Herausforderungen für die deutsche Entwicklungszusammenarbeit.* Eschborn.

Guber, D.L. and Bosso, C.J. (2013) '"High Hopes and Bitter Disappointment": Public Discourse and the Limits of the Environmental Movement in Climate Change Politics', in N.J. Vig and M.E. Kraft (eds) *Environmental Policy. New Directions for the Twenty-First Century,* Thousand Oaks, CA: CQ Press, pp. 54–82.

Guzzini, S. (2011) 'Securitization as a Causal Mechanism', *Security Dialogue* 42(4–5): 329–342.

Hameiri, S. (2008) 'Risk Management, Neo-Liberalism and the Securitisation of the Australian Aid Program', *Australian Journal of International Affairs* 62(3): 357–371.

Hannover Re (2013) Climate Change. Information, available at https://www.hannover-re.com/180650/climate-change-2013.pdf, accessed 26 September 2015.

Hänsel, H. (2010) *Stenographischer Bericht – 17068–7302, Deutscher Bundestag – 17. Wahlperiode – 68. Sitzung, 28.10.2010.* Berlin.

Harmeling, S., Bals, C., Cuntz, C., Grießhaber, L., Junghans, L., Kaloga, A.O., Kreft, S., Rommeney, D., Schwarz, R., Treber, M., Warner, K. and Zissener, M. (2012) *Der Gipfel von Doha: Aufbruch ohne Rückenwind. Anaylse der UN-Klimagipfels 2012.* Bonn, Berlin.

Harris, P.G. (2000a) 'Climate Change and Foreign Policy. An Introduction', in P.G. Harris (ed.) *Climate Change and American Foreign Policy,* New York: St. Martin's Press, pp. 3–25.

Harris, P.G. (2000b) 'Climate Change: Is the United States Sharing the Burden?', in P.G. Harris (ed.) *Climate Change and American Foreign Policy,* New York: St. Martin's Press, pp. 29–49.

Harris, P.G. (2001) 'International Environmental Affairs and U.S. Foreign Policy', in P.G. Harris (ed.) *The Environment, International Relations, and U.S. Foreign Policy,* Washington, D.C.: Georgetown University Press, pp. 3–41.

Harris, P.G. (2002) 'Environmental Security: Will Bush Follow Clinton's Lead?', *Pacifica Review: Peace, Security and Global Change* 14(2): 149–157.

Harrison, N.E. (2000) 'From the Inside Out: Domestic Influences on Global Environmental Policy', in P.G. Harris (ed.) *Climate Change and American Foreign Policy,* New York: St. Martin's Press, pp. 89–109.

Hartmann, B. (2009) *Lines in the Shifting Sand. The Strategic Politics of Climate Change, Human Security and National Defense.* Oslo.

Hartmann, B. (2010) 'Rethinking Climate Refugees and Climate Conflict: Rhetoric, Reality and the Politics of Policy Discourse', *Journal of International Development* 22(2): 233–246.
Hayes, J. and Knox-Hayes, J. (2014) 'Security in Climate Change Discourse. Analyzing the Divergence between US and EU Approaches to Policy', *Global Environmental Politics* 14(2): 82–101.
Hernández Díaz, J.I. (2009) 'Inestabilidad social y sequía en México', *Reforma*, 4 October.
Heyer, C. and Liening, S. (2004) *Enquete Kommissionen des Deutschen Bundestags. Schnittstellen zwischen Politik und Wirtschaft*. Berlin.
Hirsch, T. and Lottje, C. (2009) *Deepening the Food Crisis? Climate Change, Food Security and the Right to Food*, Stuttgart.
HM Government (2010) A Strong Britain in an Age of Uncertainty. The National Security Strategy, available at https://www.gov.uk/government/uploads/system/uploads/attachment_data/file/61936/national-security-strategy.pdf, accessed 21 September 2015.
Höhne, N., Moltmann, S., Hagemann, M., Fekete, H., Grözinger, J., Schüler, V., Vieweg, M., Hare, B., Schaeffer, M. and Rocha, M. (2012) *Climate Action Tracker Mexico. Assessment of Mexico's Policies Impacting its Greenhouse Gas Emissions Profile*. Potsdam.
Holzscheiter, A. (2005) 'Discourse as Capability. Non-State Actors' Capital in Global Governance', *Millennium – Journal of International Studies* 33(3): 723–746.
Homer-Dixon, T. (1991) 'On the Threshold: Environmental Changes as Causes of Acute Conflict', *International Security* 16(2): 76–116.
Homer-Dixon, T. (1994) 'Environmental Scarcities and Violent Conflict: Evidence from Cases', *International Security* 19(2): 233–246.
Homer-Dixon, T. (1999) *Environment, Scarcity and Violence*, Princeton, NJ: Princeton University Press.
Höppe, P. (2008) 'Naturgefahren und Klimawandel. Die Rolle der Versicherungswirtschaft', *Vierteljahrshefte zur Wirtschaftsforschung* 77(4): 110–115.
Howard, P. and Homer-Dixon, T. (1996) *Environmental Scarcity and Violent Conflict: The Case of Chiapas, Mexico*. Toronto: Project on Environment, Population and Security, American Association for the Advancement of Science and the University of Toronto.
Huebert, R., Exner-Pirot, H., Lajeunesse, A. and Gulledge, J. (2012) *Climate Change and International Security: The Arctic as a Bellwether*, Arlington, VA.
Hürriyet (2010a) 'New Edition of Turkish Red Book Shapes New Security Spheres', *Hürriyet*, 28 October.
Hürriyet (2010b) 'New Edition of Turkish Red Book Approved in Cabinet', *Hürriyet*, 23 November.
Hürriyet (2012) 'Genelkurmay SAREM'i kapattı', *Hürriyet*, 20 January.
Hürriyet (2013) 'Bakan Yıldız: Dünyayı kim kirlettiyse o temizlesin', *Hürriyet*, 16 October.
Hürriyet (2014) 'Cumhurbaşkanı Erdoğan İklim Zirvesi'nde konuştu', *Hürriyet*, 23 September.
Hürriyet (2015) 'Org. Özel Savunma ve Havacılık Dergisi'ne konuştu', *Hürriyet*, 25 March.
Huysmans, J. (2004) 'Minding Exceptions: The Politics of Insecurity and Liberal Democracy', *Contemporary Political Theory* 3(3): 321–341.
Huysmans, J. (2008) *The Politics of Insecurity. Fear, Migration and Asylum in the EU*, London: Routledge.
Huysmans, J. (2011) 'What's in an Act? On Security Speech Acts and Little Security Nothings', *Security Dialogue* 42(4–5): 371–383.

References

IASS (n.d.) Institute for Advanced Sustainability Studies, available at www.iass-potsdam.de/de/institut/die-idee.

IBB (2011) 'İstanbul Büyükşehir. BelediyesiABD'de büyük ilgi gören İklim Değişikliği Sergisi İstanbul'da', 1 October.

ICCG (2014) TTmap, a Worldwide Observatory on Climate Think Tanks, available at www.thinktankmap.org/default.aspx?, accessed 4 September 2015.

IEA (2012) *World Energy Outlook 2012. Zusammenfassung. German Translation*. Paris.

İklim Ağı (2012) *İklim değişiyor, Türkiye değişmiyor – Türkiye çözüme gerçekten ortak olsun*. Greenpeace Akdeniz (Turkey); available at www.greenpeace.org/turkey/Global/turkey/report/2012/11/Türkiye'nin%20İklim%20Karnesi.pdf.

Institute for Environmental Security (2015) Adelphi Research, available at www.envirosecurity.org/actionguide/view.php?r=118&m=organisations, accessed 5 September 2015.

Interview (2014a) Interview on climate change and security with two think tank representatives in Istanbul, 17.10.2014.

Interview (2014b) Interview with an NGO representative on climate change and security on 10.09.2014, 11.00 in Istanbul.

Interview (2014c) Interview on climate change and security with NGO experts in Mexico City, 03.04.2014.

Interview (2014d) Interview on climate change and security with NGO experts in Mexico City, 07.04.2014.

Interview (2014e) Interview on climate change and security with NGO experts in Mexico City, 08.04.2014.

Interview (2014f) Interview on climate change and security with NGO experts in Mexico City, 09.04.2014.

Interview (2014g) Interview on climate change and security with government officials in Mexico City, 14.04.2014.

Interview (2014h) Interview on climate change and security with government officials in Mexico City, 15.04.2014.

Interview (2014i) Interview on climate change and security with government officials in Mexico City, 21.04.2014.

Interview (2014j) Interview on climate change and security with an NGO representative in Essen, 23.04.2014. Essen.

Interview (2014k) Interview on climate change and security with NGO experts in Mexico City, 23.04.2014.

Interview (2014l) Interview on climate change and security with government officials in Mexico City, 24.04.2014.

Interview (2014m) Interview with an environmental activist, NGO representative and founding member of the Green Party in Berlin, 25.04.2014.

Interview (2014n) Interview with an NGO expert on climate change, security and development plicies, Bonn, 02.05.2014.

Interview (2014o) Interview with an NGO representative, 05.05.2014. Berlin.

Interview (2014p) Interview on climate change and security with think tank experts in Washington, D.C., 06.05.2014.

Interview (2014q) Interview on climate change and security with think tank expert in Washington, D.C., Center for Climate and Security, Frank Femia, 06.05.2014.

Interview (2014r) Interview on climate change and security with think tank experts in Washington, D.C., 08.05.2014.

Interview (2014s) Interview on climate change and security with think tank experts in Washington, D.C., 08.05.2014.
Interview (2014t) Interview on climate change and security with think tank experts in Washington, D.C., 12.05.2014.
Interview (2014u) Interview on climate change and security with think tank experts in Washington, D.C., 13.05.2014.
Interview (2014v) Interview on climate change and security with think tank experts in Washington, D.C., 14.05.2014.
Interview (2014w) Interview on climate change and security with NGO experts in Washington, D.C., 16.05.2014.
Interview (2014x) Interview on climate change and security with government officials in Washington, D.C., 27.05.2014.
Interview (2014y) Interview on climate change and security with government officials in Washington, D.C., 28.05.2014.
Interview (2014z) Interview on climate change and security with think tank experts in Washington, D.C., 28.05.2014.
Interview (2014aa) Interview on climate change and security with government officials in Washington, D.C., 30.05.2014.
Interview (2014ab) Interview on climate change and security with think tank experts in Washington, D.C., 03.06.2014.
Interview (2014ac) Interview on climate change and security with think tank experts in Washington, D.C., Center for American Progress, Michael Werz and Max Hoffmann, 03.06.2014.
Interview (2014ad) Interview with a climate security expert of the Federal Armed Forces and NGO representative, 25.06.2014.
Interview (2014ae) Interview with an NGO representative and general of the Federal Armed Forces, Berlin, 06.07.2014.
Interview (2014af) Interview with a journalist and diplomatic correspondent of *Die Zeit*, Berlin, 23.07.2014.
Interview (2014ag) Interview with a representative of a humanitarian aid organisation, Berlin, 23.07.2014.
Interview (2014ah) Interview with an NGO representative, Berlin, 23.07.2014.
Interview (2014ai) Interview with an IPCC representative, Bonn, 31.07.2014.
Interview (2014aj) Interview with an NGO representative in Istanbul, 27.08.2014.
Interview (2014ak) Interview with a scientist on climate change and security in Istanbul, 10.09.2014.
Interview (2014al) Interview with a scientist, Istanbul, 10.09.2014.
Interview (2014am) Interview with NGO representatives on climate change and security in Ankara, 16.09.2014.
Interview (2014an) Interview with a NGO representative on climate change and security on 17.09.2014 in Ankara.
Interview (2014ao) Interview with representatives of UNDP Turkey in Ankara, 18.09.2014.
Interview (2014ap) Interview with a scientist and expert on climate change and security in Mannheim, 07.10.2014.
Interview (2014aq) Interview with an NGO representative on climate change and security, 16.10.2014 in Istanbul.
Interview (2014ar) Interview on climate change and security with NGO experts in London, 17.10.2014.

Interview (2014as) Interview on climate change and security with a think tank representative in Berlin, 12.11.2014; 15.00.
Interview (2015a) Interview with retired general Nejat Eslen on climate change and security in Bodrum, 06.09.2015.
Interview (2015b) Interview on climate change and security with a German government official in Berlin, 09.01.2015.
Interview (2015c) Interview with a representative of the Federal Foreign Office on climate change and security, 09.01.2015. Berlin.
Interview (2015d) Interview with an NGO representative on climate change and security. Bonn, 19.01.2015.
Interview (2015e) Interview with an expert on peace and conflict studies, Hamburg, 29.04.2015.
IPC (2015a) 'Climate Change and Security in Turkey: Challenges and Opportunities – Turkish–German Expert Roundtable'. Co-organized by the Faculty of Economics, Administrative and Social Sciences, Bilkent University; Istanbul Policy Center–Sabanci University–Mercator Foundation Initiative; IOM Office Turkey; supported by the Embassy of the Federal Republic of Germany. Ankara.
IPC (2015b) 'Climate Security Roundtable'. Presentation of an expert on water and security at the IPC Climate Security Roundtable, Ankara.
IPCC (2007a) 'Climate Change 2007: Impacts, Adaptation and Vulnerability'. Contribution of Working Group II to the Fourth Assessment Report of the Intergovernmental Panel on Climate Change. Cambridge.
IPCC (2007b) *Working Group II, Impacts, Adaptation and Vulnerability Special Report Managing the Risks of Extreme Events and Disasters to Advance Climate Change Adaptation.* New York.
İzci, R. (2013) 'Turkey's Approach to Environmental Security', in E. Canan-Sokullu (ed.) *Debating Security in Turkey. Challenges and Changes in the Twenty-First Century,* Lanham, MD: Lexington Books, pp. 249–270.
Jäger, C.C. and Jäger, J. (2010) 'Warum zwei Grad?', *APuZ (Aus Politik und Zeitgeschichte)* 32–33.
Jagers, S., Paterson, M. and Stripple, J. (2004) 'Privatising Governance, Practising Triage: Securitization of Insurance Risks and the Politics of Global Warming', in D. Levy and P. Newell (eds) *Business in International Environmental Politics: A Political Economy Approach,* Cambridge, MA: MIT Press, pp. 249–274.
Jänicke, M. (2001) Ökologische Modernisierung als Innovation und Diffusion in Politik und Technik. Möglichkeiten und Grenzen eines Konzepts, available at http://edocs.fu-berlin.de/docs/servlets/MCRFileNodeServlet/FUDOCS_derivate_000000001451/rep_00-01.pdf.
Jänicke, M. (2009) Geschichte der deutschen Umweltpolitik, available at www.bpb.de/gesellschaft/umwelt/dossier-umwelt/61136/geschichte?p=all, accessed 16 October 2013.
Jänicke, M. and Jacob, K. (eds) (2006) *Environmental Governance in Global Perspective: New Approaches to Ecological and Political Modernization,* Berlin: Freie Universität Berlin.
Jensen, A. (2009) Umweltpolitik, available at www.bpb.de/gesellschaft/umwelt/dossier-umwelt/61177/umweltpolitik?p=all, accessed 16 October 2013.
Jungehülsing, J. (2010) *Las que se van, las que se quedan: reacciones frente al cambio climático. Un estudio de caso sobre migración y género en Chiapas,* Mexico City.

178 References

Kadıoğlu, M. (2012a) Türkiye'de İklim Değişikliği Risk Yönetimi, available at www.undp. org/content/dam/turkey/docs/projectdocuments/EnvSust/UNDP-TR-Iklim_ Degisikligi_Risk_Yonetimi.pdf, accessed 19 September 2015.

Kadıoğlu, M. (2012b) 'Tek ve yeni yol risk yönetimi', *Hürriyet*, 8 October.

Kaim, M. (2008) *Die sicherheitspolitischen Folgen des Klimawandels. Kanada und die Frage der arktischen Souveränität*, Berlin.

Kaim, M. (2010) 'Die sicherheitspolitischen Folgen des Klimawandels: Kanada und die Frage arktischer Souveränität', *Zeitschrift für Politikwissenschaft* 20(1): 89–108.

Kaplan, R. (1994) 'The Coming Anarchy: How Scarcity, Crime, Overpopulation, Tribalism, and Disease are Rapidly Destroying the Social Fabric of our Planet', *Atlantic Monthly* 273(2): 44–76.

Karafoulidis, T. (2012) 'Audience: A Weak Link in the Securitization of the Environment?', in J. Scheffran, M. Brzoska, H.G. Brauch, P.M. Link and J. Schilling (eds) *Climate Change, Human Security and Violent Conflict*, Berlin and Heidelberg: Springer, pp. 259–272.

Karakaya, E. and Berberoğlu, N. (2007) 'Turkey Approaching the Kyoto Protocol?', *Joint Implementation Quarterly* (July).

Kellerhoff, S.F. (2010) 'Die Grünen waren schon 1990 die "Dagegen-Partei"', *Die Welt*, 2 December.

Kibaroğlu, A. (n.d.) Özgeçmiş ve Eserler Listesi, available at www.mef.edu.tr/icerikler/ files/cvler/iibf/aysegul_kibaroglu.pdf, accessed 26 September 2015.

Kibaroğlu, A. (1996) *Prospects for Cooperation in the Euphrates–Tigris River Basin*, Amsterdam: Het Spinhuis.

King, M.D. and Gulledge, J. (2013) 'The Climate Change and Energy Security Nexus', *Fletcher Forum of World Affairs* 37(2): 25–44.

Kingdon, J.W. (1984) *Agendas, Alternatives, and Public Policies*, Boston: Little, Brown.

Kirstein, W. (2013) Die Klimakatastrophe von 1986 und was daraus wurde. Ein kritischer Rückblick zum Klimawandel, available at www.eike-klima-energie.eu/climategate-anzeige/die-klimakatastrophe-von-1986-und-was-daraus-wurde-ein-kritischer-rueckblick-zum-klimawandel/, accessed 28 August 2015.

Knebel, J., Michael, G., Wicke, L. and Zickert, K. (1999) *Selbstverpflichtungen und normersetzende Umweltverträge als Instrumente des Umweltschutzes. Forschungsbericht 29618081; UBA-FB 98-123*, Berlin: Schmidt.

KOSKI (2007) *Küresel İklim değişikliği ve cevresel etkileri. Uluslararası Küresel İklim Değişikliği ve Çevresel Etkileri Konferansı Bildiriler Kitabi*. Konya: Konya Büyükşehir Belediyesi.

Kraft, M.E. (2013) 'Environmental Policy in Congress', in N.J. Vig and M.E. Kraft (eds) *Environmental Policy. New Directions for the Twenty-First Century*, Thousand Oaks, CA: CQ Press, pp. 109–134.

Krause, K. and Williams, M.C. (1996) 'Broadening the Agenda of Security Studies: Politics and Methods', *Mershon International Studies Review* 40(2): 229–254.

Krellenberg, K. (2013) 'İstanbul, Climate Change and How to Respond', *Yeşil Gazete*, 27 August.

Krück, C., Borchers, J. and Weingart, P. (1999) 'Climate Research and Climate Policy in Germany: Assets and Hazards of Consensus-Based Risk Management', in P. Edwards and C. Miller (eds) *Changing the Atmosphere*, Cambridge, MA: MIT Press.

Kuckartz, U., Rheingans-Heintze, A. and Rädiker, S. (2006) *Umweltbewusstsein in Deutschland. Klimawandel aus der Sicht der deutschen Bevölkerung*. UBA-Studie 2006. Berlin: Bundesministerium für Umwelt, Naturschutz und Reaktorsicherheit (BMU).

Kueter, J. (2012) *Climate and National Security: Exploring the Connection,* Washington, D.C.
Kulke, U. (2013) 'Propheten der Katastrophe machen gute Geschäfte. Der Rückversicherer Munich Re warnt seit Jahren vor den Folgen des klimawandels – und verdient zugleich prächtig an der Furcht der Menschen vor Wetter- und Klimakatastrophen', *Die Welt,* 19 November 2015, available at www.welt.de/wirtschaft/article122034211/Propheten-der-Katastrophe-machen-gute-Geschaefte.html.
Kuloğlu, A. (2009) 'Küresel iklim değişikliğine ilişkin güvenlik algılamaları ve Türkiye', *Ortadoğu Analiz* 1(7–8): 80–85.
La Jornada (2008) 'Provocará el cambio climático 250 millones de refugiados ambientales para 2015: expertos', *La Jornada,* 7 November.
La Jornada (2009) 'El cambio climático global, tema de seguridad nacional para México y Centroamérica', *La Jornada,* 12 November.
Laclau, E. and Mouffe, C. (1985) *Hegemony and Socialist Strategy. Towards a Radical Democratic Politics,* London: Verso.
Langenohl, A. (2008) 'How to Change Other People's Institutions. Discursive Entrepreneurship and the Boundary Object of Competition/Competitiveness in the German Banking Sector', *Economy and Society* 37(1): 68–93.
Leggett, J. and Lattanzio, R. (2009) *Status of the Copenhagen Climate Change Negotiations.*
Leiserowitz, A. (2005) 'American Risk Perceptions: Is Climate Change Dangerous?', *Risk Analysis* 25(6): 1433–1442.
Léonard, S. and Kaunert, C. (2011) 'Reconceptualizing the Audience in Securitzation Theory', in T. Balzacq (ed.) *Securitization Theory. How Security Problems Emerge and Dissolve,* London: Routledge.
Levy, M.A. (1995) 'Is the Environment a National Security Issue?', *International Security* 20(2): 35–62.
Litfin, K.T. (1994) *Ozone Discourses: Science and Politics in Global Environmental Cooperation,* New York: Columbia University Press.
Lobo-Guerrero, L. (2007) 'Biopolitics of Specialist Risk: Kidnap and Ransom Insurance', *Security Dialogue* 38(3): 315–334.
Luege Tamargo, J.L. (2010) 'Colaborador Invitado / Agua y cambio climático', *Reforma,* 1 December.
Lütfi-Şen, Ö. (2013a) A Holistic View of Climate Change and Its Impacts in Turkey, available at http://ipc.sabanciuniv.edu/en/wp-content/uploads/2012/09/A-Holistic-View-of-Climate-Change-and-Its-Impacts-in-Turkey.pdf, accessed 22 July 2015.
Lütfi-Şen, Ö. (2013b) *Media Coverage of Climate Change in Turkey. The World Versus Turkey.* IPC-Mercator Policy Brief, June.
Lütfi-Şen, Ö. (2013c) *A Holistic View of Climate Change and Its Impacts in Turkey.* Mercator-IPC Report, SU-Istanbul.
Maas, A., Daussa, R. and Kutonova, T. (2011) *Climate Change and Food Security in Eastern Europe.* Scenario report. Berlin: Adelphi.
Maas, A. and Tänzler, D. (2009) *Regional Security Implications of Climate Change. A Synopsis.* Conducted for DG External Relations of the European Commission under a contract for the German Ministry for the Environment, Nature Protection and Nuclear Safety. Berlin: Adelphi.
Madra, Ö. (2013) *Anlatılan, bizim hikayemiz.* Açık Radyo.
Madra, Ö. (2015) 'Gezi'nin sihrini bilseydik çoktan şişelemiştik … Açık Radyo Genel Yayın Yönetmeni Ömer Madra, yazar ve aktivist Naomi Klein ile yeni kitabı İşte Bu Her Şeyi Değiştirir üzerine Cumhuriyet Sokak için konuştu.', *Cumhuriyet,* 31 May.

Madra, Ö. and Şahin, Ü. (2007) *Küresel Isınma ve İklim Krizi – niçin daha fazla bekleyemeyiz*. Agora Kitaplığı.
Masquelier, A. (2006) 'Why Katrina's Victims Aren't Refugees: Musings on a "Dirty" Word', *American Anthropologist* 108(4): 735–743.
Mathews, J.T. (1989) 'Redefining Security', *Foreign Affairs* 68(2): 162–177.
Matthew, R.A. (2013) 'Environmental Security', in N.J. Vig and M.E. Kraft (eds) *Environmental Policy. New Directions for the Twenty-First Century*, Thousand Oaks, CA: CQ Press, pp. 344–368.
Mauelshagen, F. (2009) 'Die Klimakatastrophe. Szenen und Szenarien', in G.J. Schenk (ed.) *Katastrophen. Vom Untergang Pompejis bis zum Klimawandel*, Ostfildern, Germany: Thorbecke, pp. 205–223.
Maull, H.W. (1993) 'Zivilmacht Bundesrepublik? Das Neue Deutschland in der Internationalen Politik', *Blätter für deutsche und internationale Politik* 38(8): 934–948.
McCright, A. and Dunlap, R.E. (2011) 'The Politicization of Climate Change and Polarization in the American Public's View of Global Warming, 2001–2010', *The Sociological Quarterly* 52: 155–194.
McDonald, M. (2008) 'Securitization and the Construction of Security', *European Journal of International Relations* 14(4): 563–587.
McDonald, M. (2013) 'Discourses of Climate Security', *Political Geography* 33: 42–51.
McGrady, E., Kingsley, M. and Steward, J. (2010) *Climate Change: Potential Effects on Demands for US Military Humanitarian Assistance and Disaster Response*, Alexandria, VA: Center for Naval Analysis.
MCII (n.d.) Munich Climate Insurance Initiative: Who We Are, available at www.climate-insurance.org/front_content.php?idcat=876, accessed 5 September 2015.
MDG Achievement Fund (2010) *MDG–F1680 Enhancing the Capacity of Turkey to Adapt to Climate Change. 1 MDG–F1680 Enhancing the Capacity of Turkey to Adapt to Climate Change, Erciyes Mountain from Sultan Marshes, Kayseri 2. Climate Change Impacts On Turkey*. Ankara.
Meadows, D.L. and Meadows, D.H. (1972) *Die Grenzen des Wachstums. Bericht des Club of Rome zur Lage der Menschheit*, Stuttgart: Deutsche Verlags-Anstalt.
Mederake, L. and Duwe, M. (2014) *Einfluss globaler Themen auf die deutsche Umweltpolitikforschung. Ecologic*. Berlin: Ecologic Institut.
Melillo, J.M., Richmond, Terese, T.C. and Yohe, G.W. (2014) *Climate Change Impacts in the United States: The Third National Climate Assessment*. Washington, D.C.
Mercator Stiftung (2014) '*Es kostet nicht die Welt, den Planeten zu retten*'. Anlässlich der ersten öffentlichen Präsentation des Berichtes sprechen hochrangige Vertreter des Weltklimarates und der deutsche Bundeswirtschaftsminister an der TU Berlin. Press Release.
Met Office (2011) *Climate: Observations, Projections and Impacts. Turkey*. Devon, UK.
Methmann, C. and Oels, A. (2013) 'The Vulnerable Becoming Dangerous: Rethinking the History of Environmental Security from Conflict to Resilience', in C. Daase, G. Schlag and J. Junk (eds) *Dialogues on Security: Theoretical, Methodological, and Empirical Advances and Challenges*. London: Routledge.
Methmann, C. and Rothe, D. (2012) 'Politics for the Day after Tomorrow: The Logic of Apocalypse in Global Climate Politics', *Security Dialogue* 43(4): 323–344.
Mexican Government (2007) *Plan Nacional de Desarrollo 2007–2012* [National Development Plan 2007–2012]. Mexico City.
Mexican Government (2010) *Marco de Políticas de Adaptacíon de Mediano Plazo*. Mexico City.

Mexican Government (2012) *Mexico. México quinta comunicación nacional ante la Convención Marco de las Naciones Unidas sobre el Cambio Climático.* Fifth National Communication to the UNFCCC.

Mexican Government (2013) *Plan Nacional de Desarollo 2013–2018* [National Development Plan 2013–2018]. Mexico City.

Mexican Government (2014) *Programa para la Seguridad Nacional 2014–2018. Una política multidimensional para México en el siglo XXI.* Mexico City.

Mexican Government and CICC (2007) National Strategy on Climate Change (ENACC) Mexico. Executive Summary. Mexico City.

Mexican Government and CICC (2009) *Programa Especial de Cambio Climático 2009–2012 (PECC).* Mexico City.

Mexican Government, SEMERNAT and CICC (2013) *Estrategia Nacional de Cambio Climático (ENCC) visión 10-20-40.* Mexico City.

MFA (2015) *United Nations Framework on Climate Change and the Kyoto Protocol.* Ankara.

Mignone, B.K. (2007) *The National Security Dividend of Global Carbon Mitigation,* Washington, D.C.

Mildner, S.-A., Petersen, H. and Wodni, W. (2012) 'Klimaschutz bleibt Nebensache für die USA', *SWP Aktuell* 69 (November 2012).

Mildner, S.-A. and Richert, J. (2010) 'Obamas neue Klimapolitik. Möglichkeiten und Grenzen eines klimapolitischen Wandels in den USA', *SWP Studie,* Februar 2010.

Misereor (2008) Development and Climate Justice. Policy Paper. Brussels.

Mühlenhoff, H. (2015) 'Depoliticizing the Politicized? The Effects of the EU's Civil Society Funding in the Context of Hegemonic Struggles in Turkey'. Doctoral thesis, University of Tübingen.

Müller, F. (2003) *Kyoto-Protokoll ohne USA – wie weiter?* Berlin.

Mumme, S.P., Bath, C.R. and Assetto, V.J. (1988) 'Political Development and Environmental Policy in Mexico', *Latin American Research Review* 23(1): 7–34.

Mumme, S.P. and Lybecker, D. (2002) 'Environmental Capacity in Mexico: An Assessment', in H. Weidner, M. Jänicke and H. Jörgens (eds) *Capacity Building in National Environmental Policy. A Comparative Study of 17 Countries,* Berlin and New York: Springer, pp. 311–327.

MunichRe (2015) Berlin, G7-Initiative: Klimarisikoversicherung als Beitrag zur Anpassung an den Klimawandel. So bewertet Munich Re die Zwischenschritte hin zu einem neuen Klimaabkommen, available at www.munichre.com/de/group/focus/climate-change/viewpoints/road-to-paris/berlin/index.html, accessed 26 September 2015.

Munoz, C. (2012) 'Panetta Warns Climate Change Having "Dramatic Impact" on National Security', *The Hill,* 4 May.

Mustafa Sönmez (2013) 'Istanbul and Surroundings Lure almost Three Quarters of Migration', *Hürriyet Daily News,* 13 July.

Myers, N. (1989) 'Environment and Security', *Foreign Policy* 74: 23–41.

Myers, N. (1995) *Environmental Exodus: An Emergent Crisis in the Global Arena,* Washington, D.C.: The Climate Institute.

Myers, N. (2002) 'Environmental Refugees. A Growing Phenomenon of the 21st Century', *Philosophical Transaction of the Royal Society: Biological Sciences* 357(1420): 609–613.

National Academy of Sciences (1975) *Understanding Climatic Change. A Program for Action.* Washington, D.C.

National Academy of Sciences (1977) *Energy and Climate. Studies in Geophysics.* Washington, D.C.

National Research Council (2002) *Abrupt Climate Change. Inevitable Surprises.* Washington, D.C.: National Academies Press.

NATO Transformation Command (2007) *Future Security Environment.* Norfolk, VA.

ND-Gain (2015) Vulnerability in the Gain Index, available at http://index.gain.org/ranking/vulnerability, accessed 9 September 2015.

New York Times (2007) 'China Overtakes U.S. in Greenhouse Gas Emissions', *New York Times,* 20 June.

Nicola, S. (2013) 'World Emissions May Peak Amid China Green Push, Germanwatch Says', *Bloomberg Businessweek,* 18 November.

Norck, S. (2012) 'Der Klimawandel als medial konstruiertes Risiko – Untersucht am Beispiel der Berichterstattung des Nachrichtenmagazins Der Spiegel', *Entgrenzt – Studentische Zeitschrift für Geographisches,* no. 3, available at www.entgrenzt.de/ausgaben/entgrenzt-ausgabe-3/

Nordas, R. and Gleditsch, N.P. (2007) 'Climate Change and Conflict', *Political Geography* 26(6): 627–638.

Nordbeck, R. (2002) *Nachhaltigkeitsstrategien als politische Langfriststrategien: Innovationswirkungen und Restriktionen,* Berlin.

NTV (2007) Kadiköy'de Türkiye Kyoto'yu Imzala Mitingi, available at http://arsiv.ntv.com.tr/news/406621.asp?cp1=1, accessed 17 July 2015.

Obama, B. (2008) President-elect Barack Obama to Deliver Taped Greeting to Bi-partisan Governors Climate Summit, available at http://change.gov/newsroom/entry/president_elect_barack_obama_to_deliver_taped_greeting_to_bi_partisan_gover/, accessed 28 March 2013.

O'Brien, K., Eriksen, S., Nygaard, L.P. and Schjolden, A. (2007) 'Why Different Interpretations of Vulnerability Matter in Climate Change Discourses', *Climate Policy* 7(1): 73–88.

OECD (1993) OECD Environmental Performance Review Germany, available at www.oecd.org/env/country-reviews/2448059.pdf, accessed 21 October 2013.

OECD (2008) Environmental Performance Review. Turkey, available at www.oecd.org/env/country-reviews/environmentalperformancereviewsturkey2008.htm.

OECD (2012) OECD Economic Surveys Germany – February 2012, available at www.oecd.org/eco/49616833.pdf, accessed 21 October 2013.

Oels, A. (2011) 'Rendering Climate Change Governable by Risk: From Probability to Contingency', *Geoforum* (1): 1–13.

Oels, A. (2012a) 'From "Securitization" of Climate Change to "Climatization" of the Security Field: Comparing Three Theoretical Perspectives', in J. Scheffran, M. Brzoska, H.-G. Brauch, M.P. Link and J.P. Schilling (eds) *Climate Change, Human Security and Violent Conflict. Challenges for Societal Stability,* Berlin: Springer, pp. 185–205.

Oels, A. (2012b) 'The Securitization of Climate Change: Consequences and Policy Implications.', in J. Scheffran, M. Brzoska, H.-G. Brauch, M.P. Link and J.P. Schilling (eds) *Climate Change, Human Security and Violent Conflict. Challenges for Societal Stability,* Berlin: Springer, pp. 185–205.

Oels, A. (2013) 'Climate Security as Governmentality. From Precaution to Preparedness', in H. Bulkeley and J. Stripple (eds) *Governing the Global Climate: Rationality, Practice and Power,* Cambridge: Cambridge University Press, pp. 197–216.

Oels, A. and von Lucke, F. (2015) 'Gescheiterte Versicherheitlichung oder Sicherheit im Wandel: Hilft uns die Kopenhagener Schule beim Thema Klimawandel?', *Zeitschrift für Internationale Beziehungen* 22(1): 43–70.

ORSAM (2011) 'İklim Değişiminin Güvenlik Boyutu ve Ortadoğu'ya Etkileri' [The Security Dimension of Climate Change and Its Effects on the Middle East], *Ortadoğu Analiz* 26(3): 43–52.

Özer, E. (2015) 'Ömer Madra açık konuşuyor: Şakası yok, 35 yılımız kaldı', *Cumhuriyet*, 16 August.

Öztürk, Ö. (2012) *Climate Change Efforts of Turkey.* Ankara: REC (Regional Environmental Center).

Panorama (2015) Klimakatastrophe: Wie Deutschland daran verdienen will, available at http://daserste.ndr.de/panorama/archiv/2015/panorama5622.pdf, accessed 2 September 2015.

Park, J. (2000) 'Governing Climate Change Policy', in P.G. Harris (ed.) *Climate Change and American Foreign Policy,* New York: St. Martin's Press, pp. 73–87.

Parry, M.L., Canziani, O.F., Palutikof, J.P., van der Linden, P.J. and Hanson, C.E. (eds) (2007) *Climate Change 2007: Impacts, Adaptation and Vulnerability. Contribution of Working Group II to the Fourth Assessment Report of the Intergovernmental Panel on Climate Change,* Cambridge: Cambridge University Press.

Parsons, R.J. (2010) 'Climate Change: The Hottest Issue in Security Studies?', *Risk, Hazards and Crisis in Public Policy* 1(1): 84–113.

Parthermore, C. and Rogers, W. (2010) Promoting the Dialogue: Climate Change and the Quadrennial Defense Review, available at www.cnas.org/files/documents/publications/QDR&ClimateChange_Parthemore_Rogers_Jan2010_code406_workingpaper_2.pdf, accessed 14 March 2014.

Peters, E.D. and Maihold, G. (2007) 'Die Rolle Mexikos in der globalen Strukturpolitik', Discussion Paper, *Deutsches Institut für Entwicklungspolitik* 15.

Peterson, E.R. and Posner, R. (2008) Global Water Futures. A Roadmap for Future U.S. Policy, available at http://csis.org/files/media/csis/pubs/080915_peterson_globalwater-web.pdf, accessed 30 September 2015.

Pew Research Center (2011) Crime and Drug Cartels Top Concerns in Mexico. Fewer Than Half See Progress in Drug War, available at www.pewglobal.org/2011/08/31/crime-and-drug-cartels-top-concerns-in-mexico/, accessed 8 September 2015.

Pew Research Center (2012) Tough Stance on Iran Endorsed. Public Priorities: Deficit Rising, Terrorism Slipping, available at www.people-press.org/files/legacy-pdf/1-23-12%20Priorities%20Release.pdf, accessed 27 March 2013.

Pew Research Center (2015) Global Climate Change Seen as Top Global Threat, available at www.pewglobal.org/files/2015/07/Pew-Research-Center-Global-Threats-Report-FINAL-July-14-2015.pdf, accessed 27 July 2015.

Pielke Jr, R.A. (2000a) 'Policy History of the US Global Change Research Program: Part I. Administrative Development', *Global Environmental Change* 10: 9–25.

Pielke Jr, R.A. (2000b) 'Policy History of the US Global Change Research Program: Part II. Legislative process', *Global Environmental Change* 10: 133–144.

PIK Homepage of Prof. Dr. Ottmar Edenhofer, available at https://www.pik-potsdam.de/members/edenh/dr-edenhofers-homepage?set_language=de, accessed 22 September 2015.

PIK (n.d.) PIK in den Medien — PIK Research Portal, available at https://www.pik-potsdam.de/aktuelles/pik-in-den-medien, accessed 5 September 2015.

PIK (2007) Der Klimawandel. Einblicke, Rückblicke und Ausblicke, available at https://www.pik-potsdam.de/services/infothek/buecher_broschueren/.images/broschuere_cms_100.pdf, accessed 4 September 2015.

PIK (2013a) Porträt des Instituts, available at www.pik-potsdam.de/institut/index_html, accessed 9 December 2013.
PIK (2013b) Climate Scientist Schellnhuber to Brief UN Security Council, available at https://www.pik-potsdam.de/news/press-releases/archive/2013/climate-scientist-schellnhuber-to-brief-un-security-council, accessed 15 June 2015.
PIK (2015a) Members: Hans Joachim Schellnhuber. Brief biography, available at https://www.pik-potsdam.de/members/john/kurzbiographie, accessed 26 September 2015.
PIK (2015b) Organisation – PIK Research Portal, available at https://www.pik-potsdam.de/institut/organisation, accessed 4 September 2015.
Pirages, D. (1991) 'Social Evolution and Ecological Security', *Bulletin of Peace Proposals* 22(3): 329–334.
Pirages, D. (2005) 'From Limits to Growth to Ecological Security', in D. Pirages and K. Cousins (eds) *From Resource Scarcity to Ecological Security. Exploring new limits to growth*, Cambridge, MA: MIT Press, pp. 1–19.
Pirages, D. (2013) 'Ecological Security: A Conceptual Framework', in R. Floyd and R.A. Matthew (eds) *Environmental Security. Approaches and Issues,* Abingdon and New York: Routledge, pp. 139–154.
Platzeck, M., Decker, F., Dürr, T., Ness, K., Schellnhuber, H.J., Steinmeier, F.-W., Woidke, D., Machning, M., Hassa, R. and Hüttl, R. (2008) 'Energie und Klima. Wie eine strategische Energiepolitik für Brandenburg aussehen kann', *Perspektive 21 – Brandenburgische Hefte für Wissenschaft und Politik* 37.
Pope, H. (2012) 'Erdoğan's Decade', *Cairo Review* (4): 42–57.
Pulver, S. (2006) 'Climate Politics in Mexico in a North American Perspective'. Presented at 'Climate Change Politics in North America', Woodrow Wilson International Center for Scholars, Washington, D.C.
Quiroz, C. (2012) 'Felipe Calderón promulga Ley Federal de Cambio Climático', *Excelsior*, 5 June.
Radikal (2012) 'Askerin "beyni" durdu!", 20 January.
Radikal (2014) 'İstanbul "olağanüstü kurak". İstanbul barajlarında doluluk oranı yüzde 30'a geriledi', *Radikal*, 20 February.
REC (2005) Sowing the Seeds of Success. Achievements of REC 2004–2005, available at http://archive.rec.org/REC/Introduction/CountryOffices/achievements_recturkey04_05.pdf.
REC (2008a) 2005–2008 Activity Report of REC Turkey. The Turkish National Focal Point on UNFCCC Article 6 (Education, Training, Public Awareness), available at http://documents.rec.org/topic-areas/RECTR_UNFCCCArt6_2005_2008.pdf, accessed 7 August 2015.
REC (2008b) 2005–2008 Activity Reportof RECTurkey – The Turkish National Focal Point on UNFCCC Article 6. Education, Training, Public Awareness, available at http://documents.rec.org/topic-areas/RECTR_UNFCCCArt6_2005_2008.pdf, accessed 19 September 2015.
Reforma (2010) 'Urgen atacar cambio climático', *Reforma*, 16 October.
Resmi Gazete (1983) 'Çevre Kanunu; Kanun Numarası 2872'. *Resmi Gazete*, 11 August; 18132.
Reusswig, F. (2010) 'Klimawandel und Gesellschaft. Vom Katastrophen- zum Gestaltungsdiskurs im Horizont der postkarbonen Gesellschaft', in M. Voss (ed.) *Der Klimawandel,* Wiesbaden: VS Verlag für Sozialwissenschaften, pp. 75–97.

Reuveny, R. (2007) 'Climate Change-Induced Migration and Violent Conflict', *Political Geography* 26: 656–673.

Richert, J. (2009a) *Klimawandel und Sicherheit in der Amerikanischen Politik*, Berlin.

Richert, J. (2009b) 'Sicherheit und Stabilität im Kontext des Klimawandels', *SWP Diskussionspapier* 8(3).

Richert, J. (2011) 'Klimawandel, Bedrohungsdiskurs und Sicherheitspolitik in den USA', in S. Angenendt, S. Dröge and J. Richert (eds) *Klimawandel und Sicherheit. Herausforderungen, Reaktionen und Handlungsmöglichkeiten*, Baden-Baden: Nomos, pp. 222–237.

Richert, J. (2012) 'Klimapolitik und Versicherheitlichung', *Wissenschaft und Frieden* (3): 26–28.

Risse, T. (2004) 'Kontinuität durch Wandel. Eine "neue" deutsche Außenpolitik?', *APuZ (Aus Politik und Zeitgeschichte)* (11): 24–31.

Roe, P. (2008a) 'Actor, Audience(s) and Emergency Measures: Securitization and the UK's Decision to Invade Iraq', *Security Dialogue* 39(6): 615–635.

Roe, P. (2008b) 'The "Value" of Positive Security', *Review of International Studies* 34(4): 777–794.

Rogers, W. and Gulledge, J. (2010) Lost in Translation: Closing the Gap Between Climate Science and National Security Policy, available at www.cnas.org/files/documents/publications/Lost%20in%20Translation_Code406_Web_0.pdf, accessed 12 March 2014.

Rong, F. (2010) 'Understanding Developing Country Stances on Post-2012 Climate Change Negotiations. Comparative Analysis of Brazil, China, India, Mexico, and South Africa', *Energy Policy* 38(8): 4582–4591.

Rosenberg, S., Vedlitz, A., Cowman, D.F. and Zahran, S. (2010) 'Climate Change: A Profile of US Climate Scientists' Perspectives', *Climatic Change* 101(3–4): 311–329.

Ross, M.L. (2004) 'What Do We Know about Natural Resources and Civil War?', *Journal of Peace Research* 41(3): 337–356.

Roth, R. and Rucht, D. (eds) (2008) *Die sozialen Bewegungen in Deutschland seit 1945. Ein Handbuch*, Frankfurt and New York: Campus.

Rothe, D. (2016) *Securitizing Global Warming. A Climate of Complexity*, Abingdon, Oxon: Routledge.

Saavedra, D. (2010) 'Un futuro incierto', *Reforma*, 29 November.

Şahin, Ü. (2014) Türkiye'nin İklim Politikalarında Aktör Haritası, available at ipc.sabanciuniv.edu/wp-content/uploads/2014/12/AktorHaritasiRapor_25.11.14_web.pdf, accessed 9 February 2015.

Şahin, Y. (2005) *Küresel Isınma Fetişizmi*, Ankara: Seçkin Yayınları.

Salazar, A. and Masera, O. (2010) *México ante el cambio climático. Resolviendo necesidades locales con impactos globales*. Unión de Científicos Comprometidos con la Sociedad, A.C., available at https://www.yumpu.com/es/document/view/14846711/mexico-ante-el-cambio-climatico-union-de-cientificos-, accessed 14 January 2016.

Salehyan, I. (2008) 'From Climate Change to Conflict? No Consensus Yet', *Journal of Peace Research* 45(3): 315–326.

Salter, M.B. (2011) 'When Securitization Fails: The Hard Case of Counter-Terrorism Programs', in T. Balzacq (ed.) *Securitization Theory. How Security Problems Emerge and Dissolve*, London: Routledge, pp. 116–132.

Sánchez Gutiérrez, G., Lucatello, S. and Ceccon Rocha, B. (2009) *Programa de Diálogo y Construcción de Acuerdos. Cambio Climático y Seguridad Nacional*. México D.F.

Sandıklı, A. (n.d.) *Değişen Güvenlik Anlayışları ve Türkiye'nin Güvenlik Stratejisi; rapor 02 (32 sayfa).qxd*.
Saúl, L. and León, M. (2012) 'Promulgan ley de cambio climático', *El Universal*, 6 June.
Saygın, H. (2009) *Küresel İklim Değişikliği ve Türkiye'nin Güvenliğine Etkileri*. Istanbul: BILGESAM, available at http://hasansaygin.com/tr/kuresel-iklim-degisikligi-ve-turkiyenin-guvenligine-etkileri-2/, accessed 11 February 2016.
Scheffran, J., Brzoska, M., Brauch, H.G., Link, P.M. and Schilling, J. (eds) (2012) *Climate Change, Human Security and Violent Conflict*, Berlin and Heidelberg: Springer.
Scherwitz, E. (2014) *Welche Wege führen nach Washington? Eine Analyse des EU-Einflusses auf die US-Politik*, Baden-Baden: Nomos.
Schmidt, A. (2012) 'Bewegungen, Gegenbewegungen, NGOs: Klimakommunikation zivilgesellschaftlicher Akteure', in I. Neverla and M.S. Schäfer (eds) *Das Medien-Klima*, Wiesbaden: VS Verlag für Sozialwissenschaften, pp. 69–94.
Schmidt, V.A. (2008) 'Discursive Institutionalism. The Explanatory Power of Ideas and Discourse', *Annual Review of Political Science* 11(1): 303–326.
Schreurs, M.A. (2003) *Environmental Politics in Japan, Germany, and the United States*, Cambridge: Cambridge University Press.
Schwartz, P. and Randall, D. (2003) *An Abrupt Climate Change Scenario and Its Implications for United States National Security*, Washington, D.C.
Scott, S.V. (2012) 'The Securitization of Climate Change in World Politics: How Close Have We Come and Would Full Securitization Enhance the Efficacy of Global Climate Change Policy?', *Review of European Community and International Environmental Law* 21(3): 220–230.
Seils, C. (2012) 'Angela Merkel, die Atompartei CDU und die Energiewende', *Der Tagesspiegel*, 12 March.
SEMERNAT and CICC (2009) *México Cuarta Comunicación Nacional ante la Convención Marco de las Naciones Unidas sobre el Cambio Climático*. Mexico City.
SEMERNAT and CICC (2012) *México Quinta Comunicación Nacional ante la Convención Marco de las Naciones Unidas sobre el Cambio Climático*. Mexico City.
Senado de la República (1993) *Tratado de libre comercio de America del Norte y de los acuerdos de cooperación ambiental y laboral de America del Norte. Primer Periodo Ordinario LV Legislatura Viernes, 19 de Noviembre de 1993 Diario 9*. Mexico City.
Senado de la República (1994) *Decreto que reforma, adiciona y deroga diversas disposiciones de la Ley Organica de la Administracion Publica Federal. Primer Periodo Ordinario LVI Legislatura Martes, 20 de Diciembre de 1994 Diario 17*. Mexico City.
Senado de la República (1998) *Comparecencia de la C. Maestra Julia Carabias Lillo, Secretaria del Medio Ambiente, Recursos Naturales y Pesca. Segundo Periodo Ordinario LVII Legislatura Martes, 21 de Abril de 1998 Diario 12*. Mexico City.
Senado de la República (2000) *Protocolo de Kyoto de la Convencion Marco de las Naciones Unidas sobre Cambio Climatico, firmado en Kyoto, el 11 de Diciembre de 1997. Segundo Periodo Ordinario LVII Legislatura Viernes, 28 de Abril de 2000 Diario 16*. Mexico City.
Senado de la República (2008) *Enmienda al Anexo B del Protocolo de Kyoto de la Convencion Marco de las Naciones Unidas sobre el Cambio Climatico, adoptada por la Conferencia de las Partes en el Protocolo, en la Ciudad de Nairobi, Kenia, el 17 de Noviembre de 2006. Primer Periodo Ordinario LX Legislatura Martes, 28 de Octubre de 2008 Diario 19*. Mexico City.
Senado de la República (2011a) *Iniciativa con proyecto de decreto por el que se expide la Ley General de Cambio Climatico y Desarrollo Sustentable. Primer Periodo Ordinario LXI Legislatura Martes, 11 de Octubre de 2011 Diario 12*. Mexico City.

Senado de la República (2011b) *Proyecto de decreto por el que se expide la Ley General de Cambio Climatico*. Primer Periodo Ordinario LXI Legislatura Martes, 06 de Diciembre de 2011 Diario 30. Mexico City.
Senado de la República (2012) *Decreto por el que se expide la ley general de cambio climatico*. Segundo Periodo Ordinario LXI Legislatura Jueves, 19 de Abril de 2012 Diario 24. Mexico City.
Senado de la República (2013) *Iniciativa con proyecto de decreto por el que se reforman y adicionan diversas disposiciones a la Ley General de Cambio Climatico*. Ciudad de México.
Smith, D. and Vivekananda, J. (2007) *A Climate of Conflict. The Links between Climate Change, Peace and War*, London: International Alert.
Solar4Peace (2015) Solar Energy for World Peace. 30 September. Plenary/Invited Speakers, available at www.solar4peace.org/plenary_speakers.asp.
Springer, A.L. (2008) 'The Failures of American and European Climate Policy. International Norms, Domestic Politics, and Unachievable Commitments – By Loren R. Cass', *Review of Policy Research* 25(5): 491–492.
Star Gazete (2013) '"Dünyayı kim kirlettiyse onlar temizlesin, biz kirletmedik". Ekonomi', *Star*, 17 October.
Statista and Standard & Poor's (2015) Größte Rückversicherer weltweit nach verdienten Nettoprämien in den Jahren 2012 und 2013 (in Millionen US-Dollar), available at http://de.statistik.com/statistik/daten/studie/188545/umfrage/groessterueckversicherer-weltweit-nach-nettopraemien/.
Steinmeier, F.-W. (2007) *Die transatlantischen Beziehungen im 21. Jahrhundert. Rede von Bundesaußenminister Steinmeier anlässlich der 43. Münchner Konferenz für Sicherheitspolitik*. Munich.
Steinmeier, F.-W. and Miliband, D. (2008) Europa muss sich den sicherheitspolitischen Folgen des Klimawandels stellen, available at www.auswaertiges-amt.de/DE/Infoservice/Presse/Interviews/2008/080313-klimasicherheit.htm, accessed 1 September 2014.
Stephens, T. (2015) 'Focus of Climate Change Discussions Shifts From Mitigation to Adaptation. UC Santa Cruz Climate Conference Panel Address Coastal Resilience and "Wicked Tradeoffs"'. Press Release, University of California–Santa Cruz.
Stern, N. (2006) *Stern Review on the Economics of Climate Change*, London: HMSO.
Storch, H.v. (2009) 'Klimawandel-Essay: Am Ende des Alarmismus', *Der Spiegel*, 22 March.
Stripple, J. (2012) 'The Subject of Security in a Warming World', *Brown Journal of World Affairs* 18(2): 181–194.
Stritzel, H. (2007) 'Towards a Theory of Securitization: Copenhagen and Beyond', *European Journal of International Relations* 13(3): 357–383.
Stritzel, H. (2011) 'Security, the Translation', *Security Dialogue* 42(4–5): 343–355.
SWP (2011) Klimawandel als Sicherheitsproblem, available at www.swp-berlin.org/de/swp-themendossiers/klimapolitik/klimawandel-als-sicherheitsproblem.html, accessed 4 September 2015.
T.C. İçişleri Bakanlığı (2013) *Uluslararası Sivil Toplum Araştırması*. Ankara: Turkish Ministry of the Interior, General Directorate of Associations, available at www.dernekler.gov.tr/media/templates/dernekler/images/folder/uluslararasi-sta-13temmuz.pdf, accessed 11 February 2016.
Talhelm, J. (2007) 'McCain: Address Energy Security, Warming', *Washington Post*, 23 April.
Taniguchi, H. (2011) Cambios a la Ley de Seguridad Nacional ponen en riesgo derechos humanos. Carlos Navarrete, senador del PRD, reprobó cambios que pretende realizar el

PRI en la Cámara Baja por violar garantías individuales, available at http://mexico.cnn.com/nacional/2011/04/26/cambios-a-la-ley-de-seguridad-nacional-ponen-en-riesgo-derechos-humanos, accessed 24 November 2014.

Tanlay, İ. and Yardımcısı (2010) Cancun İklim Değişikliği Zirvesi (COP16), available at www.tobb.org.tr/AvrupaBirligiDairesi/Dokumanlar/Raporlar/cop16.pdf, accessed 7 August 2015.

Tänzler, D., Vivekananda, J., Kolarova, D. and Dokos, T. (2012) *Climate Change and Conflict. Synthesis Report*, Brussels.

Tapper, J. (2007) Al Gore's 'Inconvenient Truth'? – A $30,000 Utility Bill, available at http://abcnews.go.com/Politics/GlobalWarming/story?id=2906888&page=1, accessed 18 August 2015.

Taylor, L. and Branigan, T. (2014) 'US and China Strike Deal on Carbon Cuts in Push for Global Climate Change Pact', *Guardian*, 12 November.

TBMM (1992) *no. 190140900270, B:90, O:1, 30.06.1992*. Ankara.

TBMM (2009) *Meclis Haber Bülteni – İngiltere Dışişleri Bakanı Miliband da katıldı. Çevre Komisyonunda İklim Değişikliği ile Mücadele tartışıldı.*

TBMM (2013a) *Speech of Minister of Forestry and Water Affairs, Veysel Eroğlu in Parliamentary debate on 06.06.2013. Türkiye Büyük Millet Meclisi Genel Kurul Tutanağı 24. Dönem 3. Yasama Yılı 117. Birleşim 06/Haziran/2013 Perşembe*. p. 27.

TBMM (2013b) *Speech of Member of Parliament Mustafa Serdar Soydan (CHP). TBMM 4. D.4.YY, 32. Birleşim, 15.12.2013*.

TBMM (2014a) *Genel Kurul Tutanağı. 24. Dönem 4. Yasama Yılı 48. Birleşim; Speech of Minister of Forestry and Water Affairy, Veysel Eroğlu* (Parliamentary Debate).

TBMM (2014b) *Speech of the Minister of Environment and Forestry, Veysel Eroğlu on 16.01.2014. 24. Dönem, 4. Yasama Yılı, 59 Birleşim, 11. Şubat 2014, Salı*. 15. Ankara.

TBMM (2014c) *Speech of Member of Parliament İdris Baluken (BDP Bingöl) on 19.02.2014. Türkiye Büyük Millet Meclisi Genel Kurul Tutanağı 24. Dönem 4. Yasama Yılı 64. Birleşim 19.Şubat .2014, Çarşamba*. Ankara.

TBMM (2014d) *Speech of Member of Parliament Mehmet Hilal Kaplan (CHP Kocaeli) on 19.02.2014. Genel Kurul Tutanağı 24. Dönem 4. Yasama Yılı 64. Birleşim*. 7–18. Ankara.

TBMM (2014e) *Speech of Members of Parliament Durdu Özbolat (CHP Kahramanmaraş), Mustafa Serdar Soydan (CHP Çanakkale), Rahmi Aşkın Türeli (CHP İzmir). Türkiye Büyük Millet Meclisi, Genel Kurul Tutanağı 24. Dönem 4. Yasama Yılı 71. Birleşim 01.Mart 2014*. p. 5. Ankara.

TBMM (2014f) *Request (10/912) of Member of Parliament Celal Dincer (CHP Istanbul) for a Parliamentary Research Commission on the Economic Problems of Farmers. Türkiye Büyük Millet Meclisi, Genel Kurul Tutanağı 24. Dönem 4. Yasama Yılı 79. Birleşim 22. Nisan 2014, Salı*. pp. 23–25. Ankara.

TBMM (2014g) *Speech of Member of Parliament Alaattin Yüksel (CHP İzmir) on 29.04.2014. Türkiye Büyük Millet Meclisi, Genel Kurul Tutanağı 24. Dönem 4. Yasama Yılı 82. Birleşim, 29.04.2014*. p. 15. Ankara.

TBMM (2014h) *Speech of Member of Parliament Erol Dora (BDP Mardin) in Parliamentary Debate on 30.04.2014*. pp. 59 – 60.

TBMM (2014i) *Speech of Minister of Agriculture, Mehdi Eker, in Parliamentary debate on 13.05.2014. Türkiye Büyük Millet Meclisi Genel Kurul Tutanağı 24. Dönem 4. Yasama Yılı 88. Birleşim 13/Mayıs /2014 Salı.*

Tepe, D. (2012) *The Myth About Global Civil Society*, Basingstoke: Palgrave Macmillan.

The Economist (2010) 'Is Turkey Turning Its Back on the West?', *Economist*, 21 October.

The Guardian (2011) 'Which Nations Are Most Responsible for Climate Change?', *Guardian*, 21 April.
The National Center for Public and Policy Research (1997) Byrd-Hagel Resolution, available at www.nationalcenter.org/KyotoSenate.html, accessed 28 March 2013.
The White House (1991) *National Security Strategy of the United States*. Washington, D.C.
The White House (1994) *A National Security Strategy of Engagement and Enlargement*. Washington, D.C.
The White House (2002) *The National Security Strategy of the United States of America, 2002*. Washington, D.C.
The White House (2006) *The National Security Strategy of the United States of America, 2006*. Washington, D.C.
The White House (2015a) *Findings from Select Federal Reports: The National Security Implications of Climate Change*. Washington, D.C.
The White House (2015b) *The Clean Power Plan*. mcg. Washington, D.C.
The Woodrow Wilson Center (2015) Environmental Change and Security Program (ECSP), available at https://www.wilsoncenter.org/about-ecsp, accessed 24 August 2015.
Tierney, K., Bevc, C. and Kuligowsiki, E. (2006) 'Metaphors Matter: Disaster Myths, Media Frames, and Their Consequences in Hurricane Katrina', *Annals of the American Academy of Political and Social Science* 604 (March): 57–81.
TIKDEK (2007) *Bildiri Kitabi* (Conference publication of the 1st Climate Change Congress of Turkey – TIKDEK 2007).
TIKDEK (2010) *Bildiri Kitabi* (Conference publication of the 2nd Climate Change Congress of Turkey – TIKDEK 2010).
TIKDEK (2013) *Bildiri Kitabi* (Conference publication of the 3rd Climate Change Congress of Turkey – TIKDEK 2013).
Today's Zaman (2011) 'Turkey's Civil Society Organizations Increase by 44 per cent in 10 Years', 15 June.
Topbaş, K. (2012) 'Cities and Sustainability', *Turkish Policy Quarterly* 11(2): 31–36.
Townsend, M. and Harris, P. (2004) 'Now the Pentagon Tells Bush: Climate Change Will Destroy Us', *Guardian/Observer*, 22 February.
Treverton, G.F., Nemeth, E. and Srinivasan, S. (2012) *Threats Without Threateners? Exploring Intersections of Threats to the Global Commons and National Security*, Santa Monica, CA.
Trombetta, M.J. (2008) 'Environmental Security and Climate Change: Analysing the Discourse', *Cambridge Review of International Affairs* 21(4): 585–602.
Trombetta, M.J. (2011) 'Rethinking the Securitization of the Environment. Old Beliefs, New Insights', in T. Balzacq (ed.) *Securitization Theory. How Security Problems Emerge and Dissolve*, London: Routledge, pp. 135–149.
Truman National Security Project (2015) Mission and Vision of the Truman National Security Project, available at http://trumanproject.org/about/our-story/mission/, accessed 25 August 2015.
TU Berlin (2009) Book announcement for 'Nicholas Stern: Der Global Deal (2009)'. Berlin.
Türkeş, M. (2002) *İklim değişikliği ve sürdürülebilir Kalkınma Ulusal Değerlendirme Raporu*: TTGV.
Türkmenoğlu, E. (2012) *Climate Change Policies in Turkey*. Ankara.
Ullmann, R. (1983) 'Redefining Security', *International Security* 8(1): 129–153.
Umbach, F. (2008) *German Vulnerabilities of Its Energy Security*, Washington, D.C.

UN (2007) Secretary-General's address to High-Level Event on Climate Change. New York, 24 September 2007, available at www.un.org/sg/statements/index.asp?nid=2750, accessed 7 August 2015.

UN World Commission on Environment and Development (1987) *Our Common Future: Report of the World Commission on Environment and Development*. Chapter 2: 'Towards Sustainable Development'. Genf.

UNDP (2007) *İklim Değişikliği ve Türkiye* [Climate Change and Turkey]. Ankara.

UNDP (2010) *Designing Climate Change Adaptation Initiatives. A UNDP Toolkit for Practitioners.*

UNDP Turkey (2013) Turkey Ranks 90th in the Human Development Index, available at www.tr.undp.org/content/turkey/en/home/presscenter/news-from-new-horizons/2013/03/15/turkey-ranks-90th-in-hdi.html, accessed 11 February 2016.

UNFCCC (2013c) Admitted IGO, available at http://maindb.unfccc.int/public/igo.pl?mode=wim, accessed 21 October 2013.

UNFCCC (2002) Report of the conference of the parties on its seventh session, held at Marrakesh from 29 October to 10 November 2001. Addendum: Action taken by the conference of the parties, Volume IV, Decision 26/CP7, available at http://unfccc.int/resource/docs/cop7/13a04.pdf, accessed 11 April 2015.

UNFCCC (2013) Opportunities for parties included in Annex I to the Convention whose special circumstances are recognized by the Conference of the Parties to benefit from support from relevant bodies and institutions to enhance mitigation, adaptation, technology, capacity-building and access to finance, available at www.dsi.gov.tr/docs/iklim-degisikligi/fccc_tp_2013-3-rumuzlu-teknik-belge_eng-pdf.pdf?sfvrsn=2, accessed 7 August 2015.

UNFCCC (2014) Non-Annex I national communications, available at http://unfccc.int/national_reports/non-annex_i_natcom/items/2979.php, accessed 25 November 2014.

UNFCCC (2015) The International Response to Climate Cchange. Climate Change Information Sheet 17, available at http://unfccc.int/essential_background/background_publications_htmlpdf/climate_change_information_kit/items/300.php, accessed 28 August 2015.

UNGA (2008) Resolution Adopted by the General Assembly. Protection of Global Climate for Present and Future Generations of Mankind, A/RES/62/86. New York.

UNGA (2009a) Resolution Adopted by the General Assembly. Climate Change and its Possible Security Implications, A/RES/63/281. New York.

UNGA (2009b) *Climate Change and its Possible Security Implications. Report of the Secretary-General, A/64/350 (2009)*. New York.

United Nations (1987) *Our Common Future. Report of the World Commission on Environment and Development.* New York.

UNSC (2007b) 5663 Meeting, Tuesday, 17 April 2007, 3 p.m., S/PV5663 (Resumption 1). New York.

UNSC (2007a) 5663rd Meeting, Tuesday, 17 April 2007, 10 a.m. New York.

UNSC (2011a) 6587th Meeting, Wednesday, 20 July 2011, 10 a.m. New York.

UNSC (2011b) 6587th Meeting, Wednesday, 20 July 2011, 3 p.m., S/PV.6587 (Resumption 1). New York.

UNSC (2013) Press Conference on Impact of Climate Change on Marshall Islands, available at www.un.org/News/briefings/docs/2013/130215_MI.doc.htm, accessed 13 December 2013.

UNU-EHS (2012) Press Release: 'Addressing Loss and Damage in the Context of Social Vulnerability and Resilience'. Doha.
US Army Corps of Engineers (2015) About Us, available at www.usace.army.mil/About.aspx, accessed 9 June 2015.
US Congress (1988) Global Climate Protection Act of 1987. Washington, D.C.
US Department of State (2009) Appointment of Special Envoy on Climate Change Todd Stern, available at www.state.gov/secretary/rm/2009a/01/115409.htm, accessed 8 March 2013.
US Government (1990) National Global Change Research Act of 1990. Public Law 101-606 101st Congress.
US House of Representatives (1989) The Global Change Research Act of 1989 Hon. Christopher H. Smith (Extension of Remarks October 26, 1989). Congressional Record 101st Congress (1989–1990). Washington, D.C.
US House of Representatives (1990) Sense of Congress Regarding Linkage between the Environment and National Security (House of Representatives – September 17, 1990). Congressional Record – 101st Congress (1989–1990). Washington, D.C.
US House of Representatives (1994a) Department of Commerce Justice and State the Judiciary and Related Agencies Appropriations Act 1995 – Debate on Expenses for Climate Change. Washington, D.C.
US House of Representatives (1994b) Departments of Commerce, Justice, and State, the Judiciary, and Related Agencies Appropriations Act, 1995, and Supplemental Appropriations, 1994. Washington, D.C.
US House of Representatives (1995) Omnibus Civilian Science Authorization Act of 1995. Washington, D.C.
US House of Representatives (1998a) Personal Explanation. Washington, D.C.
US House of Representatives (1998b) Departments of Veteran Affairs and Housing and Urban Development, and Independent Agencies Appropriations Act, 1999. Washington, D.C.
US House of Representatives (2005) Announcing the Introduction of the New Apollo Energy Project. Congressional Record-House June 8, 2005 (H4290). Washington, D.C.
US House of Representatives (2009a) Cap and Trade. Congressional Record – House May 13, 2009 (H5555). Washington, D.C.
US House of Representatives (2009b) Energy Independence Is a Matter of National Security. Congressional Record – House, July 21, 2009 (H8477). Washington, D.C.
US National Guard (2015) About the Guard, available at www.nationalguard.mil/AbouttheGuard.aspx, accessed 9 June 2015.
US Navy (2009) Task Force on Climate Change, available at http://greenfleet.dodlive.mil/climate-change/, accessed 8 September 2014.
US Navy (2010) *Climate Change Roadmap*. Washington, D.C.
US Senate (1989a) The Global Environment, Senate Debate, May 12, 1989. Congressional Record – 101st Congress (1989–1990). Washington, D.C.
US Senate (1989b) The Stratosperic Ozone and Climate Protection Act of 1989 (Senate – October 12, 1989). Congressional Record – 101st Congress (1989–1990). Washington, D.C.
US Senate (1990a) S.RES.316 -- Concerning the Interparliamentary Conference on the Global Environment. (Introduced in Senate – IS). Congressional Record – 101st Congress (1989–1990). Washington, D.C.
US Senate (1990b) National Defense Authorization Act for Fiscal 1990. Washington, D.C.

US Senate (1991) *Global Climate System.* Washington, D.C.
US Senate (1992a) Earth Summit. Congressional Record 102nd Congress (1991–1992). Washington, D.C.
US Senate (1992b) The Earth Summit (Senate – June 04, 1992). Congressional Record 102nd Congress (1991–1992). Washington, D.C.
US Senate (1997) The Climate Change Treaty (Senate – October 23, 1997). Congressional Record – 105th Congress (1997–1998). Washington, D.C.
US Senate (1999a) Credit for Voluntary Reductions Act. Washington, D.C.
US Senate (1999b) Forest Resources for the Environment and the Economy Act;. Washington, D.C.
US Senate (2003a) Abrupt Climate Change Research Act of 2003. Calendar no. 514 S. 1164 [Report no. 108-263]. 108th Congress 2nd Session. Washington, D.C.
US Senate (2003b) Climate Stewardship Act (October 29, 2003). Congressional Record – Senate. Washington, D.C.
US Senate (2007a) Global Warming Pollution Reduction Act of 2007. Washington, D.C.
US Senate (2007b) Congressional Record: Global Warming. Washington, D.C.
US Senate (2008a) Climate Security Act of 2008 – Motion to Proceed. Congressional Record – Senate. Washington, D.C.
US Senate (2008b) Congressional Record – Senate: S3036 – the Lieberman-Warner Climate Security Act of 2008. Washington, D.C.
US Senate (2008c) S5014 Lieberman–Warner Climate Security Act of 2008. Washington, D.C.
US Senate (2008d) Climate Security Act. Congressional Record – Senate June 5, 2008 (S5188). Washington, D.C.
US Senate (2008e) Debates on Climate Security Act. Congressional Record – Senate June 5, 2008 (S5194). Washington, D.C.
US Senate (2009) Department of Defense Appropriations Act. Congressional Record – Senate, October 6, 2009 (S10143). Washington, D.C.
Usborne, D. (2009) 'Al Gore Denies He Is "Carbon Billionaire"', *Independent*, 4 November.
USCAP (2013) United States Climate Action Partnership: Organization Homepage, available at www.us-cap.org/, accessed 8 March 2013.
USGCRP (2015) Legal Mandate of the U.S. Global Change Research Program (USGCRP), available at www.globalchange.gov/about/legal-mandate, accessed 25 August 2015.
Üzelgun, M.A. and Castro, P. (2015) 'Climate Change in the Mainstream Turkish Press. Coverage Trends and Meaning Dimensions in the First Attention Cycle', *Mass Communication and Society* 18(6): 1–23.
Üzelgün, M. and Castro, P. (2014) 'The Voice of Science on Climate Change in the Mainstream Turkish Press', *Environmental Communication* 8(3): 326–344.
Vahrenholt, F. and Lüning, S. (2012) *Die kalte Sonne. Warum die Klimakatastrophe nicht stattfindet,* Hamburg: Hoffmann und Campe.
van Munster, R. (2005) *Logics of Security: The Copenhagen School, Risk Management and the War on Terror,* University of Southern Denmark, Political Science Publications, October.
Vig, N.J. (2013) 'Presidential Powers and Environmental Policy', in N.J. Vig and M.E. Kraft (eds) *Environmental Policy. New Directions for the Twenty-First Century,* Thousand Oaks, CA: CQ Press, pp. 84–108.
Vig, N.J. and Kraft, M.E. (1984) 'Introduction', in N.J. Vig and M.E. Kraft (eds) *Environmental Policy in the 1980s: Reagans's New Agenda,* Washington, D.C.: CQ Press, pp. 3–26.

References

Vogel, C. and O'Brien, K. (2004) 'Vulnerability and Global Environmental Change: Rhetoric and Reality', *Aviso* 13: 1–8.

von Lucke, F. (2015) 'The Good the Bad and the Ambiguous: Making Sense of Different Representations of Climate Change as Security Issue', Paper prepared for the 10th International Conference in Interpretive Policy Analysis (IPA), 'Policies and Their Publics: Discourses, Actors and Power', Lille (France), 8–10 July. Tübingen.

von Lucke, F., Wellmann, Z. and Diez, T. (2014a) 'Klimakämpfe: Eine komparative Studie der Versicherheitlichung von Klimawandel', Paper presented at 'Vierte Offene Sektionstagung' der DVPW-Sektion 'Internationale Politik', 25–27 September 2014, Magdeburg, Germany.

von Lucke, F., Wellmann, Z. and Diez, T. (2014b) 'What's at Stake in Securitising Climate Change? Towards a Differentiated Approach', Special Issue: Rethinking Climate Change, Conflict and Security, *Geopolitics* 19(4): 857–884.

Wæver, O. (1995) 'Securitization and Desecuritization', in R.D. Lipschutz (ed.) *On Security*, New York: Columbia University Press, pp. 46–86.

Wæver, O. (1996) 'European Security Identities', *Journal of Common Market Studies* 34(1): 103–132.

Wæver, O. (2002) 'Identity, Communities and Foreign Policy: Discourse Analysis as Foreign Policy Theory', in L. Hansen and O. Wæver (eds) *European Integration and National Identity. The Challenge of the Nordic States*, New York: Routledge, pp. 20–49.

Wæver, O. (2004) 'Peace and Security. Two Concepts and their Relationship', in S. Guzzini and D. Jung (eds) *Contemporary Security Analysis and Copenhagen Peace Research*, London and New York: Routledge.

Wagner, J. (2008) 'Die Versicherheitlichung des Klimawandels. Wie Brüssel die Erderwärmung für die Militarisierung der Europäischen Union instrumentalisiert', *IMI Magazin*, 14–16.

Wagner, K. (2010) Der Klimaflüchtling drängt auf die europäische Bühne. Migration durch Umweltänderungen bislang kein Thema in Brüssel, available at www.ag-friedensforschung.de/themen/Migration/eu4.html, accessed 5 September 2015.

WBGU (2001) *Neue Strukturen globaler Umweltpolitik*, Berlin: Springer.

WBGU (2003) *Welt im Wandel: Energiewende zur Nachhaltigkeit. Hauptgutachten*, Berlin.

WBGU (2006) *Die Zukunft der Meere – zu warm, zu hoch, zu sauer. Sondergutachten*, Berlin: Wissenschaftlicher Beirat d. Bundesregierung Globale Umweltveränderungen.

WBGU (2007a) *Neue Impulse für die Klimapolitik. Chancen der deutschen Doppelpräsidentschaft nutzen*, Berlin: WBGU.

WBGU (2007b) *Welt im Wandel: Sicherheitsrisiko Klimawandel*, Berlin: Springer.

WBGU (2007c) *Welt im Wandel: Sicherheitsrisiko Klimawandel. Zusammenfassung für Entscheidungsträger*, Berlin and Heidelberg: Springer.

WBGU (2007d) *World in Transition. Climate Change as a Security Risk*. Summary for Policymakers. Berlin.

WBGU (2012) *Die Finanzierung der globalen Energiewende. Politikpapier Nr. 7*.

Weber, M. (2008) *Alltagsbilder des Klimawandels – Zum Klimabewusstsein in Deutschland*, Wiesbaden: VS Verlag für Sozialwissenschaften.

Weidner, H. and Mez, L. (2008) 'German Climate Change Policy. A Success Story with Some Flaws', *Journal of Environment and Development* 17(4): 356–378.

Weingart, P., Engels, A. and Pansegrau, P. (2000) 'Risks of Communication: Discourses on Climate Change in Science, Politics, and the Mass Media', *Public Understanding of Science* 9(3): 261–283.

Weingart, P., Engels, A. and Pansegrau, P. (eds) (2002) *Von der Hypothese zur Katastrophe. Der anthropogene Klimawandel im Diskurs zwischen Wissenschaft, Politik und Massenmedien,* Opladen, Germany: Leske + Budrich.

Werland, S. (2012) *Debattenanalyse Rohstoffknappheit,* Berlin.

Werz, M. and Conley, L. (2012) Climate Change, Migration, and Conflict. Addressing complex crisis scenarios in the 21st Century, available at www.americanprogress.org/wp-content/uploads/issues/2012/01/pdf/climate_migration.pdf, accessed 12 March 2014.

Werz, M. and Manlove, K. (2009) *Climate Change on the Move. Climate Migration Will Affect the World's Security,* Washington, D.C.

Wiener, A. (2007) 'The Dual Quality of Norms and Governance Beyond the State: Sociological and Normative Approaches to "Interaction"', *Critical Review of International Social and Political Philosophy* 10(1): 47–69.

Wiener, A. (2008) *The Invisible Constitution of Politics. Contested Norms and International Encounters,* Cambridge and New York: Cambridge University Press.

Williams, M.C. (2003) 'Words, Images, Enemies: Securitization and International Politics', *International Studies Quarterly* 47: 511–531.

Wilson, J. (2005) 'Novel Take on Global Warming', *Guardian,* 29 September.

WMO (1989) *Proceedings of the World Conference on the Changing Atmosphere: Implications for Global Security,* WMO, no. 710.

Wolf, S. (2007) *Klimaschutz und Energiepolitik in Mexiko, El Salvador und Nicaragua,* Mexico City.

Woodrow Wilson Center (2009) *Environmental Change and Security Program. Report Issue 13 2008–2009.* Washington, D.C.

World Bank (2008) Globe Americas Legislators Forum, available at http://web.worldbank.org/wbsite/external/news/contentmdk:21991411~pagePK:64257043~piPK:437376~theSitePK:4607,00.html, accessed 24 November 2014.

World Bank (2012a) Country Indicators: Mexico, available at http://data.worldbank.org/country/mexico, accessed 20 December 2012.

World Bank (2012b) *FONDEN. Mexico's Natural Disaster Fund – A Review,* Washington, D.C.

World Bank (2012c) *Turn Down the Heat: Why a 4°C Warmer World Must Be Avoided,* Washington, D.C.

World Bank (2013a) CO2 Emissions (kt), available at http://data.worldbank.org/indicator/EN.ATM.CO2E.KT/countries, accessed 2 April 2013.

World Bank (2013b) *Turn Down the Heat. Climate Extremes, Regional Impacts, and the Case for Resilience,* Washington, D.C.

World Bank (2014) *Turn Down the Heat. Confronting the New Climate Normal,* Washington, D.C.

World Bank (2015a) Germany. Country Data, available at http://data.worldbank.org/country/germany, accessed 5 November 2015.

World Bank (2015b) Turkey. Country Data, available at http://data.worldbank.org/country/turkey, accessed 5 November 2015.

World Bank (2015c) United States. Country Data, available at http://data.worldbank.org/country/united-states, accessed 5 November 2015.

World Bulletin (2013) Turkish Minister Meets US's Al Gore for Climate Change, available at www.worldbulletin.net/?aType=haber&ArticleID=111223, accessed 7 May 2015.

References

Wuppertal Institute (2015a) Das Wuppertal Institut in den Medien, available at http://wupperinst.org/info/presse/medienspiegel/, accessed 5 November 2015.

Wuppertal Institute (2015b) Staff – Contact – Wuppertal Institut für Klima, Umwelt, Energie, available at http://wupperinst.org/en/contact/staff/?tx_wupperinst_pi1%5B%40widget_0%5D%5BcurrentPage%5D=2&tx_wupperinst_pi1%5B%40widget_0%5D%5BcObj%5D=3682&cHash=9753d07d41f653b6ea2b421ddfea0d33, accessed 5 September 2015.

Wuppertal Institute (2015c) Wuppertal Institut für Klima, Umwelt, Energie GmbH: Die Geschichte des Wuppertal Instituts, available at http://wupperinst.org/das-wuppertal-institut/geschichte/, accessed 20 September 2015.

WWF México (2010) *Impactos y vulnerabilidad al cambio climático en México*. Mexico City.

Yamin, F. and Depledge, J. (2004) *The International Climate Change Regime: A Guide to Rules, Institutions and Procedures,* Cambridge: Cambridge University Press.

YeşilEkonomi (2015) 'Ankara'da iklim değişikliğinin güvenlik boyutu tartışıldı. Etkinlikte Türk ve Alman uzmanlar katılımı ile yuvarlak masa toplantıları gerçekleştirildi', 11 June.

Zaman (2015) 'Yeni Iklim Rejimi ve Türkiye', 15 July.

INDEX

Adalet ve Kalkınma Partisi (AKP) 121, 138, 141
adaptation 2, 17, 21–22, 24, 32–34, 36, 50, 60–61, 64, 75, 77, 89, 91, 94, 100, 104–105, 108, 114–117, 120, 137, 140, 150–151
Adelphi 74–75, 77–79, 81, 84–87, 91–94, 107–108, 111, 149
Africa 1, 48, 80, 91, 93, 132
agenda setting 19, 25
agriculture 105, 115, 128, 132
AGRIFOR 107, 111
AKP *see* Adalet ve Kalkınma Partisi
Aktaş, Emel 129–130
Albayrakoğlu, Esra 134
Algedik, Önder 122, 124, 135
American Clean Energy and Security Act, Waxman–Markey Bill 58
American Security Project (ASP) 53, 56
Annex 1 country (UNFCCC) 99, 124–125, 136
Annex 2 country (UNFCCC) 124–125, 136
anthropogenic 2, 55, 61, 71, 89
Aradau, Claudia 8–9, 31
Arbeitsgruppe Friedensforschung und europäische Sicherheitspolitik e.V (AFES) 75
armed forces *see* military
Army War College (US) 42

Askeri Tarih ve Stratejik Etüt Başkanlığı (ATASE) 129
assemblage (theory) 8
audience (Copenhagen School) 10, 18, 26–28, 52, 75, 108, 122, 126
Auswärtiges Amt (German Federal Foreign Office) 86–87

Balzacq, Thierry 7–8, 17, 28–29
Başbakanlık Afet ve Acil Durum Yönetimi Başkanlığı (AFAD) 139–140
Beck, Ulrich 9, 15
Bertelsmann Stiftung 96, 107, 117–118
Betsill, Michelle 4, 7–8, 20, 22–23, 33
Bigo, Didier 8–9, 13, 31
BILGESAM 139
Black Swan events 49
Blair, Tony 61
Brauch, Hans-Günther 7, 23, 75, 93
British Embassy (in Mexico City) 103, 108–109, 112, 117
broadening/widening of security 1, 10, 20, 31, 102
Brookings Foundation 53, 56
Brot für die Welt (bfdw) 78, 82, 85
Brzoska, Michael 1–2, 7, 33, 40, 47, 58, 60–61
Bund für Umwelt und Naturschutz (BUND) 84

Bundesministerium für Umwelt, Naturschutz, Bau und Reaktorsicherheit (BMU/BMUB) (Germany) 65, 68, 75, 79, 84, 86, 90, 93
Bundesministerium für wirtschaftliche Zusammenarbeit und Entwicklung (BMZ) (Germany) 84, 90–91
Bundesregierung (Germany) 77–78, 84, 91
Bundestag (Germany) 73–76, 78–79, 82–83, 85–86, 88–89, 93
Bundeswehr *see* armed forces (Germany)
Bündnis 90/Die Grünen *see* Green Party
bureaucracies, role in securitisation 83, 130, 141
Burgess, Peter 147
Busby, Joshua 46, 48–50, 53
Bush, George H., George W. 38–40, 44–45, 47, 51, 63, 86
Buzan, Barry 3–4, 6–8, 10–11, 14–15, 18, 25, 28–29, 31, 146, 152

Calderón, Felipe 99, 102, 106–107, 117, 119, 148
Cámara de Diputados (Mexico) 101–102, 108, 111–112, 114–116
Campbell, Kurt 46, 48, 50–51, 53, 55, 59–60, 83
CAN *see* Climate Action Network
Cancun, Conference of the Parties (COP)-16 2010 99, 102, 106
capacity 105, 128, 136, 141
Caribbean Community Climate Change Centre (CCCCC) 109
Carius, Alexander 74–75, 77, 86, 103, 108
Cartagena Dialogue 99
CDU *see* Christlich Demokratische Union
CENTCOM, US Central Command 44, 53, 60
Center for a New American Security (CNAS) 46, 51–53, 55–56, 59
Center for American Progress (CAP) 53, 56
Center for Climate and Energy (C2ES) 40–41, 47–48, 53, 56–58, 60
Center for Climate and Security (CCS) 53
Center for Strategic and International Studies (CSIS) 46, 51–53, 56, 59, 84, 90, 130

Central Intelligence Agency (CIA) 46, 61
Centro de Colaboración Cívica (CCC) 103–105, 108–111
Centro de Investigación y Seguridad Nacional (CISEN) 110, 116
Centro Mario Molina (CMM) 108, 111
Centro Mexicano de Derecho Ambiental (CEMDA) 107–108, 111–112, 118
Centro Nacional de Prevención de Desastres (CENAPRED) 111, 115
Cerit-Mazlum, Semra 137
Çevre ve Orman Bakanlığı (ÇOB) 124, 126, 139
Çevre ve Şehircilik Bakanlığı (ÇŞB) 123, 125–126, 139–140
CFR *see* Council on Foreign Relations
Chafee, John 38, 43
Christlich Demokratische Union (CDU), Christian Democrats 68, 70, 72–73, 89, 94
CIFOR 111
CIVICUS (Civil Society Index) 107, 141
civilian power 69, 80, 92
Clean Development Mechanism (CDM) 99
clean energy 58, 66
Climate
  Action Network (CAN) 82, 122
  Action Tracker 96, 122
  catastrophe 71–73, 78, 82–83, 88, 94
  Change Congress (Turkey) 128
  change, impact of 5, 7, 16, 22–23, 47, 49, 78, 81, 103, 105–108, 112, 114, 128, 132–133, 137, 140
  Change Performance Index 65, 77, 96, 122
  Change Roadmap 60
  climate change deniers, climate change sceptics 39, 44, 53–55, 58, 63, 88
  justice 82, 122, 132–133, 140, 143
  migration *see* Migration
  Network/Iklim Agi (Turkey) 122, 137
  Reality Project (Gore) 138
  refugees *see* Migration
  Risk Index 5
  security nexus 1, 3, 53
  Stewardship Act (US) 46, 57
  System Analysis and Prediction (clisap) 79

wars 127
climatisation 36
Clinton, Bill 38, 41, 43–45, 63, 148, 150
CNA (formerly Center for Naval Analysis)/ MAB (Military Advisory Board) 33, 41, 46–53, 55–56, 59–60, 84, 90, 111, 129–130, 139, 148
CNBC (Consumer News and Business Channel) 121
CNN (Cable News Network) 106, 136
CO2 emissions *see* Greenhouse Gas Emissions
Cold War 18, 41, 62, 146
Comisión Centroamericana de Ambiente y Desarrollo (CCAD) 109
Comisión de Estudios del Sector Privada para el Desarrollo Sustentable (CESPEDES) 108
Comisión Intersecretarial de Cambio Climático (CICC) 99, 104, 110–113, 114–115
Comisión Nacional del Agua (CONAGUA) 110
Communication to the UNFCCC 99, 110, 115, 128
conflict 1, 6–9, 17, 20–21, 32–33, 42, 48, 50, 63, 66, 74–75, 77, 79, 81, 85, 87, 92, 101, 103–105, 108, 117, 129–132, 142, 146
Congress (US) 38–40, 42–44, 46–47, 50, 52–55, 57–60, 63, 128, 143
contingency planning 21, 49
Copenhagen, COP-15 2009 75, 77, 79–80, 126, 130, 138, 140
Copenhagen School 3–4, 7–11, 13–17, 20, 26, 28, 31, 145, 151
Council on Foreign Relations (CFR) 46, 51, 53, 56
counter-securitisation 140

Dabelko, Geoffrey, D. 41–42, 51–52, 55, 83
Dalby, Simon 8, 20, 23, 41–42, 62
danger 14–19, 21–24, 31–33, 36, 42–50, 54–55, 57–59, 61–66, 71–76, 78–83, 88–90, 92, 94–95, 97, 100, 103, 108–109, 117, 119–120, 126, 129, 131–135, 143–153

Territorial Danger Discourse 21–22, 36, 44–45, 47–49, 54–55, 57–59, 61–64, 66, 74–75, 78–79, 81–83, 89–90, 92, 94–95, 103, 108–109, 117, 119–120, 131, 133, 143–152
Individual Danger Discourse 21–23, 48, 48–50, 74, 78, 80–81, 89, 132–134, 146, 148–151
Planetary Danger Discourse 21, 23–24, 42–42, 46, 82, 88–89, 131, 151
Deheza, Elizabeth 103–105, 109–110, 112, 115–117
Democratic Party (US) 38, 40, 55, 57–58, 63
democratisation 96, 10, 118, 142
Department for International Development (DFID) (UK) 111
Department of Defense (DOD) Pentagon (US), 44–45, 50, 52, 55–56, 60–61
Department of Energy (DOE) (US) 40, 46, 56
Department of Homeland Security (DHS) (US) 51, 56, 60–61
Department of State (DOS) (US) 44, 56
Department of Transportation (DOT) (US) 40
depoliticisation 10, 151
Deputy Under-Secretary of Defense for Environmental Security 43–44, 147
desecuritisation 10, 18, 151
Detraz, Nicole 4, 7–8, 20, 23, 33
Deutsche Kreditanstalt für Wiederaufbau (KfW) 91
Deutsche Meteorologische Gesellschaft (DMG) 71–73, 82–83, 90
Deutsche Physikalische Gesellschaft (DPG) 71–73, 82–83, 90
Deutsches Institut für Entwicklungspolitik (DIE) 74, 85
Deutsches Institut für Wirtschaftsforschung (DIW) 66, 70, 83
Deutsches Klima-Konsortium (DKK) 77, 82
Deutsches Klimarechenzentrum (DKRZ) 79
developing countries, global south 22, 32, 34, 39, 48, 61, 79, 81, 89, 91, 93–94, 96, 98–99, 119, 122
development 3–6, 9, 12–13, 22, 24, 32, 34, 44, 50, 60–61, 67–69, 73–74,

Index **199**

76–79, 81–82, 85, 88, 90–91, 94, 96–100, 106–107, 109, 114–115, 121–124, 134–137, 140–145, 147, 149
development cooperation / aid 22, 32, 34, 61, 74, 137, 141
Devlet Planlama Teşkilatı (DPT) 122–124, 139–140
Devlet Su İşleri (DSI) 112, 129, 140
Diakonie 77–78, 82, 84–85
diffuse threat 4, 8–9, 15–16, 32
disaster management/prevention 51, 61–62, 114–115, 140
discourse 3–9, 11–13, 16–18, 20–34, 36–37, 143–153
discursive entrepreneurs 3, 6, 12–13, 25–31, 37, 42, 44, 46, 51–52, 55, 64, 66, 74, 82–83, 86, 92, 94, 97, 102, 106, 108, 117, 126, 129, 135–137, 144, 147–148, 153
DOD *see* Department of Defense
Doğa, Derneği 137
Doha, COP-18 2012 87
double standard 142–143
drought, desertification 1, 7, 48, 81, 103–104, 110, 117, 125–128, 133–138
Dumaine, Carol 46
Durban COP-17 2011 122

early warning 81, 105, 108, 114
Eastern Mediterranean Climate Centre (EMCC) 122
ECOLOGIC Institute (Clico) 78, 80–81, 84, 93
ecological security 8, 20
ecosystem 9, 20–21, 23–24, 34, 49, 101, 105, 107, 115
Edenhofer, Ottmar 76
Ekolojik Toplum 138
Elbe, Stefan 4, 10, 22, 25, 31, 33
emergency measures 7, 9, 16–18, 31, 80, 151
emerging economies 5, 96, 117, 125
emission *see also* Greenhouse Gas emissions reductions 2, 39, 65, 69, 72, 89–90, 99–100, 122–123, 140, 143
management 141

Energiewende (energy turn) 79, 90, 94, 150
energy
efficiency 24, 50, 70–72, 82, 102, 104–105, 107, 114
policies 70, 79, 90, 102, 123
renewable 90, 107
security 2, 6, 46, 48, 104, 130, 135, 143, 147
Enquete Commission (Germany) 65, 72–74, 79, 86, 89
Environment, Conflict and Cooperation (ECC) 85
environmental
activists 23–24, 37, 67, 122–123, 135
conflict 7–8, 20, 74, 77, 101
law 98, 123
movement 37, 71, 92, 122, 127, 142
NGOs 51, 55, 78, 122, 148–149
sector 55, 62, 142, 149
security 2, 6–8, 11, 17, 20, 22–23, 41–44, 46, 51, 62, 71, 74, 85–86, 101, 118, 147–148
Environmental Protection Agency (EPA) 37–38, 40, 44, 55–57
Erdogan, Recap Tayyip 121, 132, 138, 141, 143
Ergenekon 129
Erneuerbare-Energien-Gesetz (EEG) 70
Eslen, Nejat 129, 135
Estrategia Nacional de Cambio Climático (ENACC) 99, 110–111, 114
EU
accession negotiations 121, 125, 128, 141, 144
acquis communautaire 125, 137
Institute for Security Studies (EUISS) 85–86
European Commission 87, 122, 140
Evangelischer Entwicklungsdienst (EED) 82
existential threat 3–4, 8–10, 15–16, 32, 90
extraordinary measures 3–4, 7, 10, 14, 16–17, 19, 26–27, 29, 32, 89, 112, 122, 146

facilitating/felicity conditions (of securitisation) 25, 28, 62, 91, 117, 142, 146

FAO *see* Food and Agriculture Organisation of the United Nations
Federal Emergency Management Agency (FEMA) 51, 56, 61
financial crisis 78, 121
Floyd, Rita 4, 10–11, 17, 25, 31, 34, 41–45
Fondo Nacional para el Desarrollo Nacional (FONDEN) 115
Fondo para la Prevención de Desastres Naturales (FOPREDEN) 115
Food and Agriculture Organisation of the United Nations (FAO) 129, 139, 141
food security 41, 82, 102, 114–116, 128, 130, 133
Foreign and Commonwealth Office (FCO) 109
forest 82, 103, 125, 127, 134
fossil fuel industry 140
Fossil of the day award 122, 135
foundations (financing)
    Heinrich-Böll-Stiftung 107, 112, 135–136
    Mercator 76–77, 93, 134–136
    Rockefeller 52–53
    Skoll Global Threats Fund 52
    Energy Foundation 52
framing 3, 8–9, 20, 26–27, 34, 51, 53–55, 58, 61–65, 71, 73–74, 76, 78, 92, 95, 101, 103, 105–106, 109, 111, 113–114, 116, 118–120, 127–128, 130–134, 137, 145–147, 149, 151–152
Fukushima 79, 90, 94
Fundación para el Ecodesarrollo y la Conservación (FUNDAECO) 109

G7/ G8 77–78, 84–86, 91
General Directorate of State Meteorology Services (MGM) 123, 139
George C. Marshall Institute 39, 53
German Federal Foreign Office *see* Auswärtiges Amt
German Institute for Development Cooperation *see* Deutsches Institut für Entwicklungspolitik (DIE)
German Institute for International and Security Affairs (SWP) *see* Stiftung Wissenschaft und Politik
Germanwatch 3, 5, 36, 65, 77–78, 80, 82–85, 87, 93, 96, 122, 139–140
Gesamtverband der Deutschen Versicherungswirtschaft e. V. (GDV), Die Deutschen Versicherer 87
Gesellschaft für Internationale Zusammenarbeit (GIZ, formerly GTZ), German Development Cooperation 78, 83, 85, 87
Gezi Park movement 122
GIZ *see* Gesellschaft für Internationale Zusammenarbeit
Global Change Research Act (GCRA) 38
Global Legislators Organisation for a Balanced Environment (GLOBE) 99, 103, 107, 111–112
global warming 1–2, 33, 41, 43, 58–59, 68, 71, 73, 75–76, 88, 93, 100, 123, 125–128, 137–138
Globe Americas Legislators Forum, GLOBE 103, 107
Goodman, Sherri 43–46, 51–52, 55, 59, 83, 147–148
Gore, Albert Al 37–38, 41–47, 55, 59, 63, 75, 101, 138, 148–149, 152
Greece 124, 138
green economy, green growth 46, 93–94, 102, 107
Green Environmental Fund (GEF) 137, 139
Green Party, Greens 66–67, 69, 72, 77, 86, 88–89, 92, 135, 137
Greenhouse Gas (GHG) / GHG emissions 2–3, 23, 34, 36, 42, 65–66, 70, 90, 99, 122, 143
Greenpeace 23, 39, 54–55, 67, 75, 77–78, 80, 83–84, 103, 105, 107, 111, 118, 127, 137, 139
Grupo de Financiamiento para Cambio Climático 112
GTZ *see* Gesellschaft für Internationale Zusammenarbeit
Gulledge, Jay 47–48, 50–52, 54, 125

Hansen, Lene 14–15, 31, 38
Hartmann, Betsy 7, 21, 33, 41, 60
health 1, 23, 49, 57–58, 98, 101–102, 112, 114–115, 131–132, 135, 143

heatwaves 104, 126, 133
Heinrich-Böll-Stiftung see Foundations
Helmholtz Centre 79, 134
Hernandez, Carolina 112
Homer-Dixon, Thomas 6–7, 21, 42, 74, 101
House of Representatives (US) 40, 43–44, 47, 54, 58
Human Development Index (HDI) 5, 121
human security 3, 7, 20, 22, 33, 79, 92, 108, 136, 146
Hurricane Katrina 49, 63, 75, 125, 135
Huysmans, Jef 7, 14, 31

İklim Ağı 122, 137
İklim Değişikliği ve Politikaları Uygulama ve Araştırma Merkezi (iklimbu) 139
individual danger see danger
individual risk, see risk
industrialised countries, developed countries, global north, west, western countries 5, 7, 18, 21, 32, 34, 65, 69, 91, 94, 99, 118–119, 124, 132, 143
industrialisation 66, 123–124, 142
Inhofe, James 39
Initiative for Peacebuilding – Early Warning Analysis to Action (ifp-EW) 108
Institute for Advanced Sustainability Studies (IASS) 68, 85
Institute for Development and Peace (INEF) 74
Instituto Nacional de Ecología (INE) 98, 100, 110–111, 114
Instituto Nacional de Ecología y Cambio Climático (INECC) 100, 109, 114
insurance, climate insurance, insurance schemes 8–9, 23, 50, 77–78, 87, 91, 94–95, 97, 105, 114–115, 147
intelligence
    sector 50, 57–61
    agencies 46, 61
Intergovernmental Panel on Climate Change (IPCC) 23–24, 39, 43, 46–47, 55–56, 63, 70–71, 73, 75–77, 80, 83–85, 110–111, 117, 138–139, 149

International Alert 85, 108
International Organisation for Migration (IOM) 136, 139
Iran, Islamic Republic of 124
Islamic State of Iraq and Syria (ISIS) IS, 144
İstanbul Büyükşehir (IBB) 133
Istanbul Policy Center (IPC) 133–137
İstanbul Teknik Üniversitesi (İTÜ) 128, 139
İTÜ Technical University Istanbul see İstanbul Teknik Üniversitesi (İTÜ)

Joint Chiefs of Staff (US) 55
Justice and Development Party see Adalet ve Kalkınma Partisi
just securitisation 10, 31

Kadıköy Bilim Kültür ve Sanat Dostları Derneği (KADOS) 137
Kadıoğlu, Mikdat 125–126, 134, 136, 138, 140
Kaplan, R.D. 42
Kerry, John 43, 53, 61
KfW see Deutsche Kreditanstalt für Wiederaufbau
Kibaroğlu, Ayşegül 129
Koch Industries, Koch Brothers 39
Konya-based Agency for Water Supply (KOSKI) 128, 132
Kuloğlu, Armağan 124, 129–130, 132, 134–135, 141
Kurnaz, Levent 136
Kyoto, COP-3 1996 44
Kyoto Protocol 2, 34, 39, 43–45, 65, 91, 99, 114, 124–125, 138, 143

Latin America 80, 96, 108
legislation 34, 36, 39–40, 43, 46, 50, 53, 57, 65, 69, 110, 126
legitimisation 3–4, 16, 25–26, 58, 97, 117, 119, 122
level of referent object 21
Ley General de Cambio Climático (General Climate Law, Mexico) 100
Liebermann, Joe 58
limits to growth 24, 41, 67–68
Locklear, Samuel L. 61

Lütfi-Şen, Ömer 125–126, 133–134, 138

Maas, Achim 78, 80, 85–86, 103, 108
macroeconomic indicators 121
Madra, Ömer 122, 126–128, 136–138
Malthus, Thomas; Malthusian, Neo-Malthusian 7, 21, 41
Marmara Üniversitesi Uluslararası İlişkiler Araştırma ve Uygulama Merkezi (MURCIR) 137
Marrakesh, COP-7 2001 75, 79, 125
Marshall Institute (US) 39, 53
Marshall, Andrew 45
McDonald, Matt 4, 7–8, 11, 20, 22, 31, 90
MDG *see* Millennium Development Goals
media
   attention 106
   discourse 106
   role of 40–41, 51, 53, 55, 68, 71–72, 76–77, 83, 86, 88, 105–106, 121, 125–126, 129, 133, 135–138
megacities 133, 143
Mercator Research Institute on Global Commons and Climate Change (MCC) 76
Mercator Stiftung *see* foundations
Merkel, Angela 69–70, 76, 86
Messner, Dirk 74, 148
Methmann, Chris 9, 14, 32–33
methodology 6, 29–30
Mexico 3–6, 12, 29, 36, 39, 77, 96–120, 135, 145, 147–148, 151–152
migration 1, 6–7, 15, 17, 21 33, 48, 78, 81, 103–105, 109–110, 115, 128, 130–134, 136, 138
militarisation 10, 42, 62–63
Military Advisory Board (MAB) *see* CNA
military
   planning 22, 33, 49, 61, 90
   reputation of 52, 62, 64–65
   role of 37, 42, 47–54, 59–63, 77, 80, 83, 90, 94, 118, 122, 126, 129, 131–132, 135, 141, 143–144, 146–150, 153
   military, armed forces (US) 36, 37, 42, 47–54, 59–63
   military, armed forces (Germany) 65–66, 77, 80–81, 83, 90, 94

   military, armed forces (Mexico) 102, 118, 120
   military, armed forces (Turkey) 129, 131–132, 135, 138, 141, 143–144
Millennium Development Goals (MDG) 141
Ministry of Environment and Forestry (Turkey) 125
Ministry of Environment and Urbanisation (Turkey) 134, 141
Ministry of Foreign Affairs (Turkey) 124
Misereor 82, 84–85
mitigation 17, 21, 23, 32–34, 36, 50, 58, 61, 72, 74–75, 81–82, 94, 99, 102, 104–105, 108, 114, 116, 120, 140, 143, 149–151
monitoring 81, 107, 114
Montreal Protocol 43, 100
Munich Climate Insurance Initiative (MCII) 77, 87, 91
Munich Re 77, 87, 91
Munich Security Conference 76, 78
Myers, Norman 2, 6, 42

NAFTA *see* North American Free Trade Agreement
National Academy of Sciences 41, 43, 54
National Aeronautics and Space Administration (NASA) 38, 43
National Climate Assessment (NCA) (US) 41
National Climate Change Action Plan (Turkey) 124
National Climate Change Coordination Group (NCCG) (Turkey) 123
National Communication on Climate Change (Turkey) 126
National Defense Authorization Act (US) 60
National Defense Strategy (US) 60
National Intelligence Estimates (NIE) (US) 50, 61
National Military Strategy (US) 60
National Oceanic and Atmospheric Administration (NOAA) (US) 54–56
National Security Council (Mexico) 116
National Security Council (Turkey) 130
National Security Document (Turkey) 140
National Security Strategy (NSS) (US) 1, 105

NATO *see* North Atlantic Treaty
  Organization
Nature Conservancy, The 54
Navy, US 51–52, 55, 60–61, 63
network citation analysis 30, 37, 55–56, 67,
  84, 97, 110–111, 123, 139
networked security 60
new security 42, 48, 62, 108, 117–118, 138
Nieto, Enrique Peña 100, 113, 116
normative consequences/implications (of
  climate change) 3–4, 6, 10–13,
  30–34, 151–152
norm entrepreneurs 26–27
North American Free Trade Agreement
  (NAFTA) 98
North Atlantic Treaty Organization
  (NATO) 81, 131

Obama, Barack 40–41, 53, 61, 150,
Oels, Angela 2, 4, 13, 27, 32–33, 36, 57,
  60, 62
Office of the Deputy Under Secretary of
  Defense – Environmental Security
  (ODUSD-ES) (US) 44, 52
Office of the Deputy Under Secretary of
  Defense – Installation and
  Environment (ODUSD-I&S) (US) 45
oil industry 40–41, 48, 58, 67, 104
Organisation for Economic Co-operation
  and Development (OECD) 84, 91
Ortadoğu Stratejik Araştırmalar Merkezi
  (ORSAM) 130, 139
Oxfam 49, 50, 78, 83–85, 111
Özal, Turgut 123
Ozone layer 37, 43, 71, 73, 100, 107

Paris COP-21 2015 86
Paris School 8, 24, 31–32
Parliamentary Commission of the
  Environment (Turkey) 124
Partido Acción Nacional (PAN) 99, 102
Partido Revolucionario Institucional (PRI)
  98, 100–101
Partido Verde Ecologista de México
  (PVEM) 102
Partîya Karkerên Kurdîstan (PKK) 124, 144

Partners for Democratic Change International
  (PDCI) 103, 105, 107–108, 110–112,
  114, 116, 119, 120
Pentagon *see* Department of Defense
  (DOD)
Petróleos Mexicanos (PEMEX) 104, 11
Pew Center on Global Climate Change *see*
  Center for Climate and Energy
  (C2ES)
PIK *see* Potsdam Institute for Climate
  Impact Research
Pirages, Dennis 8, 20, 23
PKK *see* Partîya Karkerên Kurdîstan
Plan Estatal de Acción ante el Cambio
  Climático (PEACC) 100
planetary danger, *see* danger
planetary risk *see* risk
polarisation (of political debate, US) 39, 63
policy change 32, 58, 67, 80, 150
politicisation 10, 12–13, 17–19, 32, 86, 97,
  112–114, 118–119, 122, 140
polluter pays principle 140
Potsdam Institute for Climate Impact
  Research (PIK) 69, 75–78, 80,
  83–87, 92
precautionary measures 9, 31–32, 147
precautionary principle 16, 24
preparedness 16, 120, 147
Programa Especial de Cambio Climático
  (PECC) 100, 110–111, 114–115
Programa Nacional Científico sobre
  Cambio Climático Global 98

Quadrennial Defense Review (QDR) 50,
  53, 60

RAND 53
Randall, Doug 45, 84, 130, 134
Ratify Kyoto Campaign 127
referent object 3–4, 7–10, 12–13, 15–16,
  20–23, 26, 28, 31–34, 80, 90,
  104–105, 133, 145, 152
Regional Environmental Centre (REC)
  125, 134, 137, 141
Republican Party (US) 38–39, 40, 54,
  57–59, 63, 150
resilience 8–9, 16–17, 22–24, 50, 81–82,
  85, 87, 89–90, 94, 105, 133–134

resource scarcity 1, 7, 41, 44, 103–104, 106
resource wars, resource conflicts, competition 1, 7, 9, 21, 81, 93
Rio Earth Summit (1992) 69, 71, 123–124
risk
  assessment 21–22, 60
  atlas 114–115
  dimension 16, 34, 49, 82, 100, 117
  groups 9, 16, 22, 33, 104–105
  Individual Risk Discourse 6, 21–22, 25, 62–62, 65, 82, 85, 94, 97, 99, 101–102, 105–106, 110–111, 113–120, 134, 144, 149, 151
  management 16, 49, 62, 97, 114–115, 119, 134
  Planetary Risk Discourse 21, 24, 43, 47, 101, 114, 116, 119, 145
  Territorial Risk Discourse 21, 97, 110, 116
riskification 9–10, 12–19, 21, 31, 33, 145–147
Rockefeller Foundation/Rockefeller Brothers Fund *see* Foundations
root causes 32, 94
Rothe, Delf 9, 14, 109
Royal United Services Institute (RUSI) 5, 103, 105–106, 109–117, 119–120, 148–149
Russia 81, 124

Şahin, Ümit 122–128, 135–138, 142–143
SAREM *see* Stratejik Araştırma ve Etüt Merkezi
scenario planning 16, 21, 60
Scheffran, Jürgen 79, 130
Schellnhuber, Hans Joachim 86, 148
Schröder, Gerhard 70
Schwartz and Randall 45, 84, 130, 134
Schwartz, Peter 45, 84, 130, 134
scientists, role of 24, 29, 38, 42, 54, 67–69, 72, 75, 78, 86, 88, 100, 107, 123, 126, 128–136, 138, 141–142, 148
sea level rise 1, 41, 49, 81, 103–104, 117
Secretaría de Agricultura, Ganadería, Desarrollo Rural, Pesca y Alimentación (SAGARPA) 110–111, 115
Secretaría de Energía (SENER) 104, 111

Secretaría de Gobernación (SEGOB) 115
Secretaría de Medio Ambiente y Recursos Naturales (SEMARNAT) 109–111
Secretaría de Relaciones Exteriores (SRE) 111
securitisation
  actors 12, 25, 27, 29, 33, 73, 74, 77, 80, 88, 91, 97, 119, 135
  context of 11–12, 26–31, 62–63, 91–94, 117–120, 141–143, 146–150, 152–153
  criticism 8, 10, 32, 42
  failed 58, 97, 119
  grammar of 7, 10, 15, 28
  impact of 4–6, 14, 20, 25, 32, 44, 57–62, 75, 79, 88–91, 110–117, 138–141, 149–151
  schools of 3–4, 7–11, 13–17, 20, 24, 26, 28, 31–32, 145, 151
  success conditions of 6, 13, 28–29, 62–63, 91–94, 117–119, 142, 146
  theory 3–4, 7–11, 13–17, 20, 24, 26, 28, 31–32, 145, 151
securitising move, securitisation attempt 3, 6–7, 12, 19, 24–30, 64, 71, 75, 77, 79, 81, 83, 89, 92, 100, 107, 112, 116–118, 122, 126, 130–132, 135, 138, 141, 143, 146, 1511–153
Senado de la República (Mexico) 100–102, 114–115
Senate (US) 39–40, 42–44, 46–47, 50, 52, 54, 57–61
Skoll Global Threats Fund *see* Foundations
socio-economic development 5, 96, 122–123, 143, 145
socio-economic consequences, effects of climate change 1–2, 21–23, 32–33, 43–44, 46–47, 50–52, 61–64, 73, 75, 91, 98, 103–105, 109–110, 112, 117, 128–134, 138
Sozialdemokratische Partei Deutschlands (SPD), Social Democrats 67–68, 69–70, 72, 77–78
Special Commission on climate change (Turkey) 124
speech act 3, 20–21, 25–26, 32, 106, 136, 138
State Planning Institution (DPT) 122–124, 139–140

Steinmeier, Franz-Walter 78–79, 93
Stern, Nicolas 70, 75–76, 126
Stern Report 2, 70, 80, 87, 93, 75–76, 80, 87, 93
Stern, Todd 40
Stiftung Wissenschaft und Politik (SWP) 77–79, 88
Strategic Environmental Research and Development Program (SERDP) 44
Stratejik Araştırma ve Etüt Merkezi (SAREM) 129–130, 140
surveillance 16
sustainable development, sustainable economic growth 67–69, 76, 92, 107, 114, 121–122, 124
SWP *see* Stiftung Wissenschaft und Politik

Tänzler, Dennis 78, 80, 86–87, 108
Tea Party (US) 58
territorial danger *see* danger
territorial risk *see* risk
terror, terrorism 1, 9, 15–16, 21, 33, 45, 48, 59, 137–138, 145
The Day After Tomorrow (movie) 46, 75, 125, 134
think tanks, role of 6, 27, 29, 37, 41–42, 45–48, 50–55, 57–61, 63–64, 66–67, 74–75, 77–80, 85–87, 94, 97–98, 103, 107, 109, 123, 128–129, 135, 148
threat multiplier 48, 59–60, 81
threatification 9–10, 12–19, 21, 33, 145–147
threshold (of securitisation) 19, 89, 151
TIKDEK *see* Türkiye İklim Değişikliği Kongresi
tolerable level (of risk) 22–24, 32, 34
traditional security 41, 54, 109, 113
Trombetta, Maria J. 4, 7, 11, 13, 17, 22–23, 43
TÜBITAK *see* Türkiye Bilimsel ve Teknolojik Araştırma Kurumu
TÜRÇEK 139
Türk Mühendis ve Mimar Odaları Birliği (TMMOB) 139, 143
Türkeş, Murat 123–125, 134, 136, 138
Turkish Parliament *see* Türkiye Büyük Millet Meclisi

Türkiye Bilimsel ve Teknolojik Araştırma Kurumu (TÜBITAK) 122
Türkiye Büyük Millet Meclisi (TBMM) 130–134, 142–143
Türkiye Erozyonla Mücadele, Ağaçlandırma ve Doğal Varlıkları Koruma Vakfı (TEMA) 137–138
Türkiye İklim Değişikliği Kongresi (TIKDEK) 128, 142

Umweltbundesamt (UBA) 68
uncertainty 9, 16, 22, 54, 62
UNDP *see* United Nations Development Programme
unequal livelihoods, inequality 96, 133
United Arab Emirates (UAE) 122
United Kingdom (UK) 1, 3, 5, 91, 93, 109, 113, 119, 124, 147–148
United Nations (UN)
   Conference on Environment and Development (UNCED) 2, 38
   Development Programme (UNDP) 61, 108, 121, 126, 134, 136–139, 141, 143
   Environmental Programme (UNEP) 99, 138–139, 141
   Framework Convention of Climate Change (UNFCCC) 2, 12, 38, 40, 43, 71, 74, 75, 83 85, 98–99, 110, 113, 115, 121, 123–126, 128, 135–136, 138–139, 141, 143
   General Assembly (UNGA) 2, 22, 138
   Industrial Development Organisation (UNIDO) 141
   Security Council (UNSC) 2, 22, 33, 86, 91, 116, 139
United States (US)
   Agency for International Development (USAID) 50, 56, 60, 111
   Air Force 55, 56
   Army 90
   Climate Action Partnership (USCAP) 40
   Congress 38–40, 42–44, 46
   Countries Studies Program 98
   Navy *see* Navy
Universidad Nacional Autónoma de México (UNAM) 98, 110–111

Verband Deutscher Automobilhersteller (VDA) 69
violent conflict 1, 6–7, 9, 21, 32, 79, 103, 105, 108, 117, 131–132
vulnerability
    atlas 105, 115
    human 22–23, 33, 99, 103–105, 114–115

Wæver, Ole 4, 11, 15–16, 18, 28
water
    scarcity 1, 22, 104, 128, 131–133
    security nexus 130, 133
    supply 102, 132
    wars 132–133
Water Foundation 128, 143
White House, The 1, 41, 44–45, 55, 61–62, 86
Wilson Center *see* Woodrow Wilson Center

Wirth, Timothy 38, 43–44
WMO *see* World Meteorological Organisation
Woodrow Wilson Center 42, 52–53, 56, 85
World Bank 12, 80, 103, 106–107, 110, 115
World Climate Programme (WCP) 67
World Health Organisation (WHO) 89
World Meteorological Organisation (WMO) 67–68, 84, 123, 139
World Resources Institute (WRI) 37
World Wide Fund for Nature (WWF), World Wildlife Fund 54–55, 78–79, 82–84, 103, 107, 111, 137–139
Wuppertal Institute 69, 83, 85, 92, 135

Zinni, Anthony 44, 53